easyHistory.info

The easy® family of brands photo album

sixth edition

Scan the QR code here to access the **easyHistory** website and video.

INCORPORATING

STELIOS PHILANTHROPIC FOUNDATION

WWW.STELIOS.ORG

INCORPORATING THE ANNUAL REPORT FY23

It started with a dream...

To build a world famous brand!

Dear friends 23 April 2024

of the **easy** family of brands,

Welcome to the sixth edition of easyHistory. Think of this booklet as a photo album - telling our story since 1994 when I embarked on my dream to create a world-famous brand. At the tender age of 27, I started building a family of brands centred on the word "easy" which I was determined to make a household name.

This year marks the thirtieth anniversary of the easy family of brands. Progress over the last three decades has been far from uneventful, as one would expect from such an entrepreneurial adventure.

easyHistory 1st Edition

easyHistory 2nd Edition

Some of you may have read one of the previous editions of easyHistory, or viewed the four minute video released in January 2024.

So much has happened since the first edition was signed off on the 6th February 2020. The fact that we have republished several times and are now into a sixth edition reflects the fact that so many of you seemed to enjoy and appreciate reading about the history of the easy family of brands.

The printed version has more than doubled in size since 2020 and that is no accident. We have been busy filling in the gaps and adding a lot more detail that demonstrates my vision from day one was to make the brand "easy" a household name in as many business sectors and in as many countries as possible.

Find out more

explore easy YouTube page https://youtu.be/6wqHjEAbH3M

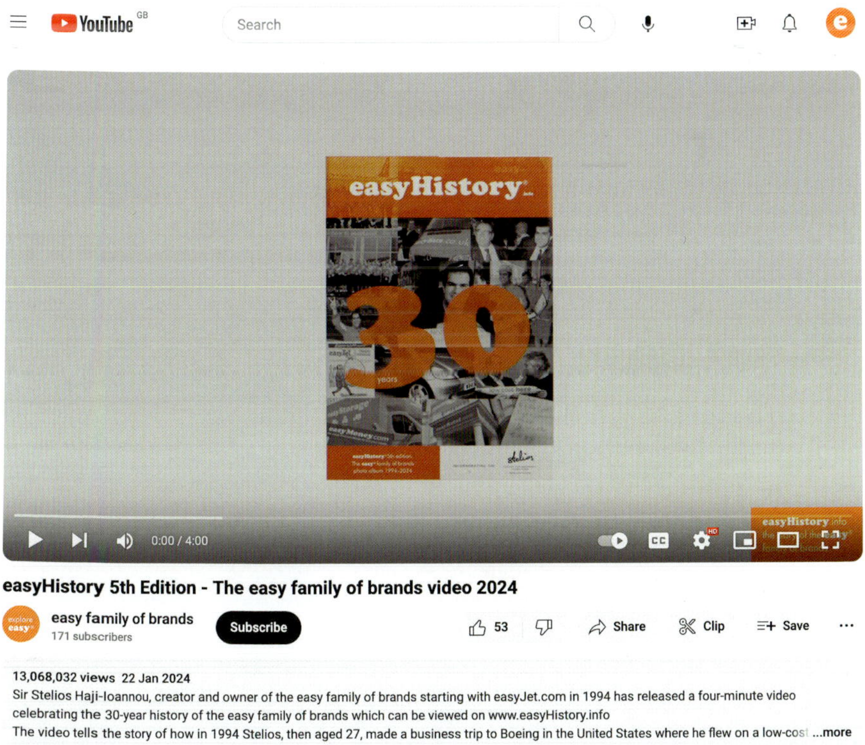

It started with a dream...

To build a world famous brand!

continued

The story goes back to 1994 when I first came across the business model of the low-cost airlines in America at a time when Europe was opening its skies up to competition and I realised that setting up an airline is a great way to create awareness and build a brand.

The brand was "easy" from day one even if, as expected, the airline easyJet became much more famous than the other members of the easy family of brands.

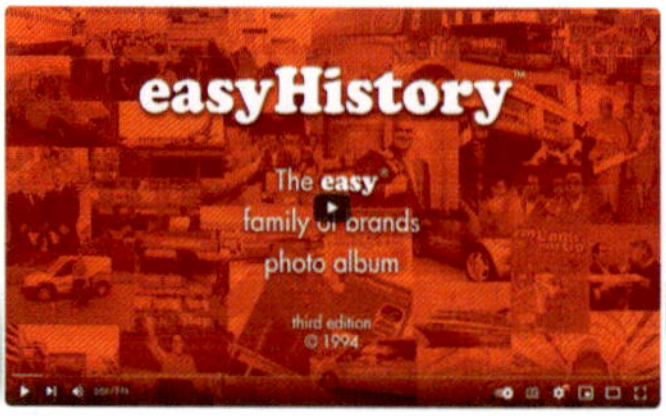

easyHistory 3rd Edition

easyHistory 4th Edition

- AND IN OTHER NEWS - 1994

AS STELIOS WAS WORKING ON HIS BIG IDEA OF CREATING A WORLD FAMOUS BRAND, THESE POLITICIANS WERE IN OFFICE

BILL CLINTON

JOHN MAJOR

ANDREAS PAPANDREOU

This is me age 28 with a big dream: to build a world famous brand.

It started with a dream...

To build a world famous brand!

continued

You could say that my best business idea in my life was to create a pioneering low-cost airline but that the next best idea was to keep the ownership of all the easy brands including easyJet in my own private company called easyGroup thus giving me more stable recurring income from royalties.

At easyGroup we have well diversified sources of income that have allowed us to manage our way through the pandemic. The royalty business model means we have income for as long as there are revenues - even without profits. This is important in challenging economic times and high stock market volatility.

So here is our story and I hope you enjoy the read. easyHistory has been organised more or less chronologically since 1994 and then by geography and by business sector right up to the present day.

Sir Stelios Haji-Ioannou
creator and owner of the **easy** family of brands
stelios@**easy**.com
www.**easy**.com

1994: A family business

Loucas Haji-Ioannou - Shipping Tycoon

A family fortune made through oil tankers

Today few people realise that the origin of the easy "family of brands" was itself another "family business". My late father Loucas Haji-Ioannou was a highly successful self-made entrepreneur, a Greek Cypriot shipping magnate who came from very humble beginnings.

In 1950 my father left Cyprus to seek his fortune, moving first to Egypt and then to Jeddah in Saudi Arabia where he developed a successful trading business. As an international trader he regularly chartered ships to transport his merchandise. But his dream had always been to become a ship owner, so he moved to London – the world centre of shipping and in 1958 he bought his first ship and named it after his wife Nedi. By the time I was born in 1967 he had moved his family to Athens, Greece from where he was running his shipping empire – Troodos (est. 1959).

Stelmar

NY Stock Exchange, opening one month after September 11
Stelmar Tankers Interim Results

My father was my first boss when I worked for the family business. In reality he's the only business boss I ever had. He taught me a lot and became my first business hero. I am eternally grateful to him for recognising my potential in business and financing my first start up business venture at the age of 25 in 1992. From that point onwards I was determined to be my own boss. That's what drives an entrepreneur!

That first start up was my own shipping company – Stelmar – with shareholdings held by my brother Polys and sister Clelia. It was floated on the New York Stock Exchange in 2001 before I sold it to a competitor near the peak of the market in 2005 at four times the IPO float price. The total value of the Stelmar exit was US$1.3 billion (including debt) and marked the end of my day-to-day involvement in a family business.

By 1993 it was already clear to me that I wanted to expand my business activities outside shipping. For two reasons: firstly, I was trying to prove myself to my father and to others. Loucas was self-made, and because of that I have always held self-made people in particularly high esteem. Since many saw me as a "daddy's boy", I got little credit for my achievements since they assumed I was merely taking instructions from "the boss".

Early image of Stelios

1994: A family business

continued

I was therefore determined to make my mark in business outside shipping. Secondly, I had enough of people not knowing what I did for a living, which is one of the problems of being in a "business to business" (B2B) industry like shipping. So I set out to create a household name. Then events took their turn.

Stelios with Sir Richard Branson 2002

In 1993 I learned that Virgin Atlantic Airways was seeking an investor for a route it was then operating between Athens and London. This led to a meeting with Richard Branson another of my business heroes. Although I never invested in that venture it sparked my interest in aviation, particularly in the United States where deregulation had led to the emergence of low-cost airlines. In the summer of 1994 I made a research trip to the US, visiting the Boeing factory in Seattle and meeting with Valujet and Southwest, then two of the fastest growing low-cost airlines in North America.

Valujet aircraft 1995

FLY SOUTHWEST AIRLINES

Southwest Airlines' Boeing 737-200 – 1990s

Boeing factory in Seattle

BOEING

Herb Kelleher - Founder Southwest Airlines

1994: A family business

continued

Polys, Clelia & Stelios Haji-Ioannou sibling portrait 1997

Southwest's founder and CEO at that time was the late Herb Kelleher who became another of my business heroes. Whilst on this US trip I stayed for the first time in my life at a budget hotel. I think it was a Motel 6. Up until then it had been mostly 5 star hotels for me. That's when it occurred to me that it was possible to extend a value brand from an airline to a hotel chain and beyond.

Haji-Ioannou family meeting at the offices of Troodos Maritime in Monaco 1997 with Polys, Clelia, Stelios and father Loucas

I later learned that Motel 6 was founded in 1962 to meet a growing demand for low-cost accommodation and got its name because it charged $6 a night for a room. Today the company now owned by Blackstone private equity has 1,430 locations and is regarded as an iconic American brand.
In 1994 airline deregulation in Europe was gathering speed and so the timing for launching a low-cost airline was ideal. I floated the idea at a business lunch with my father at Monaco's Hotel de Paris.

Low-cost accommodation
Motel 6 in the USA

By that time we had moved the Haji-Ioannou family office to Monaco since 1989. During that lunch he agreed to back my idea with his money on behalf of the family. Hence my brother Polys and my sister Clelia became shareholders in easyJet – and remain so today as well as being shareholders in easyHotel PLC. I thought the luxurious surroundings of an ultra-expensive hotel in Monaco giving birth to one of Europe's best known value brands was the biggest irony of my life.

easyHotel in South Kensington, UK

1994: A family business

continued

I became financially successful when I realised that not everyone could afford to live the way I did and that you are better off selling to the many than the few. My shipping company was called "Stelmar" (from "Stelios" and "maritime" so the working title of the airline became "Stelair" (my first brand extension) until I decided "easy" would work better than "Stel".

I had to decide between putting my own name on the planes, as the late Sir Freddy Laker had done in the 1970s or building a more versatile international brand like Virgin. I recall sitting at a bar sometime in 1994, witing different ideas on a napkin. I tried: stel, valu (as in valujet), light (as in Coke light) cheap, affordable before easy won. One of my biggest regrets was not keeping that napkin. Of course I did not know then how valuable this brand would one day become but we created a mock-up of that napkin to immortalise the moment. Also thank heavens for a moment of sanity in not allowing myself to be completely self-centred by going down the "Stel" road!

Stelios with his father Loucas Haji-Ioannou & Stelmar Ship

Freddie Laker & Laker plane

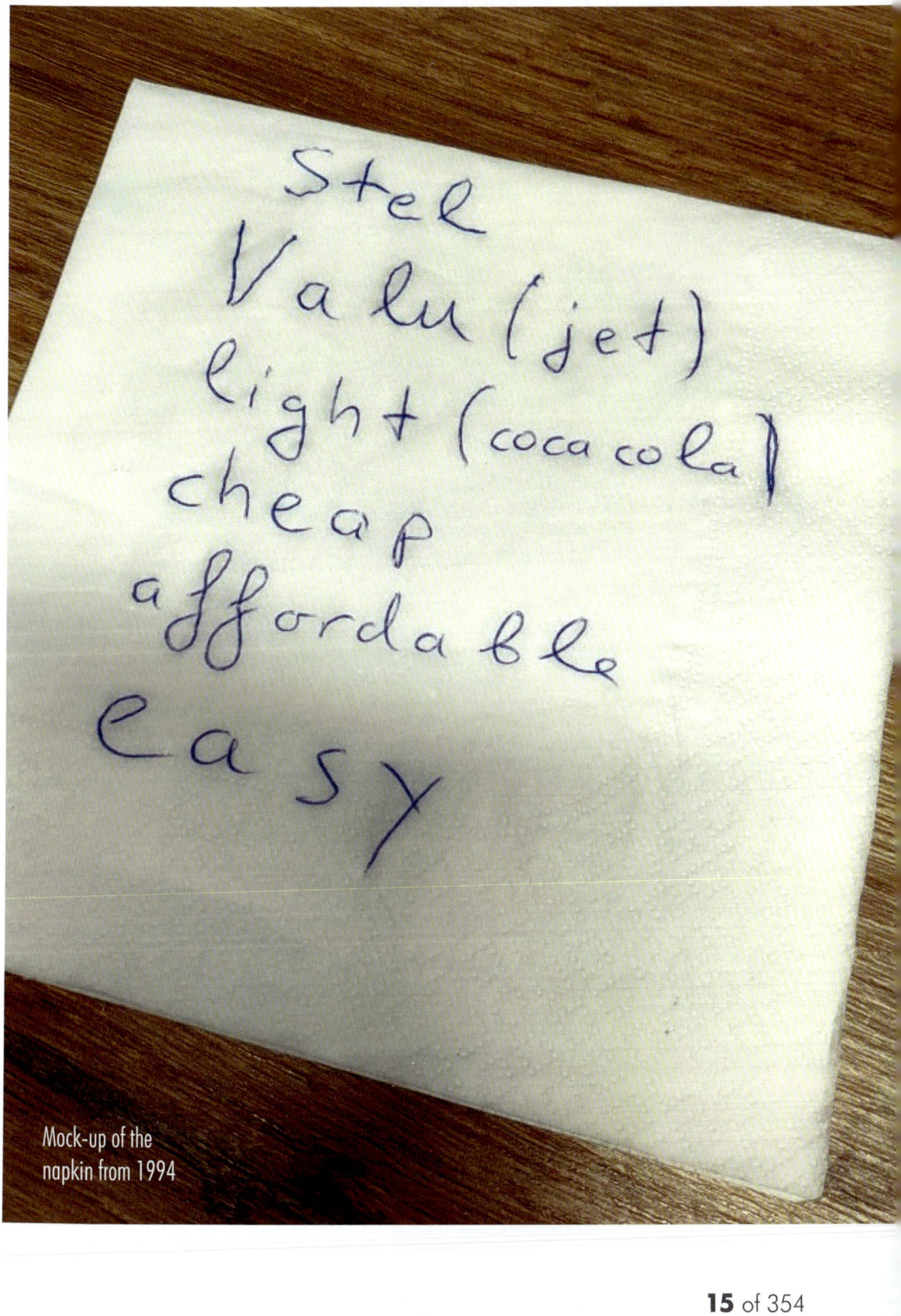

Mock-up of the napkin from 1994

the easy mission & vision

Our mission is to manage and extend Europe's leading value brand to more products and services, bringing great value to our customers whilst creating real wealth for all stakeholders.

Our vision is to develop Europe's leading value brand into a global force.

Our Brand values

1. Great value
2. For the many, not the few
3. Relentless innovation
4. Entrepreneurial
5. Taking on the big guys
6. Making a difference in people's lives
7. Keep it simple

the easy business model

Having a big airline in the easy family is a great way to build the brand. People are sometimes excited when they fly, the airline often takes them to exciting places and at the risk of sounding a bit corny: "it defies gravity".

Since 1995 Stelios has taken the brand to many other sectors starting with natural extensions and then moving onto other industries. The underlying theme is to outsource as much of the nitty gritty as possible and join forces with business partners who know their industry. The easy family of brands is not afraid to expand by trial and error. If something does not work out then we change it and try again. We keep looking for new business partners who have new business ideas to further extend the brand into as many different sectors as possible. That is how you build and consolidate a strong and distinctive family of brands. The total income earned by easyGroup UK in the financial year ended September 2023 was £23.8 m an increase of £5.5m on the previous year. That is a good income for a business that does not deploy any capital of its own. The idea nowadays is to allow the licensee companies and business partners to deploy their capital into the hard assets whilst easyGroup concentrates on managing and protecting the easy brand while earning a fair income for letting other people use the brand.

Advertising all the easy brands on the London Underground in 2016

The advantage for our business partners is that it's a lot cheaper to pay a licence fee than to spend money building and marketing their own brands from scratch. Today easyGroup owns more than 1,200 trademarks with easy either on its own or as a logo and/or as a prefix. We also own more than 4,450 internet domains.

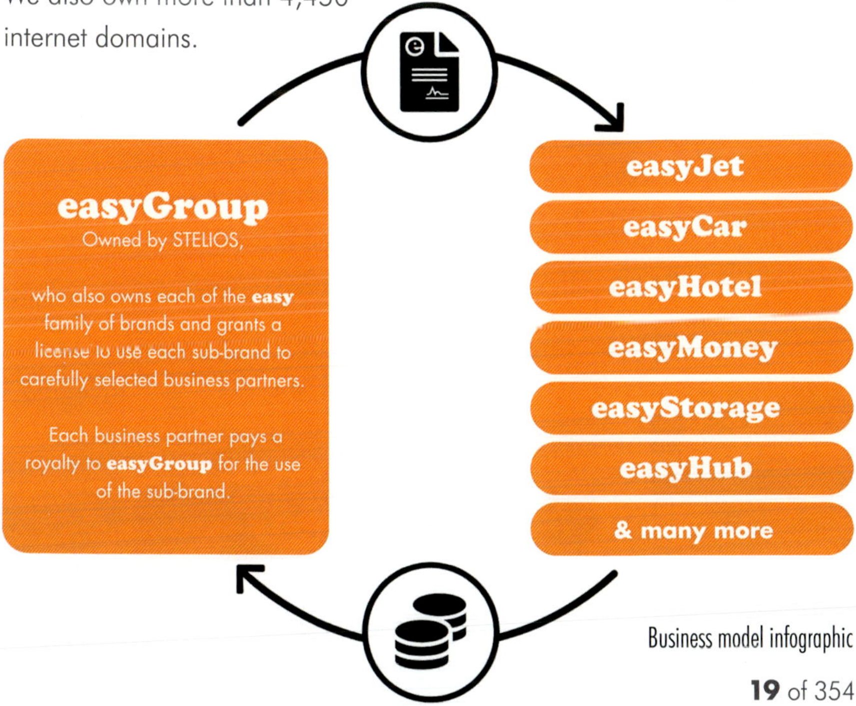

Business model infographic

New business ideas

Launching a new business idea and easy sub-brand involves four simple steps:

1. Find a suitable business partner with a novel idea and access to capital.

2. Come up with a suitable extension (suffix) after easy that matches the business model.

3. Secure the trademark and the domain.

4. Start running the business.

The legalese:

A. easyGroup is the brand owner and licenses the right to use each sub-brand to different licensee companies.

B. All IP rights in the brand and the sub-brands stay with easyGroup.

C. easyGroup have built a huge amount of reputation via prior use over the last 30 years in many countries around the world and in many different business sectors. Each sub-brand promotes the "easy" brand which itself becomes increasingly famous as more companies advertise it.

D. A trade mark is a legal monopoly for a business brand which is granted by a state via its trademark office. We own more than 1,200 of these monopolies in many countries and many different classes of business sectors.

E. We have held an EU trademark of "easy" on its own since 9th June 2000 with registration number 1699792 for the EU & UK.

F. On 15th August 2019 we obtained a UK trademark registration UK00003421566 for the colour orange per se for airline services (class 39) which means that if someone started an online travel agent or an airline in the UK using orange we could stop them. Very few companies in the world own a trademark colour!

At various points between 17 July 1995 and 28 July 1995 Stelios sat with the local designer Barry Debenham of White Knight (today called WK360) at their office. Tony Anderson, easyJet's first Marketing Director was also present. During a series of working sessions sitting together around an Apple Mac the easy visual identity gradually took shape. It was a client-led process of trial and error with Stelios directing Barry to try different design ideas on the screen until he was happy.

The easy logo design is not only protected by multiple trademark registrations around the globe but is also protected by UK copyright by virtue of the fact it is an artistic work pursuant to section 1(a) of the Copyright, Design and Patents Act 1988. As a result of various international treaties and conventions (including the Berne Convention) this copyright is recognised in a majority of countries throughout the globe. All rights in such copyright are owned by easyGroup Limited.

Stelios

Barry Debenham - White Knight Designer

Tony Anderson - Then marketing Director

Key elements of:
the easy logo & design

Among the output of the working sessions at White Knight Design in Luton in July 1995 were the following key aspects of the easy visual identity protected by copyright:

The Cooper Black font

i. Stelios did not want to use a custom design font which required a payment to its owner. He liked the Cooper Black font because it was round and "friendly". Renowned branding expert Sarah Hyndman in her book "Why fonts matter" published in 2016 states: "When I see Cooper Black I think of the easyJet logo".
Cooper Black was particularly distinctive in comparison with other airlines' choice of fonts, most notably British Airways which comprised all capital letters and was usually shown as white letters out of a blue background. Furthermore, Stelios wanted a font that would be distinctive in black and white as well as colour because he wanted to advertise the easy family of brands in newspapers which were predominantly printed in black and white.

Why fonts matter
by Sarah Hyndman

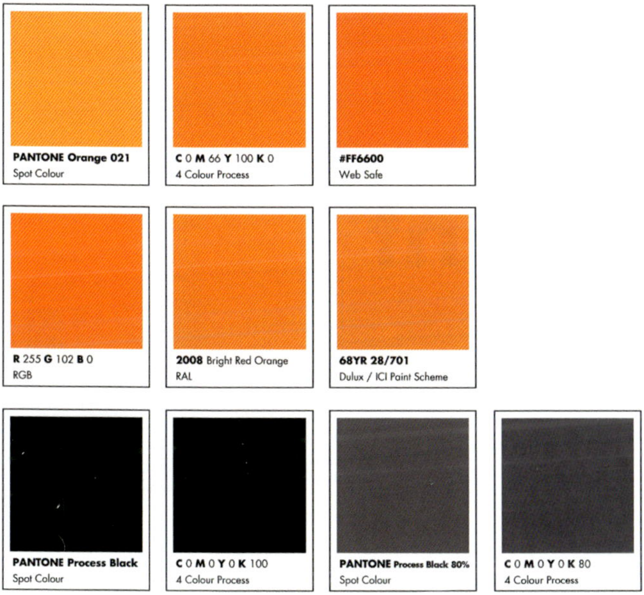

ii. The shade of orange

Stelios had already selected orange as the brand colour. At that time blues and reds were widely used for aircraft liveries while green was associated with Pakistan International Airlines which had a poor reputation. He eventually chose a particular shade of orange (pantone 021c) after flicking through a reference book of different pantone colours provided by White Knight.

iii. CAPITALISATION ...or lack of it

Stelios was considering ways in which the easy branding could work to support a brand family. He came up with the idea of capitalising the first letter of the suffix and then returned to lower case after the first letter. He wanted a logo that could be used with different suffixes to mean different things and sell different products and services. This broke with convention that companies capitalised the first letter of their logo and from that moment on Stelios insisted that easy should always be written in lower case.

Being Different

Stelios with a surviving easy uniform from 1995 in 2021

easyJet livery 1995
Photo: aeroicarus flickr

First easy crew uniform 1995

It was important to Stelios that his brand had a visual identity very different to that of its competitors. We also considered the logos of other airlines which all involved some combination of the colours white, red and blue.

These included Ryanair, British Airways, KLM and Air France all of whom as you can see below were using capital letters. Stelios wanted a distinctive logo in lower case letters associated strongly with the colour orange.

BRITISH AIRWAYS

AIR FRANCE

KLM
Royal Dutch Airlines

RYANAIR
THE LOW FARES AIRLINE

easy

Competitor airline brands 1995:
note use of capital letters

easy Brand Guidelines

easyGroup has published multiple volumes of its brand manual for the benefit of franchisees, licensees and potential business partners. Over the years the manual has evolved to suit the needs of multiple brands spanning across many different industries and sectors.

The brand manual is regularly updated to cater to the evolution of how business is made however the core values and aesthetic have remained the same. To this day, the brand manual can be downloaded from: www.easy.com/the-brand/

As a brand standard, all easyGroup brand licensees are expected to include the legend 'part of the easy® family of brands' on their website homepage. We strongly recommend this is placed in either the header or the footer of the licensee's site.

easy.com original logo 1995

easy.com logo 2005

more value for less!

easy.com logo 2022

Part of the **easy**® family of brands

easy Brand Guidelines

continued

part of the **easy**®
family of brands

Part of the eFob Badge

easy logos differentiated
through the descriptive word
(or words) after easy

easyJet.com
easyCar.com
easyValue.com
easyHotel.com
easyMoney.com
easyBus.com
easyMusic.com
easyProperty.com

Each 'easy' branded business has its own specific logo, differentiated through the descriptive word (or words) that follow "easy".

The examples shown on the right demonstrate correct and incorrect renderings of 'easy' trading names using the Cooper Black font. Whilst they do not cover every possible scenario, franchisees and licensees can formulate a good idea of what is acceptable and what is not. Some exemptions are given to some licensees to use other colours, see easyCleaning and easyFood for example.

Correct	Wrong!
easyJet	easyJet
easyJet	easy Jet
easyJet	easyjet
easyJet	EasyJet
easyInternetcafé	easy-Internetcafé
easyInternetcafé	easyinternetcafé
easyInternetcafé	easyInternetCafé
easyCar	easyCar
easyMoney.com	easyMoney.com
easyJet is great	easyJet is great
easyGroup	easyGroup
easyMoney.com	easyMoney.com
easyGroup	easyGroup
easyGroup	Easygroup
easyGroup	easyGroup
easyInternetcafé	EASYINTERNETCAFE
easyInternetcafé	EasyInternetcafé
easyGroup	easyGroup
easyValue	easyValue.
easyGroup	easyGroup
easyGroup	easyGroup

1995:

easyLand

Stelios was determined to build a strong brand around the name easy in the same way Richard Branson built the Virgin brand. On 1st March 1995 he filed the incorporation documents for EasyJet Airline Company Ltd at the UK's Companies House (at that point the name was still capitalised). The first UK trademark was filed on 5th April 1995. Later that summer he decided to base his new airline at Luton airport primarily because it was cheaper than Stansted. Everything had to be easy, low-cost and orange.

The office was far from glamorous. It was basically a large shed that had seen better days, but it was an ideal home for a start-up airline. Shortly after moving in, Stelios deliberately christened the place "easyLand" rather than "easyJet Land" and issued instructions for the building to be painted orange, including the roof. easyLand became one of the very first members of the easy family of brands alongside easyJet, easyKiosk and easyWay. Sadly, soon after installation the neon sign had to be turned off as flashing lights aren't permitted at airports.

easyLand signage 1995

FILE COPY

CERTIFICATE OF INCORPORATION
OF A PRIVATE LIMITED COMPANY

Company No. 3034606

The Registrar of Companies for England and Wales hereby certifies that
EASYJET AIRLINE COMPANY LIMITED

is this day incorporated under the Companies Act 1985 as a private company and that the company is limited.

Given at Companies House, Cardiff, the 17th March 1995

N030346069

M.LEWIS
For the Registrar of Companies

COMPANIES HOUSE

HC007B

easyJet filed incorporation document 1st March 1995

1995:

easyLand continued

First ever article in The Times
22 Jun 95 (Page right)

The location of the office, right next to the taxiway, gave the easy brand a very powerful brand presence at the airport. Over the years more than 100 million arriving and departing passengers have seen the easyLand building from their aircraft. The original building was demolished in 2015 as part of Luton Airport's redevelopment plans but the easyLand brand lives on today with centres now open in France, Cyprus, Greece & the UK selling easy branded merchandise and services. easyLand, trademark filed June 2001 with TM number 2278398. The easyLand brand is also used in partnership with Booking.com allowing customers access to worldwide accommodation via www.easyLand.travel

easyLand sign 1999

easyLand in France 2020

THE TIMES

Britain to get its own 'peanut' airline

BY HARVEY ELLIOTT

A GREEK shipping magnate is to launch a genuine cut-price domestic airline in Britain selling tickets for less than half the price of those now available from existing scheduled airlines.

Based on the American low-cost airlines, Southwest Airlines and Valujet, the new carrier — to be called Easy Jet — will offer passengers nothing but soft drinks and peanuts. If the planned three flights a day to Glasgow and Edinburgh from either Luton or Stansted prove a success, the operation will expand to include other British cities and later to many business centres on the Continent.

Stelios Haji-Ioannou, who owns Stelmar Tankers and is heir to his father Loucas's vast Troodos shipping empire, has nearly completed plans for launching the airline in early October.

"We want to test the concept first between a London airport and Glasgow and Edinburgh," he said. "Our research has shown that people in both Britain and continental Europe are crying out for an American-style operation that will give them instant access to really cheap, reliable and safe air travel."

Every aspect of the operation is designed to reduce costs. Easy Jet is playing off Luton and Stansted airports to get the lowest possible landing and handling charges. It is also scouring Britain for, initially, two modern jets — such as an Airbus A320 or a Boeing 737 — to lease. The aircraft will be painted in Easy Jet colours and tickets will be available direct only from the airline or at the check-in desk before departure. There would be no allocated seats, no inflight entertainment and the minimum number of cabin crew members to satisfy the Civil Aviation Authority's tough safety regulations.

A former Air Canada official has been appointed managing director. Other top posts have been filled by senior executives from Thomas Cook, British Airways and Jersey European Airways.

Mr Haji-Ioannou said: "By leasing the aircraft and using an existing British air operator's certificate, we can bypass most of the problems involved in starting an airline and keep costs to a minimum. Air travel is a commodity just like any other and with the liberalisation that will soon exist within Europe, anyone who has set up a no-frills operation which has become well known and is shown to work efficiently must have a chance of proving as successful as the low-cost carriers in America."

The Haji-Ioannou family, however, faces a problem in Italy, which could damage its image during the setting up of the airline. Court proceedings are still pending over shipwreck and pollution claims. The claims follow the loss of the tanker *Haven* off Genoa in 1991, in which five crew were killed and oil spewed into the Mediterranean. The potentially serious allegations are strenuously denied by both father and son.

If however, Easy Jet is successful, it could put tremendous pressure on existing airlines such as British Airways, British Midland and Air UK. A standard "walk-on" economy return fare to Glasgow or Edinburgh from London now costs £234.

The no-frills concept has been a huge success in America, driving down the cost of internal flights by at least 40 per cent and forcing many established carriers such as Continental and United to introduce their own cut-price operations. But most European scheduled airlines argue that passengers are not willing to accept such a simple service. "Europe is not ready for the peanut flight," a senior British Airways executive dismissively suggested recently.

To learn more why not visit .... easyLand today?

easyLand Croydon, 22 Addiscombe Road, CR0 5PE, UK

easyLand Park Royal, N Circular Road, London on Sep 2018. Now an easyStorage Location

To assist in future proofing its business model easyGroup Ltd of the UK decided it was a good idea to have a wholly owned subsidiary in the EU27. easyGroup Europe Ltd was registered as a company in Cyprus in 2019, (reg 562415) with local director marios.missirlis@stelios.com resident on the island which is the birthplace of Stelios' parents.

In June 2023 easyGroup IP Ireland Limited was set up as a second wholly owned subsidiary to support efforts in brand protection outside the UK.

easyLand, 28 Bvd de la Republique,
02640 Beausoleil, France

easyLand, Evripidou 10,
Athens 105 59, Greece

Find your local branch

Please visit www.easyLand.biz for details on easyLand locations.
For further information, visit our local website portals:

www.easy.co.uk

www.easygroup-france.fr

www.easy.tm.mc

www.easy.com.cy

www.easyGroup.com.gr

Exterior and interior of easyLand, Palias Ilektrikis, Nicosia, Cyprus

1995: easyWay

By late 1995 easyJet employees and other airport workers had begun referring to the short road that led up to easyLand as easyWay, rather than easyJet way. People often say that easy Street as a road name had a better ring to it, but the main airport approach road was already called airport way.

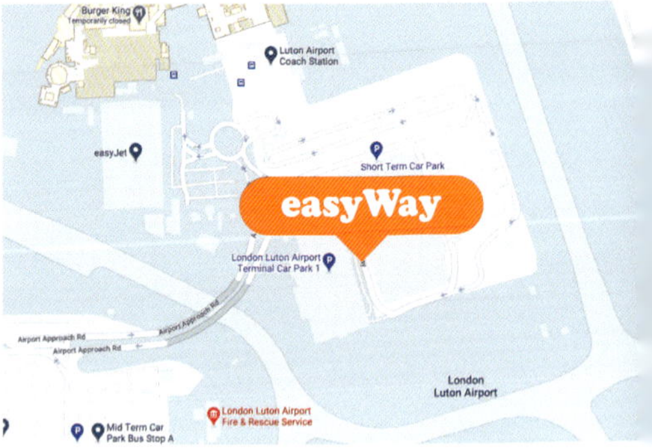

Google Maps shows location of easyWay, Luton

Anthony Rowbotham - General Manager Business Development at Luton Airport in 1995 picks up the story: "At one of our easyJet progress meetings in early summer 1995, someone asked whether we should name the short road that easyLand was situated on. One or two instantly forgettable names were suggested, probably by me, when someone came up with what some of us thought was a genius name; "easy Street". It had the brand/name, and moreover its connotation seemed to fit very well with the ethos of easyJet – laid back, cool, no worries.

Sadly, as history attests, the suggestion was over-ruled – my hunch is that it was probably believed, rightly or wrongly, that the owners of the airport at the time, Luton Council, would not see such a name fitting with their view

easyWay Feb 2020

easyWay Feb 2020

of what image the airport should project. That's how the road ended up instead becoming known as "easy Way" it didn't quite have the ring of easy Street but Stelios seemed happy!

The new name was registered in the official publication "National Address Gazeteer" and our postal address became: easyJet airline company, easyLand, easy Way, Luton Airport. Following the demolition of easyLand in 2015, easy Way now runs between two multi-storey car parks and is used by every passenger as they leave the airport by car or bus. Hardly the most glamorous location for a piece of brand history! easyWay, UK trademark number UK00003407861. You can book your holiday accommodation online via our website www.easyWay.holiday.

easyLand in 2005 with easyWay alongside (photo: P Ryan)

1995: Relentless innovation

easy yield management

Offering a fair price is central to the easy brand. Before the arrival of easyJet in 1995 British Airways and the other big European airlines had been applying their own version of yield management.

For the majority of routes departing from the UK, fares were typically higher in the summer and lower in the winter. But the prices were not set by the market because British Airways lacked serious competition on the Scottish routes and their high costs meant they were unable to offer low fares on a long-term basis. Fare rules requiring passengers to stay over a Saturday night to qualify for the lowest price were designed to stop business travellers from benefiting. The lack of true competition kept fares artificially high and allowed the big legacy airlines to rip off their passengers.

As easyJet became a more mature business the process of yield management became increasingly sophisticated and automated. But at its heart was a simple principle: that the market sets the price according to supply and demand. Sell the last seat at the highest possible price on the day of departure. This means that generally speaking the earlier you book, the less you pay. The more units that are sold, the higher the price moves reflecting the law of supply and demand.

Stelios applied similar principles of yield management to many of the new easy businesses when they first launched including: easyEverything, easyRentacar, easyCruise and easyCinema.

be different on pricing

With the launch of easyJet Stelios introduced a fundamentally different approach to pricing:

1. In the early days, prices were set in simple multiples of £10 with the lowest standard fare of £29.

2. A single fare class.

3. All fares were one-way, no Saturday night stay rule.

4. Fares could be reduced below £29 for promotional purposes.

5. Once booked, fares were strictly non-refundable

easyJet Daily Mail ad June 1996

easyEverything – Yield managing internet time 1999

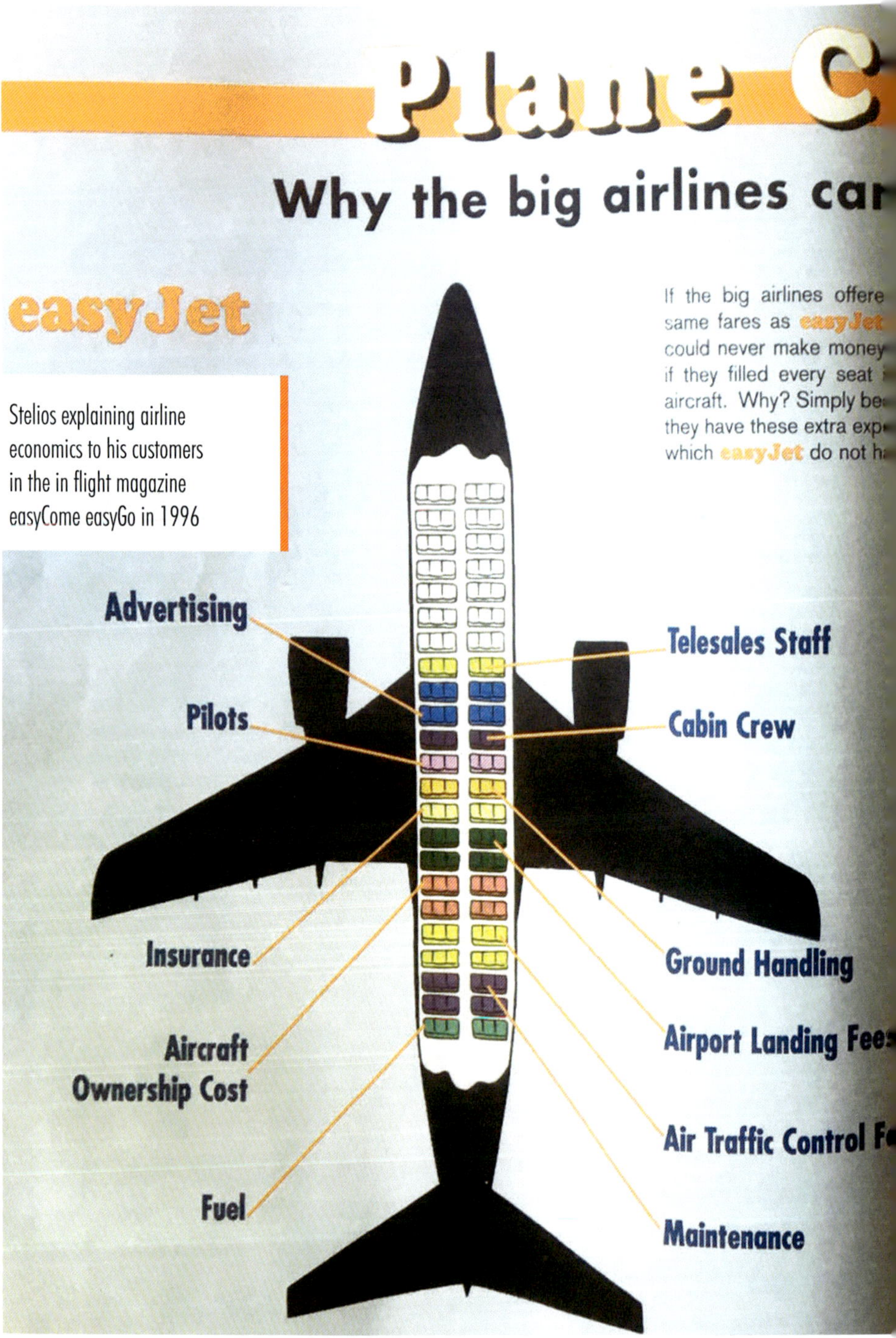

Stelios explaining airline economics to his customers in the in flight magazine easyCome easyGo in 1996

parison

pete with easyJet prices!

BIG AIRLINE

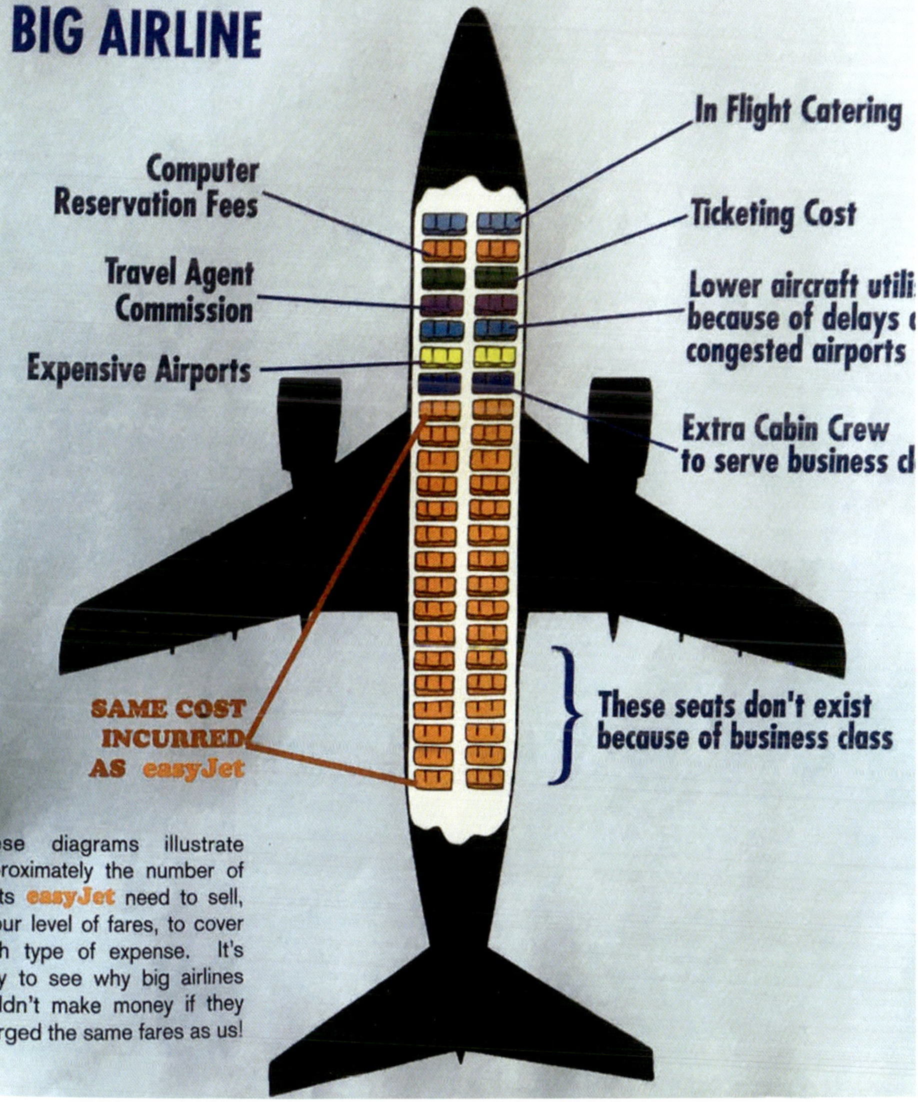

ıese diagrams illustrate ›proximately the number of ›ats **easyJet** need to sell, our level of fares, to cover ›ch type of expense. It's ›sy to see why big airlines ›uldn't make money if they ›arged the same fares as us!

1995:

Another easy world 1st
Relentless innovation

Cutting out the middle man

Selling ticketless travel direct to the public via telephone

On 18th October 1995 Stelios unveiled his idea to the world's media. The launch event took place at the Planet Hollywood restaurant in Leicester Square, London in front of a large audience of very sceptical journalists. He reasoned that because low-cost airlines had originated in the

easyJet plane with telephone number 1995

United States, taking the journalists to an American themed restaurant might help them understand the concept.

The new airline became the first in the world to completely cut out travel agents and sell 100% direct to the public. Stelios was inspired by how the then pioneering insurance firm Direct Line had cut out insurance brokers featuring a red telephone in its advertising, so he decided to paint the telephone number on the side of the plane. This was to emphasise that seats could only be booked direct by calling easyJet.

Classified ad The Scotsman 1995

FT FINANCIAL TIMES

Tycoon's airline se

EasyJet looks to provide cheap Euro

Sir Freddie Laker, one-time champion of cut-price flying, says today's passengers expect to pay for service. Mr Richard Branson, who once sold cheap seats on Virgin Atlantic, now provides high-paying travellers with an on-board manicurist.

But Mr Stelios Haji-Ioannou, 28, insists Europeans want to travel cheaply, and he intends next month to start flying them from Luton airport in Bedfordshire to Scotland on EasyJet, his new airline. Next spring, he plans to start flying to four, as yet unnamed, continental European cities.

Mr Haji-Ioannou, a second generation Greek Cypriot shipping tycoon, says EasyJet, which w
be launched next week, will
Europe's answer to cut-price
carriers such as Southwest A
lines and ValuJet. The flig
from Luton to Glasgow and Ed
burgh, in leased Boeing 737s w
an orange livery, will cost only
much as "a pair of jeans".

Mr Haji-Ioannou concedes t
does not provide a very accur
measure of what his prices w
be. "I think Giorgio Arma
makes jeans," he admits.

Prices will, however, be low
than those offered on the L
don-Scotland routes by Brit
Airways and British Midla
which sell return tickets for £

Southwest and ValuJet are t

The Financial Times announcing the arrival of cheap European flights on 14 October 1995 about one month before the first flight.

·or Luton take-off

ı flights, writes Michael Skapinker

·cess stories of low-cost travel. ·ere have been many more fail- ·s on both sides of the Atlan- including People Express and ·cer Airways, recently revived Sir Freddie as a higher-fare ·ration.

Mr Haji-Ioannou, who left his father's business to start his own ·pping company three years ·, will aim to appeal to busi- ·s people who pay for flights of their own pockets, as well leisure travellers who fly on ·pulse.

·uton is not the kind of place · travels to on impulse. Mr ·i-Ioannou says the airport is misunderstood. It is only 27 minutes by train from King's Cross station and a half-hour drive from north London.

He will announce next week what his on-board offerings will be, but he says he will provide more than peanuts. He called the carrier EasyJet because he wanted to convey how easy it would be to travel on it. There will be no tickets. Passengers will book by telephone, or via the Internet, and simply turn up.

Many in the aviation industry doubt Europe will take to such a service. Mr Haji-Ioannou says: "Twenty years ago, people said Europeans would never eat hamburgers."

1995:

Another easy world 1st
Relentless innovation

Cutting out the middle man

continued

A "flying telephone" device also featured on the first two aircraft and in some early advertising. This was soon dropped as Stelios believed the easyJet logo should be simple and uncluttered.

Stelios avoided expensive telephone number prefixes, where the receiving company pays for the call. He therefore adopted the Luton area code 01582 and looked for a suitable number.

easyJet call centre at easyLand

A local mini-cab company was using the number 01582-445566 so Stelios made them an offer to sell, which they accepted. He was attracted to 44-55-66 because it was rising (like an airplane) and Stelios could pronounce it easily on the radio commercials that he personally voiced over.

He also eliminated paper tickets (older readers may remember those carbon copy IATA coupons). All passengers had to do was take a reference number to the check-in desk. That meant more money was available for advertising and PR rather than being wasted on paying commissions to travel agents.

Stelios at the easyJet call centre - Nov 1995

Stelios in recording booth for radio commercials

Lorraine Chase - famous in the 70s for Luton connection and Campari TV ads

1995: The first easy advertisements

At the launch event held in Planet Hollywood, London Stelios stood up on a stage in front of an audience of journalists and announced easyJet would fly passengers between Luton and Scotland at fares as low as £29 one way, or as the advertising campaign put it 'the price of a pair of jeans!'

This was an incredibly low fare at the time given that BA were charging £240 for the round trip unless passengers stayed over a Saturday night. Some of the journalists present laughed when Stelios announced the £29 fare, they did not think it was possible to make money at such low prices.

Fly for the price of pair of jeans Nov 1995

THE WEEK

CAMPAIGN OF THE WEEK

EASYJET AIRLINE

Jock Wilson
Director
Propeller Marketing Communications

Forget the glamorous image of air travel. Place to the back of your mind the million-pound production budgets of the world's favourite airline. Ignore, too, the merits of chauffeur-driven trips to the airport, extra leg room, express check-ins and dedicated lounges for the cosseted high-flying executive.

Welcome instead to the prosaic world of the UK's newest – and possibly cheapest airline – EasyJet. EasyJet is the brainchild of Greek shipping tycoon Stelios Haji-Ioannou and is offering three-times-a-day flights from Luton (or London Luton as the airport's spindoctors now call it) to Scotland for the outrageously cheap price of £29 single. The campaign claims to make flying as cheap as buying a pair of jeans and at this price a journey home to Scotland would be a tenner cheaper then my last pair of 501s.

The mixed-media campaign using posters, TV and press will certainly not be a runner for any awards, and it would make the role of agency creative directors redundant. But the ads are clear, simple and to the point: you can fly to Scotland for £29 single. And this, of course, is exactly what the customer wants to know. While the airline is primarily aiming at travellers who have to dip into their own pocket to pay the airfare, canny finance directors, keen to cut the corporate travel budget, have also been targeted with ads in the *Financial Times* and *Times*.

Flying from unfashionable Luton to Glasgow and from this Friday, Edinburgh, the airline keeps its cost and airfares low. The middleman is by-passed as all seats are booked direct with the airline either by phone or over the Internet, cutting out the travel agent and his commission.

The campaign has also been produced in-house without an agency with all savings invested back into media budget.

In fact, no media opportunity has been wasted. The aircraft themselves have become part of the campaign with the direct booking line emblazoned in vivid orange the fuselage creating a cheeky direct response at the point-of-sale.

According to the fledgling airline, the Scottish route is a precursor to an assault on Europe. Good luck to them.

I will certainly be an EasyJet customer. At last it will be able to make regular trips back North of the border to sample the pleasures of watching Dunfermline Athletic without it costing the same as a trip to New York.

Ad campaign of the week Nov 1995

Having taken the decision to cut out the travel agents, easyJet needed to invest heavily in advertising to fill its aircraft. In the first two months alone Stelios spent well over £1 million on advertising. This was significantly more than had been anticipated in the business plan. Initially the focus was on press and radio advertising but by late November 1995 with British Airways heavily promoting a new low fare from Heathrow to Scotland, he decided to create a television campaign.

Anti train ad Nov 1995

1995: The first easy advertisements

continued

Clearly Stelios was already planning for route expansion because it was impossible to recoup the money spent on advertising while operating a two aircraft fleet. The messaging in the early adverts was simple and direct, always featuring the £29 price and the telephone number.

Stelios was not afraid to be controversial. He liked to poke fun at travel agents and the train companies as well as British Airways.

Evening Standard ad 31/10/95

easyJet TV ad November 1995

Stelios with early easyJet advert in Scotland

When the travel agents and the rail companies complained he ran the adverts again! The first easyJet crew uniform consisted of a pair of black jeans and a simple orange polo shirt (purchased from a Benetton store). This was embroidered on the back with the white easy logo.

1995:

Another easy world 1st
Relentless innovation

easyKiosk

Selling food & drink

easyKiosk food & drink prices 1996

Stelios' long-term ambition was to establish a family of brands employing the over-arching 'easy' prefix. He also recognised he could not be the expert at everything. For this reason, he chose to do business with different partners when launching new easy brands. An early example came in 1995 when he signed a brand licence agreement with the catering company Alpha in-flight, allowing them to sell snacks and drinks using the brand easyKiosk (again worth noting that it was easyKiosk and not easyJet kiosk). Back in 1995 most other airlines were offering 'free' in-flight meals to their passengers, resulting in higher fares and added complexity. But as Stelios liked to say 'there is no such thing as a free lunch'. This was one of his favourite expressions he'd picked up from his studies as an economist at the London School of Economics between 1984 and 1987.

Stelios still claims that he was the first person in aviation history to charge for a cup of coffee on board, something which is today commonplace, including on British Airways. easyKiosk trademark filed June 1999 number 1196138. Book travel at www.easyKiosk.travel.

easyKiosk in Flight International magazine article 01 Nov 1995

EasyJet launches with easy fares

THE EASYJET Airline Company (*Flight International*, 9-15 August) is to start scheduled services from London Luton Airport on 10 November, with three daily services (two at weekends) to Glasgow, adding similar frequencies to Edinburgh on 24 November. Services will initially be operated by GB Airways with Boeing 737-200s, until EasyJet obtains its own air-operator's certificate early in 1996, when it plans to add several European destinations to its network.

EasyJet is staking everything on a concept of direct customer sales (by-passing the travel agent), and rock-bottom, simple fares. Only single, non-restrictive fares are offered, starting at a very low £29. For the first two weeks, all seats will be available at this price.

After that, the fare structure will be based on guaranteed numbers of progressively more expensive seats for each flight: the first to be sold will be at £29, with the rest being sold at £39, £49 or one of £59 from Stansted to Prestwick — with free rail travel to anywhere in Scotland thrown in.)

The in-flight service is based on an "EasyKiosk", which offers the passenger only what he/she is willing to pay for.

The airline is owned by chairman and chief executive Stelios Haji-Ioannou, founder of the

Haji-Ioannou: what

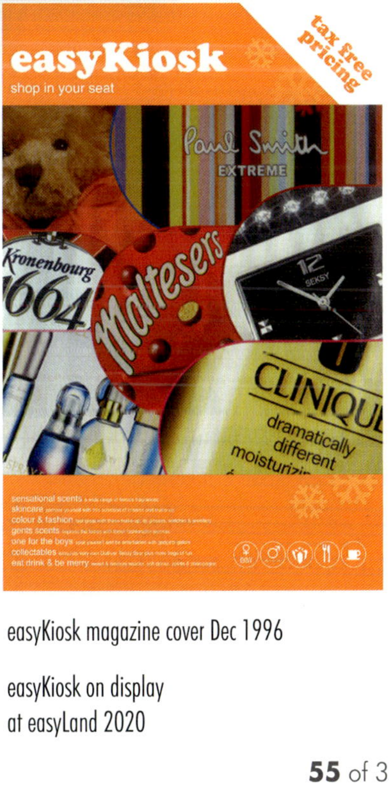

easyKiosk magazine cover Dec 1996

easyKiosk on display at easyLand 2020

1995: The first EZY flight

On 10th November 1995, just after 7am on a wet and windy morning, the first ever easyJet flight (a leased Boeing 737-200) took off from Luton Airport bound for Glasgow with the flight designation **EZY** 121 and the airlines founder in the jump-seat of the cockpit. Stelios never wanted to become a pilot and always said he left the flying of the planes to professionals but that day he sat in the cockpit because all other seats were full. For the first and only time on an easyJet flight the passengers were served a complimentary glass of champagne courtesy of

Stelios sitting in the jump seat for the first EZY flight

Evening Standard 10/11/95

Evening Standard

EVENING STANDARD *** FRIDAY, 10 NOVEMBER, 1995 19

Take-off for trip costing less than a pair of jeans

ELEVEN minutes late and in a blaze of lurid orange, a new dawn broke today in bargain basement British air travel. EasyJet, the no-frills airline, flew its first passengers from Luton to Glasgow for £29 each, boasting a service cheaper than any rival form of transport — with the exception of hitch-hiking — with a seat costing less than a pair of jeans.

Arriving at Luton before dawn to check in for the inaugural 7.20am departure of flight EZY 121, a Boeing 737, passengers were greeted by people, posters and party decorations decked out in the bright tangerine hue of the upstart airline's livery.

by DAVID TAYLOR

It would be unkind to dub this the shellsuit shuttle — there were perhaps no more than four tracksuits on board — but even the tycoons were dressing down.

Company chairman Stelios Haji-Loannou, a 28-year-old Greek shipping magnate, set the tone wearing a polo shirt and orange baseball cap.

Business travellers accustomed to cooked breakfasts may have frowned at the £2.50 "picnic pack" offering a breakfast including crisps and a Mars bar, but the emphasis is on keeping prices down.

Snacks and drinks are on sale on board and handed out by stewardesses in orange polo shirts. It is cheap and cheerful, and if first impressions are anything to go by the punters love it. First on board were Tracy Elliott and James Gould, looking distinctly red-eyed after driving two hours from Portsmouth and sleeping overnight in the airport.

The pair, junior ranks in the Royal Navy, were heading for a weekend of hill-walking around Loch Lomond. "If they keep the price low we will travel more often. This is much quicker than taking the car or the train," Tracy said.

Sister Sarah and Sister Frances, nuns from the Daughters of Charity of St Vincent de Paul convent at Mill Hill, said they were paying £126 return between them including airport tax.

Sister Sarah said. "We were going up for a meeting and I was going to drive but we discovered it was a very cheap flight and a very fast check-in."

Valerie Denaeyer, 60, of Potters Bar, was travelling up and down in a day to see her sick mother-in-law in Hamilton, outside Glasgow. "The drive takes about eight hours, but this way I'll be with her by 10am and home for midnight."

The plane touched down in Glasgow to a round of applause reminiscent of a charter flight to the Costa del Sol. The time 8.41am, 11 minutes late, but chairman Stelios was bullish.

"You can blame it on the cameramen, not the airline," he said.

He has reason to be optimistic, having sold 11,000 seats in the 22 days since the company was launched.

The airline looks set to have jets flying on average four-fifths full in the first few weeks. It has promised that at least half of the seats on its flights will be available at £29 one way, rising to a maximum of £59 for a single ticket as places fill up.

Three flights a day and two at weekends now link Luton and Glasgow, with a Luton-Edinburgh service starting on 24 November.

Lined up for success: Airline EasyJet claims only hitch-hiking is cheaper

Stelios. Tagging along for the ride was a film crew from the BBC's Money Programme who captured footage from the inaugural flight. The aircraft was in fact operated by another airline called GB Airways using the easyJet brand under licence.

Mock-up of the departure board of the first EZY flight from Luton Airport 10th November 1995

The first EZY flight just before departure with Stelios waving

1995: The first EZY flight .... continued

Stelios was doing what he has always done best since then: focusing on the brand building and leaving the operations to trusted business partners. The pilots were employed by GB Airways, but the cabin crew were hired by easyJet to be the face of the brand on board.

Glasgow Evening Times
to London?
Going up... up... and away
Easy! Give 'em what they want
01582 44 55 66 easyJet 01582 44 55 66

Glasgow Evening Times 10 Nov 1995

easyJet returns to London Luton Airport in 1995

Stelios with easyJet cabin staff in 1995

Pilots & easyJet staff take flight in 1995

They earned a basic salary plus commission from on board sales of refreshments under the easyKiosk brand. It is worth noting that from that first flight up to the present day almost 1 billion passengers have travelled holding a boarding pass with EZY on it. Every flight is announced at every gate as EZY (pronounced easy) plus the numbers. Part of the irony in the development of aviation is that in 1995 GB Airways was also a franchisee of BA whilst in 2007 GB Airways was purchased by easyJet outright (and all goodwill flowed up to easyGroup) thus ditching the BA brand.

1995: The first EZY flight .... continued

The first EZY flight was captured on film by the BBC and photographers from various media publications. Here you can see images of passengers checking-in, being greeted by Stelios and boarding the plane.

Check-in at London Luton Airport (top & left)

Stelios greets passengers

Stelios with Luton Airport CEO Richard Gooding

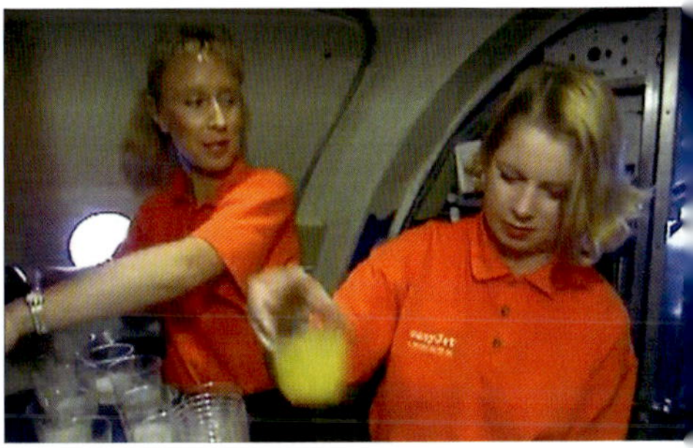

Brisk sales from the easyKiosk

Stelios arrives at Glasgow Airport (above)
Passengers boarding at Luton Airport (below)

Stelios with marketing director Tony Anderson reading Scottish newspapers at Glasgow Airport

1995: easy begins outdoor advertising

In 1995 Stelios decided that easyJet would cut out the travel agent and become the first airline in the world to sell 100% direct to the public. He realised it would require a sustained multi-million pound investment in above the line advertising across a range of European markets to build awareness of his airline. The challenge was even greater because at that time the low-cost, no-frills concept was so new. People had become accustomed to paying the high fares of the national airlines like British Airways.

easyJet poster Luton Airport 1997 Credit: P. Ryan
easyEverything Tram 1999 (below)

Other mass market easy brands like easyEverything (later easyInternetcafe) and easyCar also required substantial advertising investment to build widespread awareness. For each of these brands, outdoor advertising was to play a key role in getting their message across to the public.

Today of course the internet allows advertisers to be much more precise about their targeting, but before the internet started to become mainstream around 1999, the best way to reach the mass market was through press, radio, television and so-called 'outdoor advertising' on posters and billboards. The bright orange colour of the easy family of brands meant that outdoor advertising was particularly impactful.

easyJet London Taxi advertising 08 Aug 1996

easy London Taxis Aug 2015

1995: easy begins outdoor advertising .... continued

easyJet advertising at Spurs Stadium 1996

Stelios used a variety of different outdoor media to get his message across including buses, posters, taxis and trams.

A big advantage of outdoor advertising is that a wide campaign can provide a very strong brand presence in a particular town or city but also permits targeting of a particular strategic location through long term lease of a billboard in a specific location. Underground systems in London and other cities have been used extensively by members of the easy family of brands over the years.

easyJet branded luggage trolleys 1997 Credit: P.Ryan

easyJet outdoor London Campaign advertising 1996

easyInternetCafe advert in McDonald's Swiss Cottage 2004

easyCar advert on London Black Cabs in 2011

1995: easy in media & entertainment

Airline TV series

From day one and for nearly 30 years, Stelios has earned a reputation for using the media not as paid advertising, but to generate name awareness of the easy brand at no extra cost. That's why he allowed BBC TV cameras to film easyJet's first flight in 1995 from the inside.

Since then the easy brand has been featuring regularly on global television. 'Airline' a fly-on-the-wall TV docu-soap featuring staff and passengers of easyJet started filming with Stelios in 1998 and was first broadcast on the UK's ITV channel in 1999. It ran until a 9th series in 2007 with a total of 205 episodes. In 2003 'Airline' was the most popular factual programme on ITV with up to 12.6 million viewers per episode placing it just behind EastEnders and Coronation Street in the national TV ratings The Airline theme tune 'Come fly with me' brings instant recall of easyJet. Repeats were still being broadcast as recently as December 2019 on CBS Reality in Europe, the Middle East and Africa.

The series has been sold and broadcast into many countries around the world including New Zealand, Australia and Japan, increasing the global profile and awareness of the easy brand.

In 2018 ITV in partnership with easyJet produced a TV series called "Inside the cockpit" narrated by Stephen Fry. The series showed close up the training of a professional pilot from selection to flying their first paying passengers. The popularity of the show led to a second season airing in 2019.

easyJet on prime time TV

1995:

easy in media & entertainment

continued

The airline series was not the only docusoap to feature a member of the easy family of brands.

In 2005 in partnership with Sky TV, Stelios produced a TV series called 'Cruise with Stelios', featuring the passengers and crew of the newly launched easyCruiseOne. The programme ran for three seasons in the UK and was also broadcast on the Travel Channel in the United States under the title "Cruiseline".

Evening Standard

Cruise with Stelios
Sky One, 9.00 pm
This entertainingly follows the man who helped revolutionise air travel as he attempts to do the same on the high seas. Not content with planes, cars and internet cafés, Stelios Haji-Ioannou explains the thinking behind EasyCruise which, he says, will revolutionise cruising,

easyCruise show time Evening Standard 29/04/ 2005 easyCruiseOne at sea (below)

Jeremy Clarkson interviews Stelios 1998

Stelios himself has made innumerable TV appearances on news channels and factual documentaries. In November 1998 he was interviewed by TV personality Jeremy Clarkson for the Clarkson show broadcast on BBC2. The episode had the second highest audience of the series attracting over 3 million viewers.

Promotional material for easyJet on-board movies 2011

1995: easy in media & entertainment

continued

easyCinema Milton Keynes entrance

On 30th October 2001 Stelios informed the Financial Times that he was planning to open a movie theatre to be known as easyCinema. Two years later the cinema opened in Milton Keynes, showing movies to cinemagoers from as little as 20p. The cinema operation was highly innovative for example it was the first in the UK to allow entry using barcode scanning.

Unfortunately, the film distributors opposed the disruption that easyCinema was causing to the industry and in particular the fact that it was lowering prices for customers, so they refused to release the latest films to Stelios.

Evening Standard

Stelios has no-frills cinema in the frame

EasyJet tycoon joins Notting Hill demo to promote latest venture

easyCinema launch in Evening Standard 03 Mar 2004

The Guardian

Stelios plans to make the big screen cheaper

Richard Adams

Serial entrepreneur Stelios Haji-Ioannou has plans to make it big in the movies – using the same formula he has applied to EasyJet airline seats and EasyCar rental cars.

The Guardian 8 Apr 2002

This led to Stelios finding an alternative use for the brand and from 2005 the easyCinema brand was applied to an online DVD rental business run in partnership with Lovefilm who acquired the business before being bought by Amazon.

In 2011 easyJet launched a service in partnership with media company Mezzo to provide passengers with devices allowing them to view blockbuster movies and TV series during their flight.

Evening Standard

Stelios's cinemas zoom in on London

By Robert Lea

EASYJET multi-millionaire Stelios Haji-Ioannou is planning to bring his struggling cinemas venture to the capital in a bid to prove his revolutionary ticket-pricing business model can work in this sphere.

With his pilot easyCinema project in Milton Keynes failing to take off — its billing of "second-run" films are showing to 80%-empty movie theatres at its multiplex in the new town — Haji-Ioannou believes his only chance

tem of book early-save money is working.

"It is the industry side that's not good, with the distributors not giving us first run films. That means we are only trading at the industry average of being 20% full."

Haji-Ioannou is convinced that his website-based "yield management" techniques, honed at easyJet, for attracting larger volumes of customers by offering them cheaper tickets the earlier they ... to the movie

... the losses on ... have so ... than £1 ... nou is ... invest-

... expert- ... it stop- ... ia] was ... id the

The Economist

Economics and reality

The Big Easy

Stelios Haji-Ioannou is attempting to bring the dismal science to undismal life—with mixed results

IT IS perhaps fitting that micro-economics should have one of its most interesting ideas tested in Milton Keynes, a smallish town north of London which combines (by accident) the names of two of the last century's greatest economists. The 600-odd people who went to the opening showing of easyCinema there last Friday were doubtless more interested in seeing a film cheaply (prices started at 20p) than in being guinea pigs for the theory of marginal pricing.

But it is this that fires the imagination of Stelios Haji-Ioannou, multi-millionaire, self-publicist and founder of easyCinema, easyJet, a budget airline, easyCar, a car-rental outfit, easyInternetcafé and others. As demand goes up, he argues, so should prices. So people who buy early, or choose slack times of day, get better deals. For example, charges at his internet cafés rise as the seats fill up. The more people that hire his cars, the greater the cost to the remaining customers. The first seats sold on easyJet flights are cheap, the last few the most expensive.

I'm starring in my epic

Evening Standard 9 Dec 2003 (top)
easyCinema article The Economist 31 May 2003

easyCinema Poster (right)
easy outside the movie theatre in Athens 2023 (below)

easyCinema in Greece and Cyprus

View of the Acropolis from Cine Paris Jan 2021 (bottom)
Cine Paris Entrance 2024 (left)

For a number of years, the easyCinema brand was used in partnership with the Cine Paris open air movie theatre in Athens, Greece. Tickets could be purchased via the easyCinema.com website and signage was displayed prominently outside the building.

Cine Paris is located in the historic Plaka neighbourhood of Athens on Kydathineon 22 and offers a magnificent view of the Acropolis and Parthenon. It was opened in the 1920s by a Greek who had made Paris his home for many years and due to the cinema's heritage and magnificent setting it has become a cultural icon. In 2017 Stelios bought the building where the Cine Paris is located and gifted it to his charity, the Stelios Philanthropic Foundation. The whole building has since been refurbished to a high standard in keeping with its heritage.

The Foundation operates a conference hall within the building that it makes available to charities and educational institutions and the cinema is scheduled to officially reopen in May 2024.

easyCinema.gr partnership with Cinobo

Stelios with Dafni Bechtsi 2023

In July 2023 easyGroup reached an agreement to license the easyCinema.gr brand to a Greece based streaming service called Cinobo.

Cinobo was set up in 2020 during the pandemic by a young Greek entrepreneur and film lover called Dafni Bechtsi. Dafni saw a gap in the market for a streaming service that makes available independent and arthouse movies to audiences in Greece and Cyprus who are passionate about quality cinema.

All films are available with subtitles in the Greek language providing access for non-English speakers.

Through easyCinema.gr and easyCinema.com.cy users can sign-up and subscribe to a high-quality streaming service that they can access via mobile devices or at home.

easyCinema.gr Website 10 Apr 2024

1995: continued

easy in media & entertainment

TOP TV SUNDAY PEOPLE

				Million
1	(1)	Coronation St	ITV	17.48
2	(2)	EastEnders	BBC1	14.21
3	(4)	Airline	ITV	12.56
4	(3)	Emmerdale	ITV	11.47
5	(-)	Midsomer Murders	ITV	11.36
6	(-)	Stars In Their Eyes	ITV	10.36
7	(-)	Animal Hospital	BBC1	10.03
8	(-)	Peak Practice	ITV	9.84
9	(6)	National Lottery Live	BBC1	9.81
10	(4)	Changing Rooms	BBC1	9.75

easyJet Airline TV Ratings
The Sunday People 05 Apr 1998

It is inevitable that when you become such a strong brand you invite humour and parody. So it's important not to take yourself too seriously. Stelios decided in 1998 to overrule his advisers and let ITV cameras into the heart of his business empire to film the airline series. He knew that the show would include some mishaps and feature angry customers. Sometimes Stelios himself was filmed trying to placate them by offering free drinks onboard.

1 CORONATION ST.

2 EastEnders

3

One episode of the Airline TV series on ITV in April 1998 attracted 12.6 million viewers.

campaign

EasyGroup entrepreneur Stelios to star in Post Office TV ad

EasyGroup entrepreneur Stelios Haji-Ioannou is to star in the latest Post Office TV commercial, as the network unveils its 'Kids Go Free' travel insurance offer. The 20-second ad, created by Publicis, shows Stelios relaxing on a Spanish beach, surrounded by children playing in the sand and water. He tells viewers that he has had a great idea, that kids should get free travel insurance, and that if anybody else has had the same idea, he will eat his hat. At dinner, Stelios, who appeared in a previous Post Office ad last year, is presented with his garnished hat ready for consumption. Media planning and buying is handled by Carat. The TV campaign will be supported by in-store marketing materials created by Joshua.

Campaign Magazine 06/06/02

Ultimately his decision was vindicated when the show became a huge success and massively boosted the easy brand recognition. Stelios even starred as himself in a mainstream TV commercial paid for by the UK's Post Office in 2002 that used the easy brand values to sell travel currency and travel insurance.

Stelios advertising for The Post Office - 2002

Filming inside his internet cafes and surrounded by easy branded rental cars, it was an amusing way to engage with people through television and to gain name and face recognition.

1995: easy in media & entertainment

easy on YouTube

continued

easyHistory 5th Edition video on the explore easy YouTube page with over 13 million views in three months

When the easy story began in 1994 the internet was still several years from becoming mainstream. Stelios relied on PR and advertising to build his family of brands (with help of course from the Airline TV series!)

In easyJet's early years the best way to reach the mass market was by advertising on national television but this was expensive and poorly targeted.

The arrival of the internet changed everything. Today Stelios still invests millions of pounds every year to build awareness of his brands, but this can be much more effectively targeted than back in the 1990s.

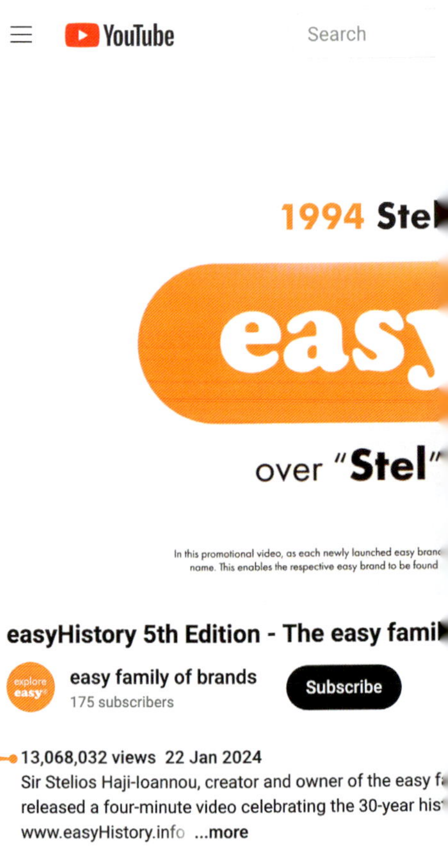

Google pay-per-click (PPC) advertising is one means of attracting customers and easyGroup has been spending on PPC to promote several of its long standing and strategic brands.

Platforms easyGroup uses to promote its brands

Google

Meta

LinkedIn

More recently Stelios has decided to invest money in creating videos as a means of building awareness through social media platforms. The most obvious example is the easyHistory.info video which was launched at the end of January 2024 and by the end of April had already attracted over 13 million views in just three months.

Brand adverts available on the explore easy YouTube channel 2024

Stelios realised that promoting videos on YouTube is a way to build mass market awareness in a cost-effective way and so he instructed his marketing agency to produce a range of videos for different members of the easy family of brands.

Screenshots of a selection of these videos can be seen on these pages. Why not check out the easyHistory channel on YouTube for yourself.

1995: easy in media & entertainment

continued

David Walliams as "Omar Baba" pretending to be Stelios

Since the very early days there have been cartoons featuring easy in a wide range of publications. Stelios himself has been parodied in the 'Come Fly with Me' TV series broadcast by the BBC in 2010 and 2011. This featured an airline called 'Fly Lo' and its boss 'Omar Baba' played by well-known comedian David Walliams of "Little Britain" fame.

David Walliams as normal

easyJet Rising by Tony Anderson

It is a huge compliment to the brand that it works with both cartoon humour and parody on television. It means it is famous enough for the average reader or viewer to get the joke.

There have been books written about us including 'easyJet Rising' by Tony Anderson, who worked for the easy family of brands between 1995-2000.

The Guardian cartoon 21/02/16

The Guardian cartoon 19/11/13

'The Chase' TV Quiz Show February 2020

Barrysbanterbus Instagram
May 2020

1995: easy in internet and telecoms

From time to time, easyGroup acquires the rights to brands from other companies and incorporates them into the easy family. In November 1995 a company called Easy Networks based in Portsmouth was established by an entrepreneur called Richard Gwilliam. They offered internet, network and telecom services to businesses in Portsmouth and the surrounding area. As part of an agreement dated 25th January 2019 all brand rights including those for prior use since 1995 were purchased by easyGroup. The company is now a member of the easy family of brands using the easyNetworks (TM 18060442) brand under licence. Visit easyNetworks.co.uk for more details.

Stelios visits easyNetworks office - April 2019

easyNetworks Signage in Portsmouth

easyNetwork branded Tesla vehicles below

easyNetworks Vuns on location 2022

1995: easy in internet and telecoms

continued

In 2004 Stelios decided to disrupt the telecoms sector by launching easyMobile offering a market leading low-cost tariff in partnership with a Danish telecoms company.

Stelios promoting easyMobile 2004

THE TIMES

EasyGroup ventures into mobile phone deal

By Peter Klinger

STELIOS HAJI-IOANNOU, the serial entrepreneur, has added a mobile phone venture to his easyGroup stable after striking a deal with TDC, the Danish telecoms group.

Mr Haji-Ioannou said easyMobile should be running in the UK by the end of the year. The venture could, however, run into immediate trouble with one of its competitors.

Mr Haji-Ioannou said easyMobile would adopt the easyGroup brand's distinctive orange colour. That prospect has attracted threats of legal action by Orange, the mobile phone business owned by France Télécom.

Mr Haji-Ioannou said any such claims would be without foundation.

Unlike his control over previous ventures, including internet cafes and a car rental business, he will let TDC operate easyMobile, lending it only his brand name.

EasyMobile will be targeted at price-conscious phone users, and will offer pre-paid contracts over the Internet to

The Times - 11/08/04

FT FINANCIAL TIMES

COMPANIES UK

EasyMobile ready to dial up discord

Robert Budden finds that EasyGroup's latest venture, based on a low-cost Danish model, could seriously upset the mobile phone industry

EasyGroup's imminent entry into the mobile phone arena, partnering with T-Mobile, marks the latest grand ambition of Stelios Haji-Ioannou to shake up an established market.

His attempts to break into other industry sectors have been mixed. EasyJet, the low-cost airline, has helped transform the airline business model, forcing established carriers to take a closer look at their costs. But other ventures, such as EasyInternetcafé, have been far less successful, indicating that the Greek entrepreneur is not infallible when it comes to spotting business opportunities.

Mobile operators, which are already coming under pressure from new entrants such as 3 and Virgin Mobile, must be hoping that this latest mobile phone venture will fall into the less-successful category.

However, it may be the likes of Vodafone and Orange that have the most to fear from EasyMobile, judging by the record of Telmore, the low-cost Danish mobile operator that has formed the blueprint for Mr Haji-Ioannou's venture.

"In a relatively short space of time you saw quite a sharp deterioration in margins in Denmark," says one analyst. "At its worst point TDC, the incumbent operator, had ebitda margins in the high 20's. This is pretty much unheard of for a number one operator in a western European market."

Telmore caused a mini price war among its rivals in Denmark as it gained customers on the back of cut-price voice tariffs. One of its strengths was that it sold phone services online, allowing it to cut distribution costs significantly.

However, it also sold just SIMs, the smart-cards that slide inside phones, allowing it to avoid paying the hefty subsidies that mobile operators usually pay to phone manufacturers for supplying phones.

Having suffered at the hands of Telmore, TDC eventually bought the new entrant and the market has since stabilised.

It is unclear how aggressive EasyMobile will be in the UK. Some in the industry expect it to position itself with cut-price deals in a move that could have a significant negative effect on mobile operator profitability.

"If this launch is done well it could be dramatic," says Fred Knops, vice-president of Booz Allen Hamilton, a strategy consulting firm.

"The average acquisition cost of a mobile customer is between £150 and £250, with most of those costs coming from the information technology related to provisioning and sales, plus the subsidy of the handset itself.

"On this basis, it typically takes 9 to 12 months for a customer to have a positive impact on a mobile operator's finances. If EasyGroup can trim the distribution costs by doing its sales online, plus sell phone services without subsidising a handset, it could radically shorten this 9-to-12 month pay-back period. That is the power of it."

The potential impact of a slimmed-down operator with an established brand seeking to gain customers with cut price tariffs explains why mobile operators have been reluctant to do a wholesale deal with EasyMobile.

Having spent £22.5bn in the UK buying 3G licences at the height of the telecommunications boom, the last thing mobile operators want is a renewed price war on voice calls. Voice calls make up more than 80 per cent of mobile operators' revenues with text messaging making up the the bulk of the remainder.

Instead, mobile operators are seeking to take the mobile phone experience upmarket with the launch of services such as live video calling or music video clips downloaded on to phones.

But the arrival of a low-cost brand from outside the mobile market could potentially do more than just alter the business models of the established operators.

Some also believe that EasyMobile could kick-start a gradual revolution in mobile phone distribution as more mobile customers are won online. This explains why retailers such as Carphone Warehouse are watching developments just as closely as the established mobile operators.

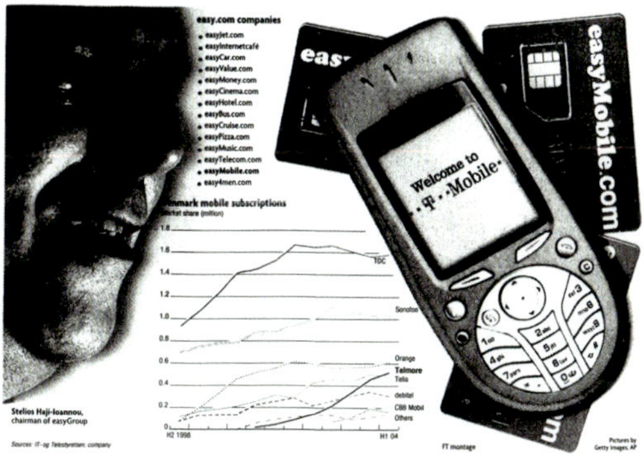

Stelios Haji-Ioannou, chairman of easyGroup

Sources: IT- og Telestyrelsen; company

FT covers the launch of easyMobile Nov 2004

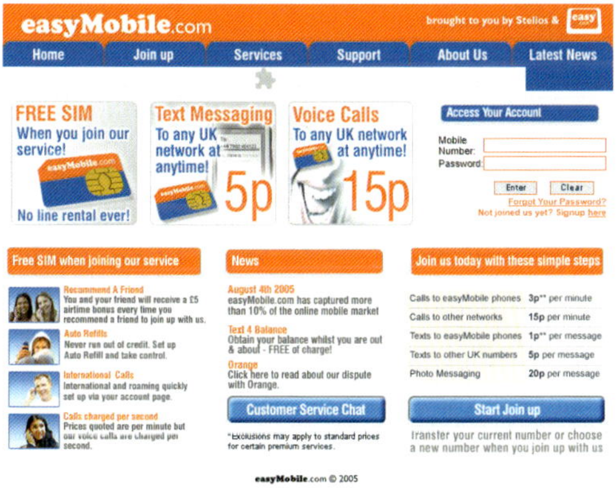

easyMobile.com homepage 2005 (right)

FT FINANCIAL TIMES

Easy Group signs up with T-Mobile

By Robert Budden, Telecommunications Correspondent

Easy Group yesterday confirmed that it has signed a deal with T-Mobile to offer mobile services in the UK as it targets a formal launch of EasyMobile in March next year.

The move, which marks the first foray of entrepreneur Stelios Haji-Ioannou into mobile telephony, is likely to intensify price competition in the UK.

Under the agreement, which is a joint venture between Easy Group and TDC, the Danish telecommunications operator, consumers will sign up to a low-cost mobile service over the internet.

Voice calls will be carried over the UK network of T-Mobile, Deutsche Telekom's mobile arm.

EasyMobile is seeking to strip out expensive distribution costs by just selling SIM cards – the smart cards that slide inside phones – and by restricting sales to the web. A similar venture in Denmark by Telmore – now part of TDC – led to significant price declines across the Danish market.

TDC refused to outline its tariff plans for next March but the company said that its UK pricing model would be similar to its tariff plan in Denmark. There the company charges a simple DKr0.8 (7.5p) per minute for a voice call, one of the cheapest tariffs on the market.

Users are required to spend at least DKr30 a month on voice calls.

There are fears at rival operators that the new tariff plan, backed by the Easy brand, could heighten competition further in the market. The UK boasts five mobile operators with their own networks as well as several other "virtual" operators, such as Virgin Mobile, which piggy-back on the network of an established operator.

TDC said EasyMobile would not aim to be the cheapest on the market but that it would be highly competitive for voice calls.

Stelios visits easyNetworks office Apr 2019 (above)

FT covers easyMobile partner Nov 2004

1995: easy in internet and telecoms

continued

easySim.global

In 2023 Richard Gwilliam, the founder and licensee of easyNetworks launched a new telecoms proposition using the easySim brand available at easySim.global

easySim.global provides travel eSIMs, which can cut the cost of using a mobile phone when travelling abroad. It is available to anyone in the world, travelling to anywhere else in the world.

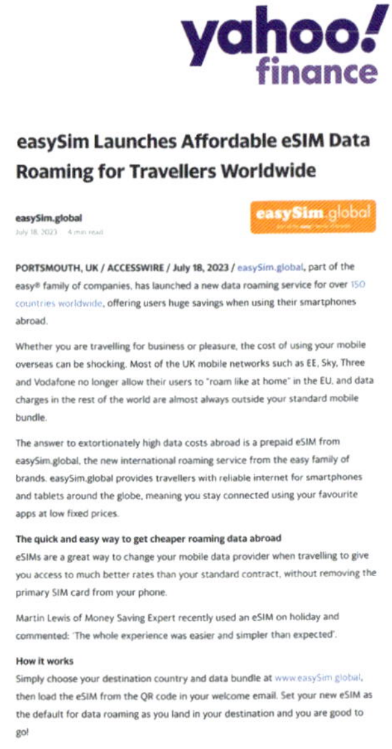

yahoo! finance

easySim Launches Affordable eSIM Data Roaming for Travellers Worldwide

easySim.global
July 18, 2023 · 4 min read

PORTSMOUTH, UK / ACCESSWIRE / July 18, 2023 / easySim.global, part of the easy® family of companies, has launched a new data roaming service for over 150 countries worldwide, offering users huge savings when using their smartphones abroad.

Whether you are travelling for business or pleasure, the cost of using your mobile overseas can be shocking. Most of the UK mobile networks such as EE, Sky, Three and Vodafone no longer allow their users to "roam like at home" in the EU, and data charges in the rest of the world are almost always outside your standard mobile bundle.

The answer to extortionately high data costs abroad is a prepaid eSIM from easySim.global, the new international roaming service from the easy family of brands. easySim.global provides travellers with reliable internet for smartphones and tablets around the globe, meaning you stay connected using your favourite apps at low fixed prices.

The quick and easy way to get cheaper roaming data abroad
eSIMs are a great way to change your mobile data provider when travelling to give you access to much better rates than your standard contract, without removing the primary SIM card from your phone.

Martin Lewis of Money Saving Expert recently used an eSIM on holiday and commented: 'The whole experience was easier and simpler than expected'.

How it works
Simply choose your destination country and data bundle at www.easySim.global, then load the eSIM from the QR code in your welcome email. Set your new eSIM as the default for data roaming as you land in your destination and you are good to go!

easySim Global online Advertising (below)

easySim in Yahoo Finance 18 July 2023 (above)

Advertising value to travellers in 2024 above and below

easySim.global Website in 2024

Most mobile phones and tablets support eSIMs, which work in tandem with a normal SIM card, so customers keep their existing mobile number. easySim enables travellers to take advantage of this technology, to save money.

The eSIM is simple to install and works in over 150 countries, offering savings of up to 95% on home network roaming charges. This allows customers to stay connected, without the fear of a massive bill, when they arrive home.

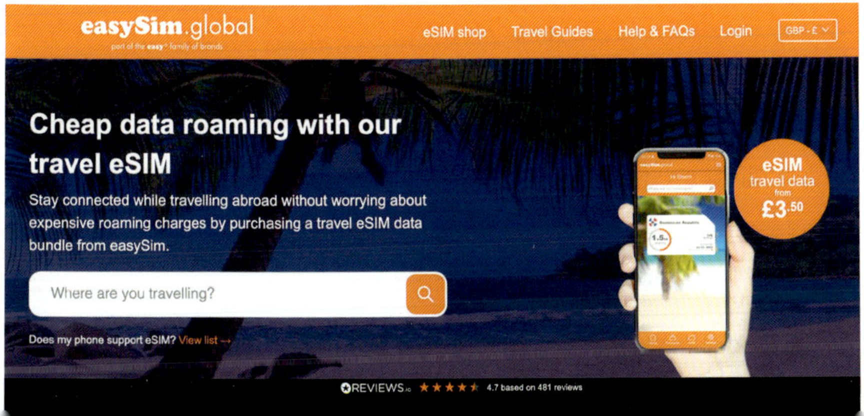

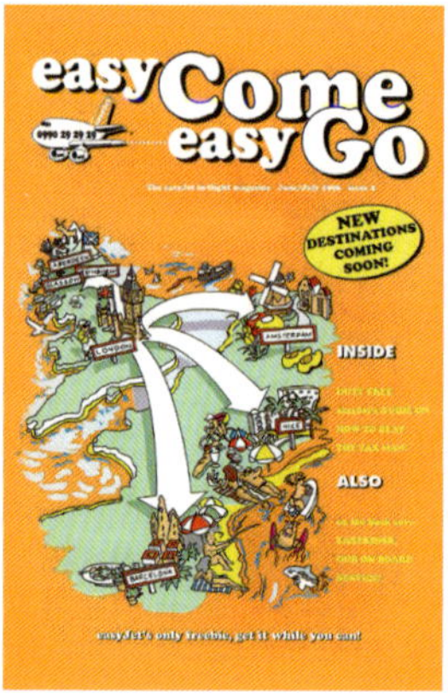

1996 Pages from the second edition of the 'easyCome, easyGo' catalogue from June

1997 easyUpdate Newsletter

1998 easyExtras advertising on booking confirmation letter 12/08/98

1996: Relentless innovation

easy & retail catalogue services

The sale of products on board easyJet flights started in 1996 with each passenger provided with a catalogue, generally in the seat pocket in front of them. Various easy brands have been associated with these retail catalogues over the years including paid advertisements of all the easy family of brands in recent editions.

The first catalogue formed part of the inflight magazine 'easyCome, easyGo'. The catalogue was produced under licence by Alpha Sky Retailing who had special permission to use the 'easy' brand. Even back then the catalogue offered a wide range of goods including perfumes, cosmetics, watches, sunglasses, confectionery and toys.

In 1997, a licence agreement was signed with a company called Travel Extras allowing the sale of ancillary facilities such as hotels and car rental services under the brand 'easyExtras', trademark number 16119869 now seen at www.easyextras.biz. Not only were these ancillary services promoted on easyJet flight confirmation letters which were sent out before the internet became established, the easyExtras brand was also promoted in the retail catalogue alongside the various retail goods being offered (as well as in special promotions with national newspapers such as the Daily Mirror and the Sunday People).

1998 easyKiosk front cover

1998 easyJet Flight confirmation letter

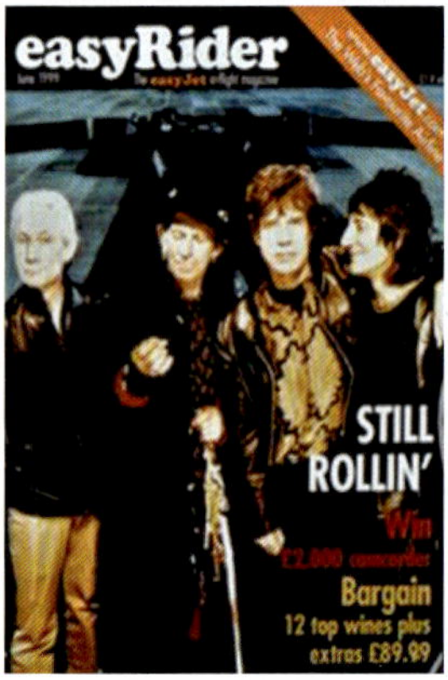

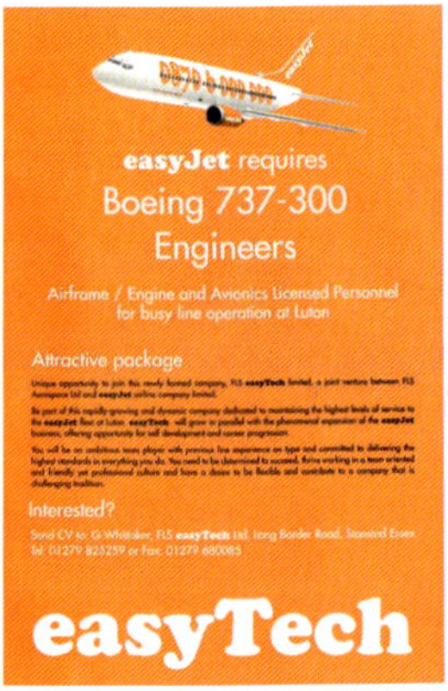

1998 easyRider magazine

1999 easyRider cover June

1999 easyTech job ad 11/05/99

2021 easyJet Boutique Feb 2021

1996: Relentless innovation

easy & retail catalogue services continued

In or around 1997, the inflight magazine was renamed easyRider, seen today at www.easyrider.online and the catalogue was renamed easyKiosk (to bring it in line with the food and drink offering on board which had always been called easyKiosk from the outset).
=The easyUpdate brand also featured regularly as a newsletter within the easyJet In-flight catalogue, now at www.easyupdate.net. easyTech, trademark number 1128743 was a joint venture company set up in 1998 to provide maintenance services to easyJet aircraft. FLS Aerospace were the licensees for the easyTech brand, online at www.easytech.info.

Today, goods are made available to purchase via easyJet's inflight catalogue 'easyJet Boutique' (the latest print edition released October 2019 has a mere 184 pages to explore and offered a much wider variety of goods compared to the first edition of the catalogue promoted under the easyCome, easyGo name). The easyJet Boutique catalogue is now available to browse online via https://buyonboard.easyjet.com. Passengers are able to purchase goods online for collection on board.

easy brands now working with Booking.com

Stelios likes to say that easy brands never die, in fact every easy brand ever created remains in use today. It is of course in the nature of entrepreneurship that not all business ideas work out, some licensees will not be successful and Stelios does not like to see trademarks and domains standing idle.
Through an established partnership with the online travel agent Booking.com easyGroup has found a way to monetise the goodwill in some long-standing easy brands and domains.

easyHostel.com and other easy brands are available in 220 countries offering over 28 million listings of places to stay.

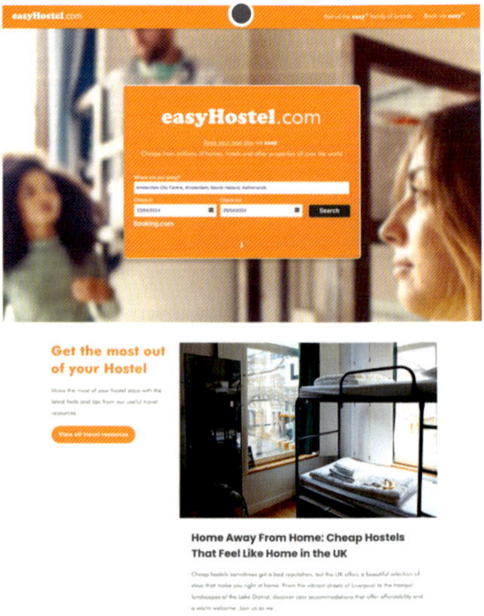

easyHostel.com allowing users to book accommodation via easy.

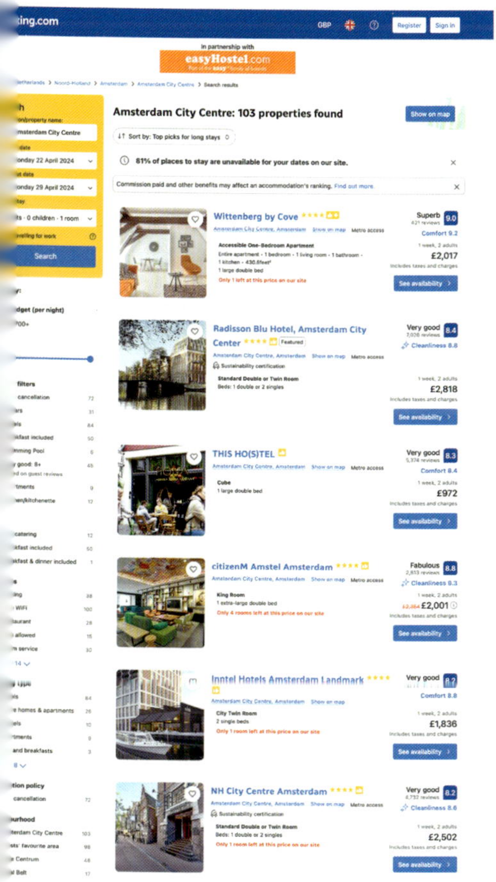

easyHostel Co-branded page on Booking.com

The total transaction revenue (TTV) generated from easy brands listed here working with Booking.com is currently running at over €4 million p.a.

Book your next stay via easy

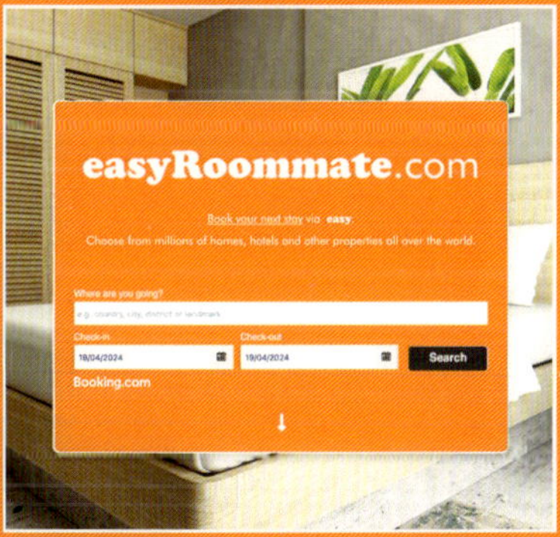

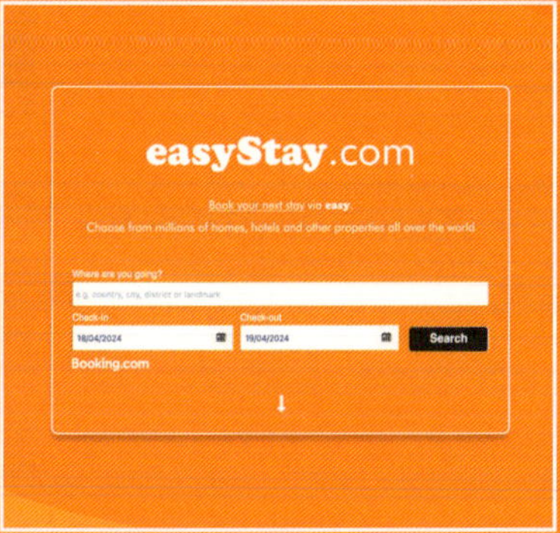

1996: Relentless innovation

easy newspaper promotions

Sell more newspapers using cheap flights

Before the arrival of easyJet, newspaper promotions had been used by airlines including British Airways as a means of shifting seats that would otherwise go unsold, typically in off-peak periods such as the post-Christmas period. Prices would be heavily discounted and were offered for sale well in advance of the travel date to avoid revenue dilution.

This type of promotion usually required customers to collect tokens. These would be printed in successive editions of a newspaper to boost their sales. What Stelios did was to take the idea of the flight promotion and supersize it, taking the volume of seats and the level of discounts to a new level.

The Daily Telegraph

Fantastic flights with easyJet

The Daily Telegraph has teamed up with easyJet, the web's favourite airline, to offer readers fantastic discounts on flights to a host of UK and European destinations.

Edinburgh **£30** rtn

Madrid **£40** rtn

Nice **£42.90** rtn

Athens **£61.20** rtn

Through this offer you can fly to one of 15 exciting cities from just £20 return. There are 25,000 seats available through this promotion which is valid for travel between Monday, September 18 and Saturday, October 28. Full details of the routes, fares and destinations are published below.

easyJet

As one of the key pioneers of e-commerce, easyJet leads the way on the net in the airline industry, reinforcing its position as the web's favourite airline. The company has sold over three million seats online and consistently sells over 70% of all seats over the Internet – no other airline in the world comes close to selling a similar proportion of seats online.

easyJet is at the forefront of Internet innovation and was the first airline to introduce discounts for Internet bookings. All passengers who book their seats online receive a £5 discount on every return trip (£2.50 discount each way).

Bookings for flights departing more than two months ahead can only be made online. And because fares generally increase as the departure date gets closer, this means that the best fares are first available to those who log-on to easyJet.com.

How to book

Bookings for this offer may only be made via the Internet at easyJet.com using the eight letter password published in The Telegraph today. Bookings can be made until midnight on Monday, August 7. For readers who do not have access to the Internet, why not visit an easyEverything Internet shop? There are now six stores in the UK, five in London (Trafalgar Square, Kensington High Street, Victoria, Tottenham Court Road and Oxford Street) and one in Edinburgh (Rose Street). **When you access the easyJet.com site, the promotional flights will be marked by the words 'promo fare'. Other seats marked 'web fare' will also be available. As the number of seats is limited, certain flights and certain dates have already been booked, so please be flexible with your travel arrangements.**

easyJet password: easysale

To take advantage of this offer you need to visit the easyJet.com website and enter the eight letter password published today.

easyJet.com

Flight prices

London Luton to	Telegraph rate single	Telegraph rate return
Liverpool	£15	£20
Aberdeen	£20	£30
Glasgow	£20	£30
Edinburgh	£20	£30
Inverness	£20	£30
Belfast	£20	£30
Amsterdam	£25	£42.30
Geneva	£22.50	£35
Zurich	£32.50	£45
Nice	£25	£42.90
Madrid	£25	£40
Palma de Mallorca	£25	£40
Barcelona	£25	£40
Malaga	£30	£50
Athens	£30	£61.20
Liverpool to	**Telegraph rate single**	**Telegraph rate return**
London Luton	£15	£20
Belfast	£17.50	£25
Amsterdam	£25	£42.30
Geneva	£22.50	£35
Nice	£25	£42.90
Madrid	£25	£40
Palma de Mallorca	£25	£40
Barcelona	£25	£40
Malaga	£30	£50
Gatwick to	**Telegraph rate single**	**Telegraph rate return**
Geneva	£22.50	£35
Stansted to	**Telegraph rate single**	**Telegraph rate return**
Geneva	£20	£30

The Daily Telegraph promotion Aug 2000

Daily Mirror Promotion 1998 (above)

The Times promotion 1999 (below)

The first easyJet promotions were run in 1996 and they soon became an important part of the airline's marketing plans. By 1997 easyJet had established a strong working relationship with the Daily Mirror which at the time had a printed circulation of over two million copies. As well as generating significant revenue, newspaper promotions allowed Stelios to build the easy brand by securing huge amounts of front-page exposure across a range of national newspapers. To get an equivalent amount of advertising space would have cost millions of pounds.

1996: Relentless innovation

easy newspaper promotions continued

Sell more newspapers using cheap flights

ECHO

Liverpool Echo, Thursday, October 16, 1997 5

• Changing times . . . for Barbara Dickson at the Playhouse
Pictures: STEPHEN SHAKESHAFT

Barbara on the button

By Joe Riley, arts editor

IT'S a triple triumph for Barbara Dickson as she shows off three outfits from her new solo show.

But that's less than half the story.

The Scottish-born singer is transporting herself through The 7 Ages of Woman, which opens at the Playhouse tonight .

Edge

The musical journey, with songs by Stephen Sondheim, Kurt Weill and Leiber and Stoller, has a distinctly Liverpool cutting edge.

For there is also music by Lennon and McCartney and Willy Russell.

It was in Russell's 1974 musical, John, Paul, George, Ringo and Bert at the Everyman that former folk singer Barbara became famous and launched a career that included several Top 10 hits.

She later created the role of the mother in Willy Russell's musical Blood Brothers at the Playhouse.

"Liverpool is definitely my musical home," said Barbara prior to curtain-up. "I've really enjoyed putting this show together."

The production has been devised and directed by Chris Bond, a former artistic director of both the Everyman and Playhouse theatres.

Due to demand, an extra Sunday performance of the show has been arranged on October 26 (7pm).

LIVERPOOL ↔ BELFAST

NORSE IRISH FERRIES

norse 'n' easy

FARES TO REMEMBER THIS NOVEMBER

CAR & UP TO 4 PASSENGERS £99 one way

ALL FARES INCLUDE:
• 4 Course evening meal
• Ensuite berth
• Full Breakfast

FOOTPASSENGER 5 DAY RETURN £59

Two die in rage attack

POLICE are hunting a driver who deliberately rammed into another car three times – killing a young couple in a suspected road rage attack.

Toby Exley, 22, and his 20-year-old girlfriend Karen Martin, died after their car crossed the central reservation of the A316 Great Chertsey Road, in Twickenham, west London.

A witness told police that an unidentified second car was following the couple's Ford Fiesta on the westbound carriageway, and slammed into the back of it three times.

On the third collision, the Fiesta was forced over the reservation onto the eastbound carriageway.

The couple suffered multiple injuries when their car was hit by a Vauxhall Cavalier on the other carriageway.

The mystery car failed to stop.

AMSTERDAM £35

NICE £39

The only way to fly.

Liverpool - Amsterdam from £35

Liverpool - Nice from £39

easyJet

Fly our NEW daily non-stop service from Liverpool to Amsterdam and Nice from 27th October

call 01582 700022 anytime

easyJet Ad for new Amsterdam route
Liverpool Echo1997

Before the arrival of the internet, fulfilling these sales via telephone through the easyJet call centre was a huge operational challenge. The sheer volume of calls meant that customers would often have to wait for an agent to be available to take their booking and waiting was never popular.

From 1999 onwards customers could book promotional flights online but of course the arrival of the internet had a devastating impact on the printed newspaper circulation.

easyFood Magazine Covers (left to right) June-July 2022, January-February 2023 & July-September 2023

Under the terms of their licence some easy brands are permitted to promote their goods or services in other colours. A good example is easyCleaning who feature a variety of colours across their product range. This is because cleaning products are often differentiated and categorised by the colour of their bottles and containers.
Here are some examples of easy brand promotion or advertising that do not feature the colour orange

easyJet Telegraph advert
05 Jun 1996
(white logo on black)

easyCleaning products
and advertising Apr 2024

Aural rendering of the easy brand

When Stelios chose EZY as the flight code for his new airline in 1995 he did so because he wanted to embed the word easy in the minds of his customers.
What Stelios could not have predicted at the time was the huge growth of voice as a means of people engaging with technology, including the prevalence of voice assistants like Alexa and Siri.
According to an October 2023 article in the influential website techreport.com

- **41% of US adults use voice search on a daily basis.**
- **The number of voice assistants will reach over 8.4 billion in 2024.**
- **90% of people say voice search is easier and faster than regular search.**

In light of such statistics, the continued growth of voice search and the goodwill built up over many years of millions of people speaking the names of members of the easy family of brands it is unsurprising that Stelios wants to exercise his rights not only with regard to easy in its written form but also its aural equivalents including:

eazy.biz and ezy.group for booking hotel accommodation in partnership with Booking.com

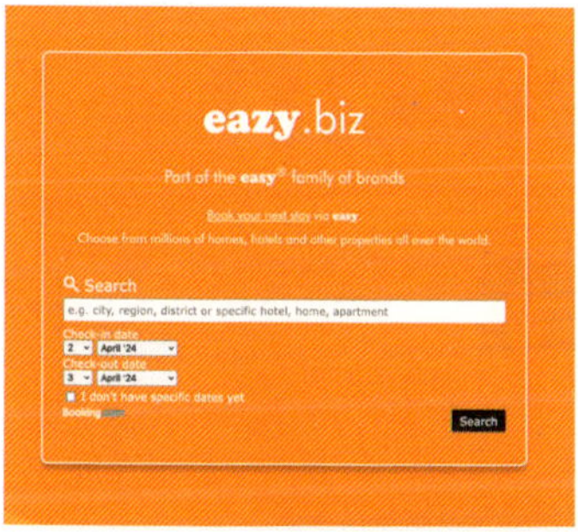

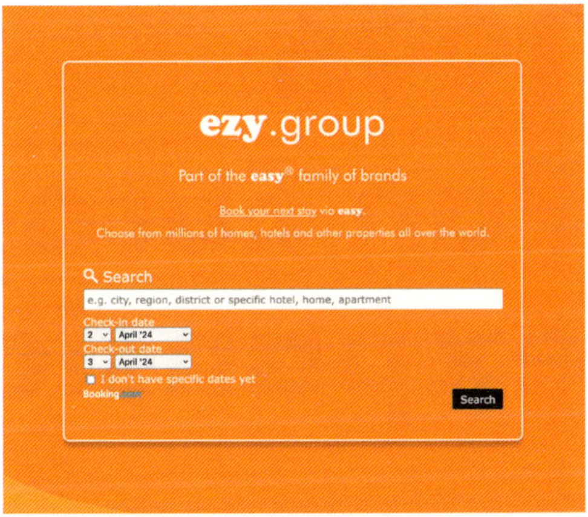

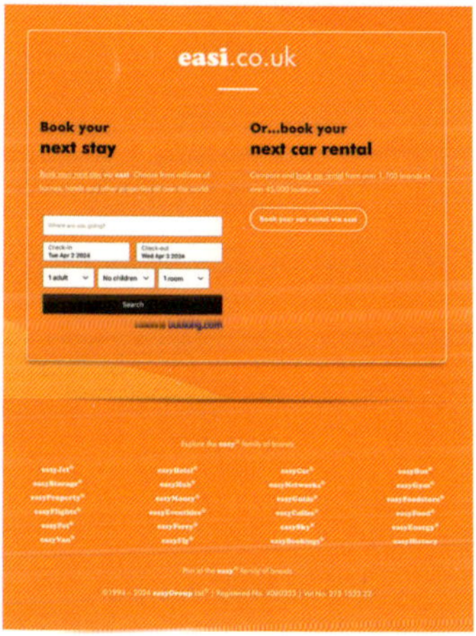

easi.co.uk for accommodation and car rental

eaziGroup.com for easy branded merchandise (right)

Voice assistant technology now common in household devices

1996: Pan European expansion

The easy family of brands including easyJet was intended to be international from the start. The UK is simply too small to support a solely domestic airline and let's face it, people all over the world are attracted by the prospect of a great deal.

easyJet ad, The Economist 1996

The easyJet business plan envisaged operating between London and Scotland for a few months before extending the concept into continental Europe. Stelios wanted to adopt what he called a 'cookie-cutter' approach to European expansion. Virtually every European country had a national carrier like British Airways that had been ripping off the travelling public with high fares and limited serious competition. The brand strategy was to pick a fight with the national carrier, invest heavily in advertising and aim to generate as much free publicity as possible.

Amsterdam launch promotion Apr 1996

The first international route flown by easyJet was between London and Amsterdam. The Dutch city was a popular UK short break destination. Stelios believed there was significant opportunity to grow the market by lowering fares and offering the flexibility of a one-way ticket.

The management of Schiphol airport in Amsterdam wrote to Stelios advising him to fly elsewhere but fortunately he was not deterred.

FT article - 07/08/96 FT FINANCIAL TIMES

EasyJet writ for KLM

The Sun MONEY £

250 jobs at Littlewoods

POOLS and shopping giant Littlewoods is creating 250 jobs in its mail order business.

The firm, which recently appointed former Cable & Wireless chief James Ross as chairman, is staffing up its new Index Extra catalogue.

Based in Sunderland it aims to sell £100million worth of clothes and household goods.

£8m sure is handy!

POCKET computer maker Psion yesterday announced a [illegible] jump in profits

CLOGFIGHT

No frills . . . Easyjet has axed meals to cut fares

Cheapo airline's fare war with Dutch giant

easyJet v KLM article The Sun 02/08/96

The new route was launched in April 1996 on the back of a national promotion with the Mirror newspaper and a major advertising campaign in the UK press.

easyJet's first new Boeing 737-300 at Luton Airport Apr 1996

1996: easy in the NETHERLANDS

For an airline route to be profitable it needs to generate traffic from both ends. This meant that easyJet would need to attract Dutch as well as English customers to fill its planes. Without the travel agents to sell seats that meant building a brand from scratch in the Netherlands.

Stelios's strategy was to take easyJet into a major David versus Goliath battle with the Dutch national airline KLM. The confrontation led to huge levels of brand awareness among the Dutch public. Despite the small size of the Netherlands in comparison with other European countries, KLM was a large international airline and Amsterdam Schiphol had become a major hub for transatlantic flights. Some commentators questioned the wisdom of easyJet picking a fight with what they saw as something of a Dutch national institution.

DeMorgen.

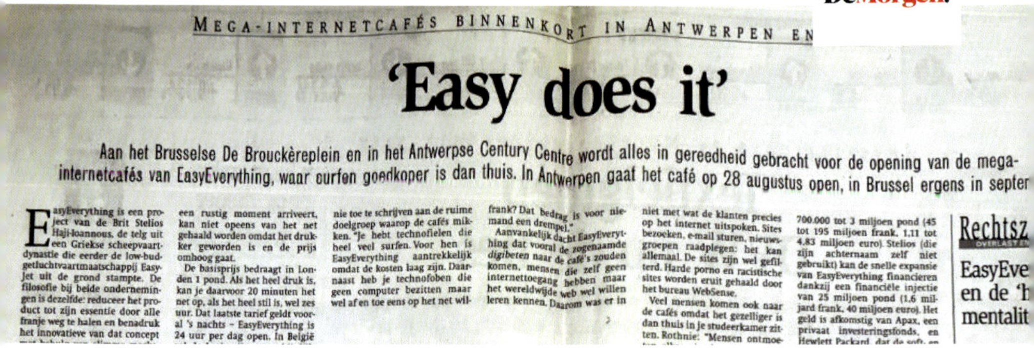

MEGA-INTERNETCAFÉS BINNENKORT IN ANTWERPEN EN

'Easy does it'

Aan het Brusselse De Brouckèreplein en in het Antwerpse Century Centre wordt alles in gereedheid gebracht voor de opening van de mega-internetcafés van EasyEverything, waar surfen goedkoper is dan thuis. In Antwerpen gaat het café op 28 augustus open, in Brussel ergens in septer

EasyEverything is een project van de Brit Stelios Haji-Ioannous, de telg uit een Griekse scheepvaartdynastie die eerder de low-budgetluchtvaartmaatschappij EasyJet uit de grond stampte. De filosofie bij beide ondernemingen is dezelfde: reduceer het product tot zijn essentie door alle franje weg te halen en benadruk het innovatieve van dat concept

een rustig moment arriveert, kan niet opeens van het net gehaald worden omdat het drukker geworden is en de prijs omhoog gaat.

De basisprijs bedraagt in Londen 1 pond. Als het heel druk is, kan je daarvoor 20 minuten het net op, als het heel stil is, wel zes uur. Dat laatste tarief geldt vooral 's nachts – EasyEverything is 24 uur per dag open. In België

nie toe te schrijven aan de ruime doelgroep waarop de cafés mikken. "Je hebt technofielen die heel veel surfen. Voor hen is EasyEverything aantrekkelijk omdat de kosten laag zijn. Daarnaast heb je technofoben die geen computer bezitten maar wel af en toe eens op het net wil-

frank? Dat bedrag is voor niemand een drempel."

Aanvankelijk dacht EasyEverything dat vooral de zogenaamde *digibeten* naar de café's zouden komen, mensen die zelf geen internettoegang hebben maar het wereldwijde web wel willen leren kennen. Daarom was er in

niet met wat de klanten precies op het internet uitspoken. Sites bezoeken, e-mail sturen, nieuwsgroepen raadplegen: het kan allemaal. De sites zijn wel gefilterd. Harde porno en racistische sites worden eruit gehaald door het bureau WebSense.

Veel mensen komen ook naar de cafés omdat het gezelliger is dan thuis in je studeerkamer zitten. Rothnie: "Mensen ontmoe-

700.000 tot 3 miljoen pond (45 tot 195 miljoen frank, 1,11 tot 4,83 miljoen euro). Stelios (die zijn achternaam zelf niet gebruikt) kan de snelle expansie van EasyEverything financieren dankzij een financiële injectie van 25 miljoen pond (1,6 miljard frank, 40 miljoen euro). Het geld is afkomstig van Apax, een privaat investeringsfonds, en Hewlett Packard, dat de soft- en

Rechtsz

EasyEve
en de 'h
mentalit

easyEverything article De Morgen 10/08/2000

However Stelios believed that the Dutch public, in common with passengers across other European countries had been overpaying for air travel for too long, so he embarked on a controversial PR and advertising campaign. It wasn't only KLM who were opposed to easyJet's new flights from Luton to Amsterdam. The management of Schiphol Airport actually sent Stelios a fax to try and persuade him not to start the new route. The message was of course ignored but not before it had been shared with the press.

De Telegraaf
Nov 2000

De Telegraaf

Dutch Press
ad 2001

easyJet Press
ad 1999

De Telegraaf

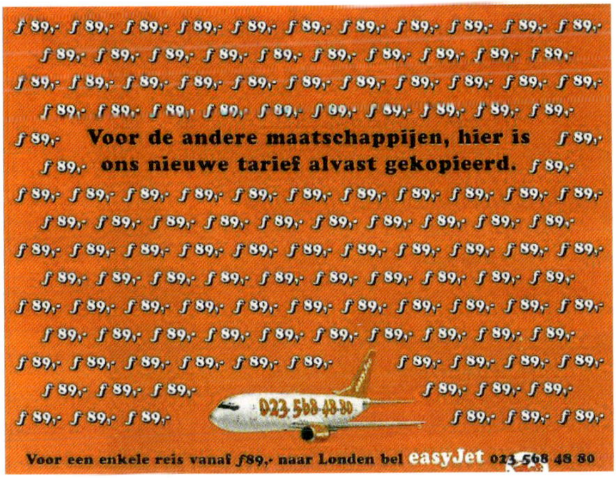

De Telegraaf August 1998

easyJet Amsterdam Poster 1996

1996: easy in the NETHERLANDS

continued

The two leased Boeing 737-200 aircraft used by easyJet to fly to Scotland did not comply with Schiphol's noise regulations. Stelios bought his first new aircraft, a 737-300 to operate the Amsterdam route.

From this point onwards easyJet was committed to purchasing new aircraft and having one of the youngest fleets. This policy helped to dispel concerns from customers who expected low-cost airlines to operate older and potentially less safe aircraft.

Stelios gives major interview to Dutch magazine de Volkskrant in 2000

deVolkskrant

EasyJet-baas Stelios

Een kapitalist die volksheld wilde worden

Hij is jong en schatrijk, en hij heeft een voornaam om als een *one name celebrity* de geschiedenis in te gaan. Toen de Griekse rederszoon Stelios vijf jaar geleden een *low budget airline* begon, werd hij uitgelachen. Maar het pesten van de concurrenten is inmiddels zijn favoriete hobby. EasyJet is een begrip, evenals de internetketen EasyEverything. "Mijn vader vertegenwoordigde de duistere kant van het kapitalisme. Ik wilde het vriendelijke gezicht ervan laten zien."

easyJet poster Amsterdam 2010

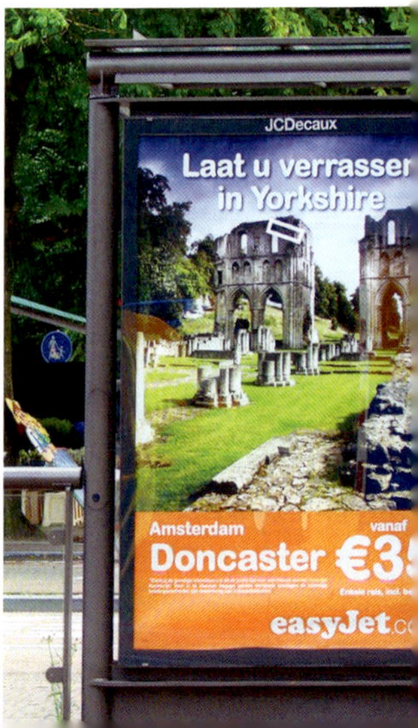

De Telegraaf

easyJet Press ad 1999 (left)

KLM advert from 1995 (below)

As a publicity stunt Stelios personally delivered a sack full of letters from easyJet passengers complaining about KLM's high fares to the airline's head office in Amsterdam. The letters were personally addressed to Mr Bouw, the CEO of KLM at the time. The Dutch TV stations had been tipped off and came along with Stelios to record the stunt.

easyJet also adopted the same confrontational style of advertising that had proved successful against British Airways. Over the years KLM had built an association with swans and often featured swans in their advertising and easyJet ran an ad saying (in Dutch) 'Hunting season has begun'!

1996: easy in the NETHERLANDS continued

The large advertising investment by easyJet and significant media coverage both on Dutch TV channels and in the press resulting from the airline's PR activities, soon started to show results. Both the easyJet brand and Stelios himself achieved huge levels of awareness among the Dutch public. The positioning of easyJet as David versus KLM, with the Dutch airline in the role of Goliath, seemed to really resonate in the country. The high profile of Stelios and easyJet made the task of launching new easy brands into the Dutch market, starting with easyEverything in 1999, much easier as consumers in the Netherlands already associated the easy brand with low-cost.

easyEverything Tram July 2000

easyCar ads 2004

The cities of Amsterdam and Rotterdam became awash with orange advertising including posters and trams in preparation for the launch of easyEverything and easyRentacar. It helped that orange was the colour of the national football team. There was also extensive coverage in the Dutch newspapers and in particular the business press.

In 1999 easyEverything opened its Amsterdam store near the Rembrandtsplein in the heart of the city. When it opened it became for a short time the largest internet café in the world with over 600 seats, before being overtaken in 2001 by easyEverything in Times Square, New York. A store in Rotterdam together with a second easyEverything in Amsterdam reinforced the presence of the easy brand.

Stelios opens easyEverything
Amsterdam June 2000

1996: easy in FRANCE

Evening Standard

Paris plan by easyJet after Air Liberté fails

From Ross Tieman in Toulouse

EASYJET hopes to use Paris as a second major operating base after the collapse of France's second biggest airline, Air Liberté.

EasyJet, Europe's second largest no-frills airline after Ryanair, wants to base 10 Boeing 737-700 and B737-300 aircraft at Orly Airport, providing cheap flights to European cities.

easyJet in France Evening Standard 22 Jun 2001

Stelios owned a home in Monaco and had strong family links to the Principality, so he was happy that the launch of an easyJet route from Luton to Nice in June 1996 meant that he would no longer have to pay BA's ridiculous prices when he travelled home from Luton at weekends.

easyJet outdoor advertising

easyJet to France Evening Standard 11 Jul 1996

Second home owners were an important target market for easyJet and the British expatriate community living in the South of France were targeted with local English language media including Riviera Radio. Word quickly got around about the new low-cost alternative to British Airways and it didn't take long for easyJet to become established on the route.

easyJet Billboard in Paris 2002

1996: easy in FRANCE

continued

easyEverything ad 2001 (above)
easyJet in Le Nouvel Economist October 2002

After the early success, capacity on the London route was increased and within a year the airline launched a new service between Nice and Liverpool and also between Amsterdam and Nice. easyJet established a major brand presence in Nice with poster sites at key locations and sponsorship of festivals and street events.

Le nouvel Economiste

Bienvenue à easyLand, le pays de la vie moins chère

Pour les clients comme pour les salariés, la compagnie aérienne easyJet cul les valeurs d'économie et de débrouillardise. Voici un voyage dans la « cultu orange », la couleur de la marque déclinée tous azimuts.

Sept heures quarante. Pour découvrir easyJet, entreprise siégeant à l'aéroport secondaire de Luton (Grande-Bretagne), il convient de s'embarquer sur un de ses fameux vols (à partir de 60 euros l'aller-retour Paris-Londres). Tout commence à Roissy au terminal T9. A 8 heures, sur le tarmac, les passagers se ruent vers la passerelle de l'avion. Logique : la compagnie n'offre ni business class ni sièges numérotés : premier arrivé, premier assis. Le Boeing 737 est presque plein. Les hôtesses, qui viennent tout juste de nettoyer l'avion, sourient.

As in other countries the arrival of easyJet attracted some national media coverage especially in the business press.

The real breakthrough for the easy brand came when easyJet took over slots at Paris Orly airport in 2001. This followed the 9/11 attacks in the US and the subsequent collapse of the French airline Air Liberté. It was a bold move by easyJet to expand when other airlines across Europe were cutting back their capacity.

easyCar ad 2003

easyJet ad in Paris Metro 2001

1996: easy in FRANCE

continued

nice-matin

A bord d'Easycruise, le premier paquebot « low cost »

easyCruise article Nice-Matin 2006

The easy brand presence in France was further reinforced by the opening of two easyEverything stores in Paris in 2000 and the launch of easyRentacar as well as the launch of easyCruise whose first voyage started from the port of Nice in 2005 and attracted significant media coverage. Today Nice has its own easyHotel and a further easyHotel has opened near Charles de Gaulle airport in Paris.

easyJet Paris Outdoor Advertising 2002

easyGym Palais Royal, France, today (top)
easyLand, 28 Boulevard de la République, 06240, Beausoleil, France, today

nice-matin

Vols « low cost »

Paris à 22,5 € de Nice

Nice : le p
en baiss

L'annonce en a été faite, hier, lors du conseil de la con
à la suite de l'accord conclu entre la ville et la Géné
3,02 € (19,82 F) à 2,55 € (16,77 F). Soit un gain de 0

The fast-expanding fitness chain easyGym has nine gyms open in France including five in Paris with plans to open more. The brand easyVoyages is a major player in online travel search in the French market and has further boosted awareness of the easy family of brands in the country.

easyJet in Nice-Matin, The largest daily newspaper to cover the South of France, June 2001 (left)

1996: easy in ITALY

easyJet 6th millionth passenger Turin July 2005

easyJet poster Rome Metro 2014

The easy brand became familiar to many Italians in 1996 because the easyJet story captured international media attention and furthermore there is a sizeable Italian presence either living in the UK or travelling there on a regular basis. Furthermore, the fact that Nice Airport is located close to the Italian/French border meant the easyJet brand became familiar to many Italians living in the north-west of Italy from 1996 when easyJet began flying to the South of France.

On 19th May 1998 the first easyJet flight, then under the Go banner, began operating from Stansted to Rome and from that point on the airline started to develop Italy as a significant market. The acquisition of British Airway's low-cost subsidiary Go by easyJet in 2002 further fuelled the airline's growth in Italy.

easyJet press advert 2005

easyJet poster Milan 2016

1996: easy in ITALY

continued

easyInternetcafe Rome postcard 2002

The opening of an easyInternetcafe located in the centre of Rome in Piazza Barberini on 15th December 2000 strengthened the easy brand presence in the Italian capital. In 2006 easyJet opened its first Italian base in Milan Malpensa airport operating flights to a series of new European destinations. Further bases have since been opened in Naples and Venice as the airline has continued to develop its Italian presence.

Beerlino Italy Advertising November 2005

easyJet Italia 2005 (above)

easyJet Corriere della Sera article 13/5/2002
easyEverything in La Stampa 09/01/2001

LA STAMPA

SBARCA A ROMA «EASYEVERYTHING»

Nuovo, molto Internet e poco caffè

Offre accessi ad alta velocità e presto aprirà a Milano e a Firenze

Maria Grazia Bruzzone

ROMA

Dal fast food al fast web. I passanti sbirciano dalle vetrine e restano perplessi. I colori vivaci delle ragazze alle casse e i tabelloni luminosi possono trarre in inganno. Ma al posto dei soliti branchi di ragazzotti allegro ufficio, aperto giorno e notte. Di Internet Café a Roma ne era già spuntato qualcuno, ma sembravano bar con l'aggiunta di qualche computer. Questo, appena inaugurato dalla catena inglese «easyEverything», si ispira a una filosofia diversa: molto Internet a poco caffe. Panini, snack, bibite e 350 postazioni (ciascuna dotata di webcam) su tre piani, così fitte da scoraggiare - volutamente - i gruppetti. Un luogo pubblico riservato più che agli incontri sociali, a passatempi solitari. Eppure è pieno.

«E' il sintomo della difficoltà a sono sei e il costo dipende dal traffico. Per risparmiare devi andarci nelle ore più strane». Marco, Ylenia e Barbara ci hanno provato a stringersi in tre davanti allo schermo. Hanno 15 anni e un'aria smarrita, è il loro primo contatto col Web. Cliccano su «Superfighetto & Megatipina», un gioco che sembra andare per la maggiore, a giudicare dai tanti che ci stanno sopra. «Mi ha imparato mia sorella, che ha un'amica col computer» spiega sgrammaticato Marco, che tiene il mouse come uno scettro mentre le ragazze guardano.

ne di più. «I medici non ti spiegano e ti dicono quello che vogliono loro».

Fra tanti ragazzi spiccano le teste grigie. Una è di Raimondo, professore di tedesco. «Vengo da Cinecittà a fare ricerche o spedire e-mail. Alla mia scuola i computer ci sono ma la burocrazia rende tutto difficile. Di questi posti dovrebbero aprirne in ogni quartiere. Ma il pubblico è indietro, così ci pensano i privati».

Infatti. Gli «easyEverything» li ha inventati un imprenditore greco, lo stesso che ha creato «easyJet», compagnia aerea a basso costo e

1996: easy in ITALY

continued

easyNoleggio equipment available for hire in Italy

More recently easyNoleggio (translates as easyHire) has begun operations in Italy offering the rental of construction equipment to individuals and businesses and is expanding fast in the Italian market.

1996: easy in SPAIN

Spain has always been a popular destination for UK outbound travellers both for summer holidays and shorter city breaks, so it was not a surprise when easyJet announced its first flights to the country would operate from Luton to Barcelona starting 12 June 1996. Barcelona like Amsterdam was a route where there was huge potential for growing the market by lowering fares. The lowest non-promotional price offered by easyJet at the Spanish end of the route was 9,900 pesetas or around £49.

easyJet Madrid press conference 1996

LA VANGUARDIA

ECONOMÍA

EasyJet lanza la primera empresa de alquiler de coches por Internet

El nuevo "rent a car" operará sólo con la clase A de Mercedes

DOLORS ÁLVAREZ

BARCELONA. – EasyGroup, la cabecera de la popular compañía aérea de tarifas reducidas EasyJet, ha puesto en marcha un nuevo negocio: el alquiler de coches mediante una compañía que ofrecerá sus servicios sólo por Internet. La nueva empresa, EasyRentacar, alquilará únicamente el modelo clase A de Mercedes, a casi la mitad de precio que los "rent a car" tradicionales. Barcelona, Glasgow y Londres son las tres ciudades elegidas para lanzar el negocio, con el objetivo de ir extendiéndolo en los próximos años por toda Europa.

Según explicó ayer Stelios Haji-Ioannou, presidente y propietario de EasyGroup, se trata de trasladar al negocio del alquiler de coches la misma idea que ha inspirado la compañía aérea: simplificar el servicio para poder dar mejores precios y aprovechar la operativa de Internet para reducir al máximo los costes. "Utilizaremos vehículos nuevos de la casa Mercedes porque es una marca de calidad, que tiene un valor de reventa en el mercado de se- está prevista la adquisición de otros 30.000 coches, 2.000 de los cuales se ofrecerán en alquiler en España.

Barcelona es la primera ciudad española en la que se lanzará el negocio, a finales de abril. Para el depósito de los coches, se ha llegado a un acuerdo con Saba para arrendar varios centenares de plazas de su parking de Arc de Triomf, una ubicación que se ha elegido por estar conectado directamente con el aeropuerto mediante el tren y a la que también se llega en metro. La reserva y el contrato de alquiler solamente podrán realizarse por Internet, aunque se prevé abrir alguna oficina en el centro de la ciudad con ordenadores disponibles para solicitar el servicio.

La utilización de la red rebajará al máximo la necesidad de personal. También para reducir costes, el servicio tiene una serie de limitaciones: el coche debe devolverse en el mismo lugar donde se alquiló y habrá que pagar un plus extra si se quiere ampliar la cobertura del seguro que incluye la tarifa estándar. El Mercedes clase A se podrá alquilar a partir de 2.500 pesetas día más una tasa de 1.500 por contrato, independientemente de la duración del mismo. Al igual que ocurre con EasyJet, los precios variarán en función de la demanda, es decir, serán más caros en temporada turística, aunque en ningún caso se espera rebasar las 5.000 pesetas, según Miguel de Lucas, director de EasyRentacar España.

En cuanto a EasyJet, una compañía nacida hace cuatro años que factura unos

ARCHIVO

Stelios Haji-Ioannou

easyRentacar launches in Spain 09/03/2000

easyJet Outdoor Ad Madrid 1999

1996: easy in SPAIN

continued

The new route soon proved a success and was quickly followed by Madrid and after that by services to Malaga and a range of other Spanish destinations. Without the help of travel agents to promote easyJet, building the brand in Spain required another big investment in advertising, mainly in the national newspapers and outdoors.

easyEverything article La Vanguardia 30/04/2000

LA VANGUARDIA

DOMINGO, 30 ABRIL 2000 — VIVIR EN BARCELONA | 3

BARCELONA VIVE LA **ECLOSIÓN** DE LOCALES CON **ACCESO PÚBLICO A INTE**

Los cibercafés se preparan para la llegada del gigante easyEverything el 23 de junio

PATRICIO SIMÓN

El Café de Internet, en la Gran Vía, fue el primer cibercafé que abrió en Barcelona. En junio cumplirá cinco años

–continúa– y desde entonces hemos marcado la pauta a seguir a la hora de montar establecimientos de este tipo en Barcelona. Creo que seguiremos siendo una referencia."

La calidad es el sello de distinción de El Café de Internet. "Somos más caros que la gran mayoría pero ofrecemos mejor calidad." Torrente es un convencido de que lo barato acaba siendo caro: "El nuestro es, por el momento, el único café ISP (proveedor de acceso a Internet) de la ciudad; es decir, que no contratamos los servicios de otro servidor y esto se nota en lo más importante para un internauta: la rapidez en la navegación".

Este local sigue una fórmula mixta: café e Internet al 50%. En la planta baja está el café, que, de hecho, es un restaurante. En el piso de arriba se halla la sala de navegación, con 18 pantallas. Para el usuario, ambas plantas son lo mismo pero en realidad se trata de dos negocios separados. Torrente destaca que la empresa sea totalmente española, a difeeasyInternetcafe Madrid 2002

LA VANGUARDIA

EasyEverything abrirá este año un nuevo local en la Rambla con 500 ordenadores

VIENE DE LA PÁGINA 1

y te puedes llevar la información en un CD". Ciberopción ofrece cincuenta puntos de conexión y prevé una ampliación hasta 150.

Pero si hay un local que se alimente del turismo es el gigante EasyEverything (se le conoce simplemente como Easy). María González, responsable de estrategia de negocio en España de esta cadena de "Internet shops", estima que la mitad de sus clientes son turistas, una cifra que en pleno verano llega al 70%. "Los turistas siempre han contado para nosotros", reconoce González. Las incisivas estrategias publicitarias de EasyEverything lo corroboran. El naranja de esta firma persigue a los turistas allá por donde llegan y por donde se mueven: en el aeropuerto, en las estaciones de autocares y de trenes, en los taxis, en el metro, en los autobuses, en las cabinas de teléfono, en los

PATRICIO SIMÓN

Interior del EasyEverything de la ronda Universitat

easyEverything article La Vanguardia 01/09/2000

1996: easy in SPAIN

continued

The Spanish public became very familiar with the easy brand over the years as easyEverything opened one of its first international stores on Barcelona's busiest shopping street, Las Ramblas, while easyCar also developed a major presence in the country starting with the opening of a rental site in Barcelona in April 2000 followed by a large site in Malaga. Today Barcelona is home to the largest easyHotel in the world with 206 rooms while additional Spanish sites are now open in Malaga and Madrid. Further expansion is anticipated including the opening of a new easyHotel in the Spanish city of Valencia.

easyAlquiler items for hire

easyEverything promotional postcard 2000

easyHotel Barcelona 2018

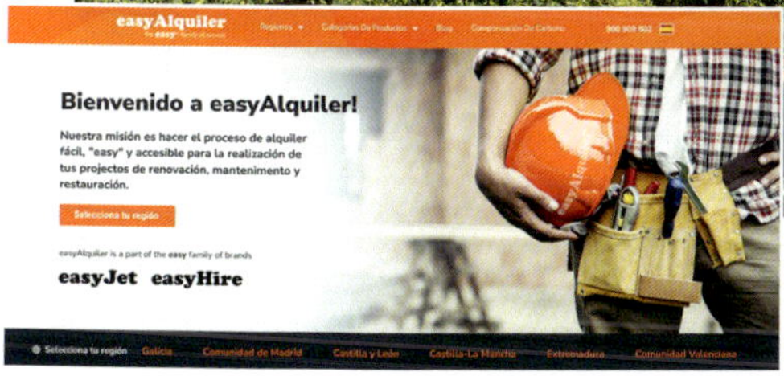

easyAlquiler.com website 2022

easyAlquiler team 2022

In 2021 the presence of the easy brand in Spain was further strengthened by the launch of easyAlquiler an equipment hire business using the same platform as easyNoleggio in Italy bringing low-cost equipment hire to businesses and customers throughout Spain. Visit easyAlquiler.com.

1996: easy transport by bus and coach

Travelling to Luton airport by bus and coach was very important in the early days of the easy brand as the direct railway links between Luton and London were poor and the train station at Luton was struggling to cope with the volume of easyJet passengers. easyBus filed for UK trademark on 15th October 1996 with number 2112956 and EU number 2900926 filed on 17 October 2002.

FT FINANCIAL TIMES

EasyJet founder plans to expand by bus

By Lucy Smy

Stelios Haji-Ioannou founder of the EasyGroup of companies, plans to add to his empire next year with the launch of EasyBus – a low-cost inter-city coach operator.

FT article - 24/11/05

Stelios sold many bus tickets to people travelling to and from Luton and went on to paint all the buses between the train station and the airport with the famous orange livery.

Later, a piece in The Guardian published on 31st December 2002 asked famous people to share their New Year resolutions. Stelios said he was considering his own easyBus operation.

easyBus at Luton airport 1997

easy transport by bus, coach & train

The Guardian

Stelios Haji-Ioannou
Founder and former chairman of EasyJet airlines

This year I plan to start two new businesses, one being EasyCinema. I haven't decided what the other one will be yet but I am considering EasyDorm, EasyBus, EasyFitness or Easy-Cruise. I also want to turn a profit at EasyCar

The Guardian article - 31/12/02

easyBus website - 2024

A press conference in August 2004 generated significant media attention with easyBus once more on the side of the consumer, reducing fares for the many and not the few. easyCoach was launched as a sister brand in September 2016.

By the start of 2020 easyBus.com was selling more than one million low-cost bus seats per year, online on many hundreds of routes all over Europe and beyond in partnership with a variety of reputable operators (including the British Airways of the sector called National Express) contributing about £1m pa in profits to easyGroup.

The easyBus.com website is now powered by the global bus travel online retailer distribusion.com. For more information email vladimir.klunic@distribusion.com. Through easyBus you can book tickets on

Evening Standard

Evening Standard ad 03 Aug 2015

bus journeys through Europe and beyond, hence the easyBus.com slogan "book here, go anywhere". The easy brand has been associated with rail travel since the earliest days of easyJet as so many of easyJet's passengers arrived by train at Luton railway station and then took a short journey on a branded easyBus to the airport. In 2023 Stelios launched easyTrain.com also in partnership with distribution.com allowing customers to purchase rail tickets initially in Italy, Switzerland and the Netherlands.

Stelios has proven that when you own a strong brand, you don't need to spend the money to purchase vehicles around the world to operate yourself when others are happy to carry customers on your behalf. As Stelios puts it "Outsourcing and focusing on the brand works!"

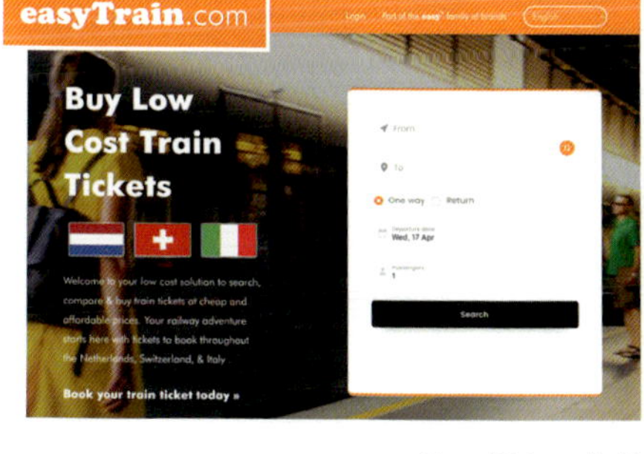

easyTrain Website (left)
easyBus Liverpool route 2018

1997: easy in accommodation

If your starting point is setting up a low-cost airline, then offering budget accommodation is a natural brand extension. Stelios had become familiar with the customer experience as he often stayed at the budget IBIS hotel at Luton Airport in the early years of easyJet. The airline's "easy come easy go" in-flight magazine contained many adverts for hotels and hostels so it made sense to offer this service under the easy brand. In 1997 the easyExtras brand was sub-licensed to a local Luton businessman to sell a range of ancillary services including hotel rooms.

easyExtras remains in use today providing access to low-cost accommodation through easyExtras.biz

easyExtras.biz website 2024
Independent easyDorm article 24 May 03

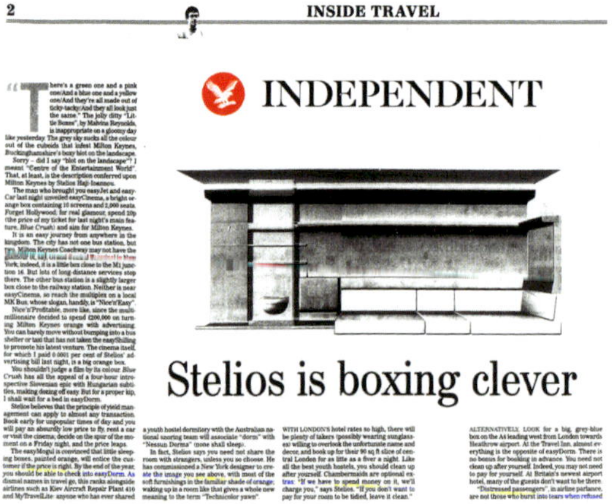

2 INSIDE TRAVEL

INDEPENDENT

Stelios is boxing clever

"There's a green one and a pink one/And a blue one and a yellow one/And they're all made out of ticky-tacky/And they all look just the same." The jolly ditty "Little Boxes", by Malvina Reynolds, is inappropriate on a gloomy day like yesterday. The grey sky sucks all the colour out of the cuboids that infest Milton Keynes, Buckinghamshire's boxy blot on the landscape.

Sorry – did I say "blot on the landscape"? I meant "Centre of the Entertainment World". That, at least, is the description conferred upon Milton Keynes by Stelios Haji-Ioannou.

The man who brought you easyJet and easyCar last night unveiled easyCinema, a bright orange box containing 10 screens and 2,000 seats. Forget Hollywood; for real glamour, spend 20p (the price of my ticket for last night's main feature, *Blue Crush*) and aim for Milton Keynes.

It is an easy journey from anywhere in the kingdom. The city has not one bus station, but two. Milton Keynes Coachway may not have the glamour of, say, [illegible] in New York; indeed, it is a little box close to the M1 junction 14. But lots of long-distance services stop there. The other bus station is a slightly larger box close to the railway station. Neither is near easyCinema, so reach the multiplex on a local MK Bus, whose slogan, handily, is "Nice'n'Easy".

Nice'n'Profitable, more like, since the multi-millionaire decided to spend £200,000 on turning Milton Keynes orange with advertising. You can barely move without bumping into a bus shelter or taxi that has not taken the easyShilling to promote his latest venture. The cinema itself, for which I paid 0.0001 per cent of Stelios' advertising bill last night, is a big orange box.

You shouldn't judge a film by its colour. *Blue Crush* has all the appeal of a four-hour introspective Slovenian epic with Hungarian subtitles, making dozing off easy. But for a proper kip, I shall wait for a bed in easyDorm.

Stelios believes that the principle of yield management can apply to almost any transaction. Book early for unpopular times of day and you will pay an absurdly low price to fly, rent a car or visit the cinema; decide on the spur of the moment on a Friday night, and the price leaps.

The easyMogul is convinced that little sleeping boxes, painted orange, will entice the customer if the price is right. By the end of the year, you should be able to check into easyDorm. As dismal names in travel go, this ranks alongside airlines such as Kiev Aircraft Repair Plant 410 and MyTravelLite: anyone who has ever shared a youth hostel dormitory with the Australian national snoring team will associate "dorm" with "Nessun Dorma" (none shall sleep).

In fact, Stelios says you need not share the room with strangers, unless you so choose. He has commissioned a New York designer to create the image you see above, with most of the soft furnishings in the familiar shade of orange; waking up in a room like that gives a whole new meaning to the term "Technicolor yawn".

WITH LONDON'S hotel rates so high, there will be plenty of takers (possibly wearing sunglasses) willing to overlook the unfortunate name and decor, and book up for their 90 sq ft slice of central London for as little as a fiver a night. Like all the best youth hostels, you should clean up after yourself. Chambermaids are optional extras: "If we have to spend money on it, we'll charge you," says Stelios. "If you don't want to pay for your room to be tidied, leave it clean."

ALTERNATIVELY, LOOK for a big, grey-blue box on the A4 leading west from London towards Heathrow airport. At the Travel Inn, almost everything is the opposite of easyDorm. There is no bonus for booking in advance. You need not clean up after yourself. Indeed, you may not need to pay for yourself. At Britain's newest airport hotel, many of the guests don't want to be there.

"Distressed passengers", in airline parlance, are not those who burst into tears when refused

"I believe the concierge at the Kensington EasyHotel booked us a table."

easyHotel cartoon Evening Standard 01 Aug 05 (above)

1997: easy in accommodation

continued The Times article 02 Aug 05

THE TIMES

THE TIMES TUESDAY AUGUST 2 2005 NEWS

A room without a view – £20

By Alan Hamilton

DON'T even think about trying to swing a cat. You could barely hold a gerbil at arm's length in one of London's cheapest and smallest hotel rooms.

For the grand total of £20, two people can have a double bed with a duvet and one pillow each, a flat-screen television that costs £5 extra to watch, a tiny private bathroom and just enough room to park their boots. And nothing else.

Really. Nothing. No swimming pool, porter, restaurant, bar, wardrobe, bedside light or room to pull off your pants except standing at the end of the bed or on it. But for the price of one night at the Connaught, you could spend the best part of a month at the easyHotel.

Stelios Haji-Ioannou, founder of easyJet, the budget airline, has gone into the accommodation business in what you might call a small way.

He bought a tired old bed and breakfast near Gloucester Road in West London for £2 million, spent a further £1 million refurbishing it and yesterday opened it as the first easyHotel. Where there were once 20 rooms, there are now 34, categorised as "tiny" (60 sq ft), "very small" and "small" (80 sq ft).

Stelios said: "There is a gap in the market between the unbranded bed and breakfast, and the branded chain hotels. The consumer is prepared to sacrifice space for a low price, and I am offering private and reliable accommodation, with all the rooms of the same standard; there are no surprises."

Oh, but yes there are, you ain't never seen hotel rooms this small. You could, Stelios admitted, get a cheaper bed in London, but it would be in a room shared with strangers in a hostel. And, he emphasised, his rooms can only be booked on the internet and are not available by the hour.

Stelios owns this property but plans to put future hotels out to franchise; a Swiss entrepreneur is already preparing to open one in Basle later this year.

Nothing, of course, is ever quite what it seems. The £20 rate for a double room could increase to £50 depending on when it is booked.

You will also pay a premium for a window; only three rooms in the hotel have one. "It's the least-desirable aspect, but I don't think people are too worried about windows. It doesn't unduly bother them in the cabins of my cruise ship. And anyway, the air conditioning works."

Stelios denied there was any similarity with Japan's "capsule" hotels. "In my hotel, you have a private bathroom and room to stand up," he said.

The rooms are plain, except for the doors and floors of the tiny bathrooms, which have been painted in the brand's familiar colour. Claustrophobics who can't stand orange should really look elsewhere.

Pius and Peter Fan, brothers from Melbourne, Australia, were the first guests to check in yesterday. They had viewed the website every day until it opened for bookings.

Their check-in was not quite as smooth as it might have been at the Connaught. They were shown to their room, only to find a television cameraman standing on the bed trying to capture the tiny dimensions with a fish-eye lens.

They were shown to another room, to discover the lights were broken. They were soon fixed and, at the price they were paying, the Fan brothers decided not to make a scene.

The first guests at the easyHotel in West London, Peter and Pius Fan, after checking in to one of the 60sq ft budget rooms

EASY STREET

Stelios Haji-Ioannou: 38, son of Greek shipping tycoon Loucas Haji-Ioannou
Educated: Greece, LSE
First company: aged 25 set up Stelmar Tankers
Breakthrough: setting up easyJet in 1995
Empire: 40% shares in easyJet; easy empire embraces mobile phones, cinemas and cruises
Wealth: £480 million
Marital status: eligible

On 14th October 1997 in an interview with the Scottish Daily Record newspaper, Stelios first announced he was considering offering accommodation under the easy brand.

On 21st September 2000 Stelios registered the easyHotel trademark number 1866706. Then in 2003 Stelios revealed in an interview with the respected travel journalist Simon Calder that he was exploring an easyDorm design using a futuristic easy-to-clean and easy-to-maintain bedroom and bathroom design, in orange of course. The easyDorm.com website provides customers with access to low-cost accommodation around the world through the partnership with Booking.com
In February 2004 Stelios confirmed he had purchased the freehold property of a hotel in Lexham Gardens, London W8 which was to be refurbished (i.e. painted orange!). Stelios himself stayed in a tiny windowless room overnight on the 1st August 2005 at the first branded easyHotel property in London. The hotel was fully booked for its first week.

The easyDorm property 150 Old Brompton Road, London

Also in 2019 the IP rights to the brand easyRoommate, which was set up in the 1990s to promote accommodation and property letting and sharing services across several countries, were acquired by easyGroup. The brand easyRoommate.com also forms part of the partnership with Booking.com for travellers on low-budgets who are willing to consider sharing their room to reduce cost.

Evening Standard 13 May 04

Evening Standard

CHEAP ROOMS FOR TOURISTS ARE LATEST VENTURE FROM EASYJET FOUNDER

Sleep tight ... there's no other way in this £5 hotel

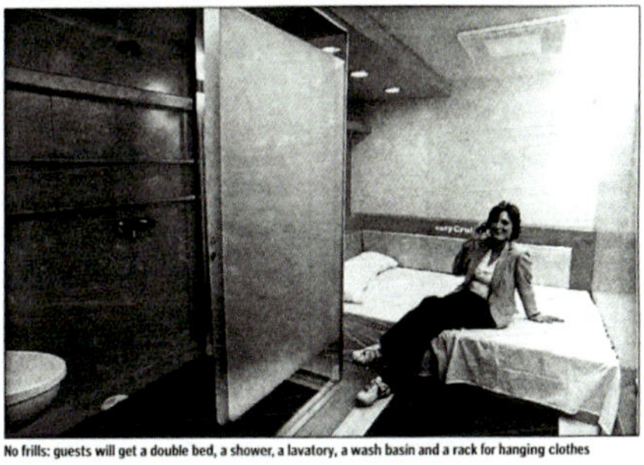

No frills: guests will get a double bed, a shower, a lavatory, a wash basin and a rack for hanging clothes

Growth and success of easyHotel

easyHotel Shoreditch in The Sun 2021

THE Sun travel Edited by LISA MINOT

EASYHOTEL, LONDON SHOREDITCH

WHAT'S IT LIKE? A no-frills budget choice with basic rooms in a prime location in trendy East London. Despite the bargain price, the hotel doesn't scrimp. It's spotless throughout, the rooms have all you need for a good night's sleep and customer service is top class.

ROOMS ANY GOOD? All are air-conditioned, fully heated and have en-suite showers. Beds are really comfy, towels are soft and there are bedside USB charging ports. The curtains keep out the light but you can also choose a room without a window. The hotel must have good insulation as we didn't hear a peep from other guests or the street.

EAT HERE OR GRAB A PIZZA? The hotel doesn't have a bar or restaurant facilities but there are plenty of brilliant restaurants on the doorstep. Contemporary Italian restaurant Officina 00, just a few hundred yards away, serves delicious pasta dishes. And over the road, traditional cafe Fast Break serves all-day breakfasts on plates bigger than your head.

WHAT ELSE? The hotel is close to Old Street underground station and a prime spot for retail therapy. It's a short walk from the trendy nightlife hotspots of Shoreditch and Dalston and within walking distance of The Barbican Centre.

SO YOU'D GO BACK? Yes. It's an ideal location for sightseeing or visiting loved ones. You would be hard pressed to find a cheaper hotel without scrimping on quality.

WHAT'S THE DAMAGE? If you book before January 28, 2021, rooms at easyHotel Shoreditch are available from £34.99 until November 30, 2021. For other easyHotel deals see easyhotel.com.

EMMA PIETRAS

REST EASY . . . interior

In 2014 the company's shares were floated on the London Stock Exchange whilst easyGroup retained all IP rights to the easyHotel brand. The business was taken private in 2019 and today the majority shareholder in easyHotel is financial investment group ICAMAP with Ivanhoe Cambridge, although Stelios and his family have retained their 22% stake. The company is headed by ICAMAP's Harm Meijer as Chairman and Karim Malak as CEO. In October 2022 easyHotel acquired eight franchised hotels in the Netherlands and Belgium from Crossroads Real Estate at a price of €145 million.

Franchising is key to its growth strategy with franchises available for suitable property owners who want to trade their hotel under the easy brand. If you have an opportunity for an easyHotel site or want more information about becoming a hotel franchisee, please email Gwenaelle.Pouy@easyhotel.com

Harm Meijer - easyHotel

Karim Malak - CEO easyHotel

Alexandre Aquien - Chairman

Manchester City Centre

Glasgow

Reading

Croydon

Belfast

London City Shoreditch

Liverpool

Newcastle

Leeds

Sheffield

Ipswich

Milton Keynes

Edinburgh

London Paddington

London Victoria

London South Kensington

Birmingham

Oxford

easyHotel going global

Brussels

Sofia

Nice

Berlin

Dublin

Paris CDG

Budapest

Amsterdam Arena

Amsterdam City Centre

Madrid

Rotterdam

The Hague City Centre

The Hague Scheveningen Beach

Maastricht

Lisbon

Basle

Zurich City Centre

Valencia

Marseille

Alicante

Barcelona Meridiana

easyHotel Low-Carbon room in 2024

easyHotel going global continued

Total assets on easyHotel balance sheet FY 2023
£405 million

easyHotel Liverpool interior

easyHotel continues to go from strength to strength as it expands across Europe and beyond. The company has grown its portfolio to 47 owned/leased and franchised hotels in 11 countries. The increased presence outside the UK is testimony to the international awareness of the easy brand.
The pipeline of new easyHotels continues to develop well with construction underway in Valencia, Marseilles and Alicante as well as a second hotel in Barcelona.

One of the largest easyHotel today is a 200 room purpose built freehold property in Barcelona

Locations

UK
Belfast
Birmingham
Cardiff
Croydon
Edinburgh
Glasgow
Ipswich
Leeds
Liverpool
London City Shoreditch
London Paddington
London South
Kensington
London Victoria
Manchester
Milton Keynes
Newcastle
Oxford
Reading
Sheffield

BELGIUM
Brussels

BULGARIA
Sofia

FRANCE
Nice
Paris CDG
Paris Nord Aubervilliers

GERMANY
Berlin

HUNGARY
Budapest

IRELAND
Dublin

NETHERLANDS
Amsterdam Arena
Boulevard
Amsterdam City Centre
Amsterdam Zaandam
Maastricht
Rotterdam
The Hague City Centre
The Hague
Scheveningen Beach

PORTUGAL
Lisbon

SPAIN
Barcelona
Madrid
Malaga

SWITZERLAND
Basel
Zurich City Centre
Zurich Limmatplatz
Zurich Main Station
Zurich West

COMING SOON
Alicante
Barcelona Meridiana
Marseille
Valencia

1997: easy in SWITZERLAND

Switzerland is an attractive market for European airlines as overall demand for air travel is highest in the summer months. Stelios believed that operating flights to Switzerland during winter would allow easyJet to significantly grow the ski market. So in December 1997 easyJet began flights between Luton and Geneva.

Observer ad 18/10/98 Geneva Display ad 1999

Campaigning against Swissair 1999

The new route proved very successful and it became clear that in addition to skiers, easyJet was also attracting UK business travellers who were fed up with paying British Airways prices.

Swissair plane from 1999

easyJet Swiss telephone number livery

easyJet poster 1999

1997: easy in SWITZERLAND

continued

Even more interestingly easyJet was also attracting fliers from the Swiss end of the route. Stelios was very encouraged that the Swiss who have a reputation for being selective in their choice of airlines were prepared to fly with easyJet and to ditch the national carrier Swissair.

easyJet branded tram Geneva 2017

easyBus to and from Geneva Airport 2018

He therefore decided to operate the route year round with additional flights during the winter months and in November 1998 easyJet introduced a new route between Luton and Zurich which attracted significant business traffic as well as skiers.

1997: continued easy in SWITZERLAND

Because the Swiss population is concentrated in a small geographic area, outdoor advertising is a very effective way of reaching customers and potential customers. Here you can see some of the creative advertising used by easyJet in Switzerland.

easyJet Branded Train in Switzerland

easyBus Geneva 2014

1998: Doing battle with swissair

Taking on the big guys

After the success of the flights between Luton and Switzerland, Stelios had his eyes on a much bigger prize. In March 1998 easyJet acquired a stake in a Swiss charter airline called TEA that later become a wholly owned subsidiary called easyJet Switzerland. In 1999 Stelios announced plans to fly from Geneva and Zurich to other European cities, a move that was strongly opposed by the national carrier Swissair.

ÉCONOMIE

EasyJet se frotte à Swissair. Au cœur du conflit, la ligne Genève-Madrid

AVIATION • Philippe Vignon, porte-parole d'easyJet, accuse la compagnie Swissair de tenir un double langage et de s'appuyer sur une «loi bâtarde» pour parvenir à ses fins.

Geneva article - 1998

24heures Economie

AVIATION ■ LA COMPAGNIE BON MARCHÉ NE LÂCHERA PAS LE MORCEAU

Swissair-EasyJet: la guerre continue

Le conseiller fédéral Moritz Leuenberger devrait trancher cette semaine.

Campagne publicitaire peu correcte

24 heures 13/7/99

On the eve of the first flight between Geneva and Barcelona the Swiss Transport Minister ruled that Swissair had a protected monopoly causing Stelios to refund passengers so the easyJet flight could operate. He actually passed a bucket around the aircraft asking for donations and received half the money back!

Orange tent pitched outside Barcelona

easyJet Anti-Swissair livery - 1998

In order for the airline to meet a legal requirement that easyJet Switzerland provide flights together with accommodation, Stelios instructed staff to buy a number of orange tents which were pitched on a hill outside Barcelona where passengers could stay for free. Despite their dirty tricks Swissair was unable to compete with easyJet on short-haul European routes and on 1st April 2002 the airline went out of business.

easyJet has continued to grow in Switzerland since the demise of Swissair and the awareness of the easy brand was boosted by the launch of an easyBus service transporting skiers from Geneva airport to the ski slopes.

1998: easy in IRELAND

The substantial Irish population in the UK and the strong social, economic and cultural links between the two countries means there is a high level of awareness of the easy brand in Ireland.

easyJet began flying to Belfast in 1998 and last year celebrated its 25th anniversary since its first flight. Today easyJet flies from two Belfast airports to 38 destinations in the UK and Europe. A high proportion of passengers are travelling to and from the South of Ireland including Dublin which has good transport links to Belfast. Rental cars can be booked throughout Northern and Southern Ireland via easyCar which is powered by the Irish company CarTrawler.

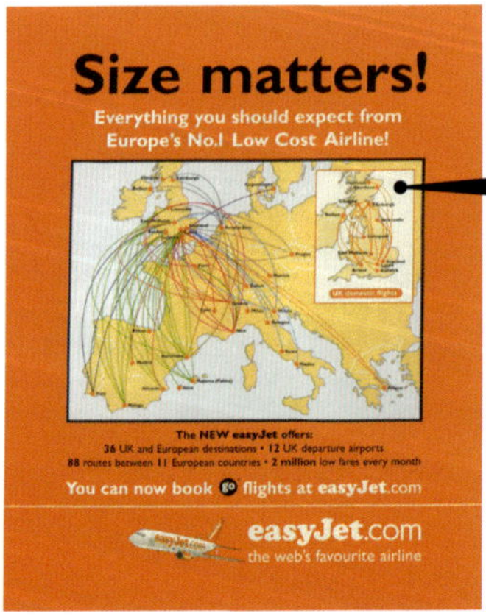

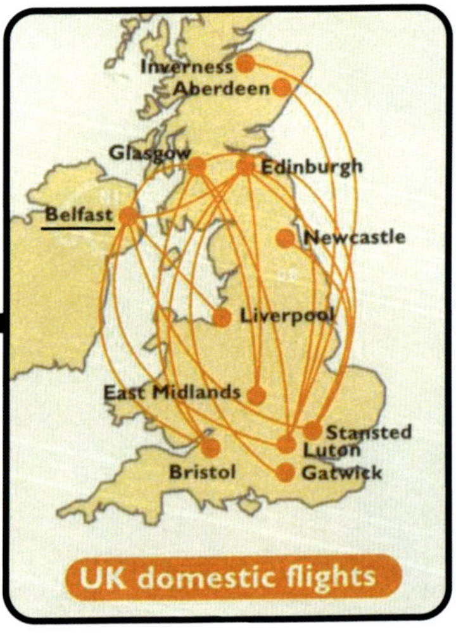

easyJet in the Economist 23 Nov 2002 advertising European and UK domestic flights including Belfast

easyFood.ie is Ireland's most widely read food magazine available on news stands across the country.
In 2023 a 160 room easyHotel opened in the popular Smithfield area of Dublin bringing its affordable low-carbon accommodation to the Irish capital.
easyCleaning products are available for purchase in the famous Irish store chain Dunnes which is one of the country's best-known retailers.
In 2023 easyTaxi.app began a trial of its affordable on demand booking app connecting users with local taxi and private hire companies in the cities of Dublin and Cork.
Through easyCharging.app drivers can charge their electric vehicles at locations throughout Ireland including 19 in Dublin.
Watch out for more easy brands coming to Ireland in the future!

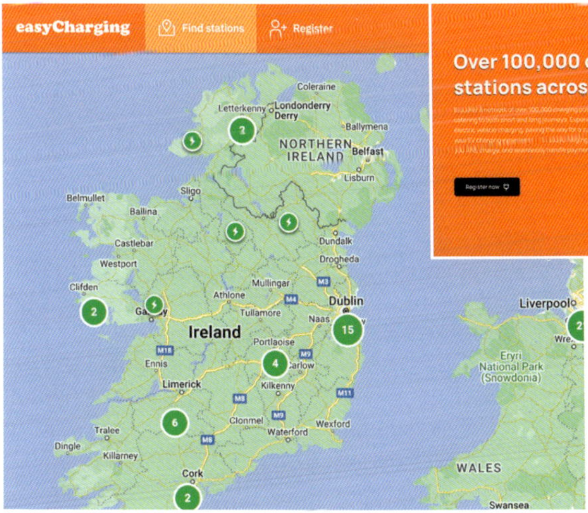

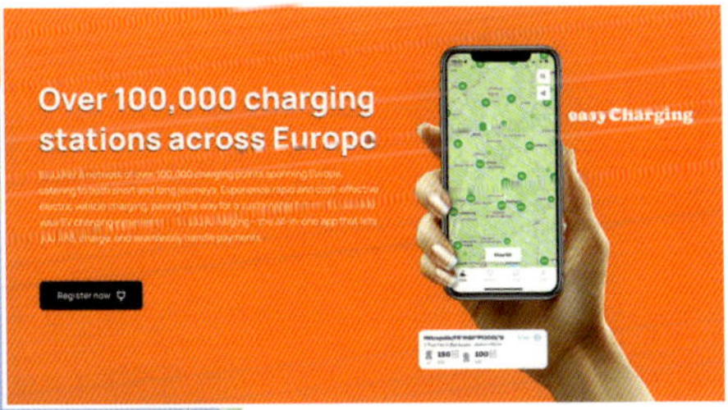

easyCharging coverage of Ireland Apr 2024

easyCleaning now available in Dunnes Store (top left)
easyHotel Dublin City Centre interior 2024 (top right)

1998: easy in GERMANY

easyJet ad Berliner Zeitung 09/03/19

Despite the large size of the German market, easyJet (under the Go banner) did not begin flying to the country until 25th November 1998. At the time easyJet first launched credit card penetration was relatively low in Germany compared to other European countries which for the first couple of years limited the opportunity. Of course the Germans wanted low-fares just as much as everyone else.

On 11th October 2000 the first easyEverything store opened in Munich's Hauptbahnhof with 550 terminals, the biggest in Germany. This was followed by a second store in Berlin on 16th December 2000 with 350 terminals.

easyJet poster Dortmund 2005

The arrival of easyEverything was extensively covered in the German press and media The first easyHotel opened in Berlin in 2010 offering rooms from just €10 per night.

easyHotel Berlin 2019

easyJet outdoor Berlin 2017

easyJet tram Freiburg 2018

easyHotel BernKastel 2018

1998: easy in GERMANY continued

easyJet Germany poster 2011

There has been substantial growth for easyJet in Germany since 1998. The first period of expansion was in 2004 when the airline opened a base at Berlin Schönefeld airport and began flying to 11 new destinations.

Then in 2017 easyJet acquired some of the assets of bankrupt carrier Air Berlin and began operating domestic routes for the first time which significantly increased brand awareness within Germany. Today easyJet is the largest airline operating from Berlin's new Brandenburg airport.

The Guardian

EasyJet to take over BA's German airline

Fast expanding low-cost carrier lashes out at Ryanair for its 'flights to nowhere'

Andrew Clark

EasyJet's plans for expansion moved into overdrive yesterday, as the low-cost airline agreed to buy British Airways' German offshoot, Deutsche BA, and confirmed that it was "within days" of a deal to pur- that its policy of using 'secondary airports meant "every time they announce a new destination you have to get a map out to find out where it is".

EasyJet plans to turn Deutsche BA into a German version of its Luton-based operation. The carrier, which trol by paying between €30m and €39m by July 2003.

Mr Webster said: "We want to make sure Deutsche BA is seen as a European airline, operating as part of the EasyJet brand. We would be the first to admit we've got a lot of work to do in learning how to run an

Alongside its spending spree, EasyJet announced it had made a profit during the quiet winter months for the first time. It produced a first-half pretax profit of £1m, against a loss of £10.2m, with passenger numbers up 36% to 4.3m.

EasyJet had hoped to fi- and did not want to be part of the combined business. Ms Cassani would have preferred Go to remain independent and is unhappy that Go's backer, 3i, has opted to sell.

Mr Webster committed EasyJet to operating from both its own hub at Luton and Go's to time and we will pop them." Go yesterday said its profits had jumped from £4.2m to £17m in the year to March. Job losses under any takeover are expected to be "very few", with surplus ground staff redeployed to new roles as EasyJet opens more routes.

The Guardian 09 May 2002

easyJet Berlin Brandenburg Airport

Germany banner advert Aug 2022

easyJet poster Berlin 2020 (above)

easyEverything Berlin 2001
interior & booking code (bottom)

1998: Doing battle with BRITISH AIRWAYS

Taking on the big guys

Stelios believed the best way to build a brand as consumer champion was to pick a fight with the large established companies in the industry. That's why it's no surprise that taking on the big guys remains one of the easy brand values.

BA Aircraft 1998 (above)
easyJet 'Stop Go' livery
1998 (below)

Go Aircraft 1998

The Guardian 21/12/01 (right)
Evening Standard 11 May 1998 (below)

Evening Standard

EasyJet takes no-frills challenge to High Court

by MARTIN DELGADO

SKY WARS moved to the High Court today as BA faced a legal challenge to its no-frills carrier Go.

Rival EasyJet is seeking an injunction to prevent the company offering return tickets for £100 to its first three destinations – Rome, Milan and Copenhagen.

The Guardian

URGENT MEMO
to Financial Directors/CEOs

Stop your staff wasting company money!

20% of top UK companies use British Airways as their preferred airline for European business travel. They justify this policy on price!

Who are they kidding?
(maybe we should get them a calculator!)

easyJet: Amsterdam from **£22.50** single
BA: Amsterdam from **£267.90** single

easyJet.com
the web's favourite airline

The Economist

BA CHEAPO

VS

easyJet

Does "the world's favourite airline" really want a low cost carrier?

1. Confused customers wouldn't know what "frills" to expect.
2. Their mainstream business will be hit as customers switch to BA CHEAPO.
3. The unions will hate it.
4. Travel agents may boycott their long haul flights if cut out by BA CHEAPO.
5. They will screw it up and lose a fortune, so making money can't be the objective!
6. The only possible reason for starting BA CHEAPO is to eliminate smaller competitors.
7. And then increase their fares again!
8. This is against the consumers' best interests and illegal.

Fly **easyJet** from London Luton to Amsterdam - Barcelona - Nice - Palma de Mallorca - Aberdeen - Inverness - Edinburgh - Glasgow, also new daily services from Liverpool to Amsterdam - Nice

www.easyjet.com

British Airways had earned a reputation for resorting to dirty tricks in their dealings with Laker Airways and Virgin who competed with them on trans-Atlantic routes.

In January 1998 after first initiating and then calling off talks with Stelios to take a stake in easyJet, British Airways announced they were setting up a "copycat" low-cost airline of their own.

The Economist 01/11/97

1998: Doing battle with

BRITISH AIRWAYS

continued

The easyJet clone was called 'Go'. The move triggered a huge legal, advertising and PR campaign by Stelios to prevent BA from succeeding in its aim to put easyJet out of business. As part of the campaign easyJet painted the message "Stop BA Stop Go" on the side of one of its aircraft and flew it to Brussels with a planeload of easyJet staff and their families to lobby the European Commission. Once again, the brand received huge amounts of PR coverage.

It is interesting to note that British Airways' decision to set up Go validated the low-cost concept in the mind of the average European consumer. The rationale being that if BA was prepared to set one up, then low-cost airlines must be as safe as legacy airlines.

Anti-BA ad - 1998

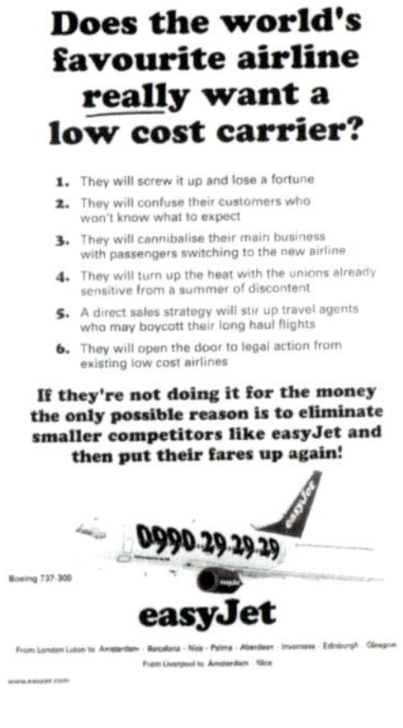

Anti-BA ad - 1998

Evening Standard

MONDAY, 6 NOVEMBER 2000

Rod Eddington: taking the long view

Selling off Go is right for British Airways

Evening Standard
06 Nov 2000

Stelios lobbying
in Brussels - 1998

1998: The most famous easy PR stunt

Taking on the big guys

The battle with British Airways gave rise to one of Stelios' most famous PR stunts. On the morning that Go's flights went on sale, Tony Anderson, easyJet's marketing director at the time, booked ten seats on their inaugural flight from Stansted to Rome. Unfortunately, the distinctive name "Stelios Haji-Ioannou" was spotted by a Go booking agent, so it wasn't a complete surprise for the new airline when easyJet's founder turned up for the first flight. But Go's CEO Barbara Cassani and her team had no idea what was about to hit them.

On 22nd May 1998 Stelios and a group of easyJet employees checked in for Go's inaugural flight wearing bright orange boiler suits with matching baseball caps. The outfits were easyJet branded and each had a single letter printed in white on the reverse.

The Times 29 October 2003

THE TIMES

PART 3 The final extract from Go: An Airline Adventure

'Stelios had won: they sold us out for a quick profit'

In the eyes of BARBARA CASSANI 3i was a shrewd investor, but one that let £600 million of potential return go begging because it needed to offset failures elsewhere

When the team stood in a line they spelled out "Go easyJet" which made for great photographs. Someone from Go's PR team called in the airport police, but of course easyJet were doing nothing illegal and were permitted to board. During the flight Stelios handed

The easyJet "hi-jack" team assemble 22/05/98

Airport police arrive

Barbara Cassani tries to stop Stelios handing out easyJet flight vouchers on-board

out vouchers for free easyJet flights to Go passengers and gave interviews to journalists at the back of the aircraft. The stunt, described as a "hijacking" was widely covered in the UK press and attracted significant media attention including national TV coverage on ITV News. It was ironic that a few years later in 2000 BA sold Go to the venture capital company 3i who then sold it on to easyJet in 2002.

THE Sun

The Sun 23/05/98

CHEAP JET 'HIJACKED

BRITISH Airways' new low-cost airlin Go made its first flight yesterday – an was "hijacked" by the boss of it fiercest competitior.

Stelios Haji-Ioannou, of no-frill rival easyJet, and six of his uniforme staff bought £100 tickets to be amon the 147 passengers on the Boeing 73 from Stansted, Essex, to Rome.

Mr Haji-Ioannou – embroiled in legal war with BA – then accused it c trying to put his firm out of busines by letting Go make a £29million los

He said: "Look at BA's track recor to see how predatory they are."

Go's chief Barbara Cassani – also o board – ignored his stunt. She sai "This is an exciting day for travellers

THE TIMES

The Times 23/05/98

Get set, Go: airline fares war takes off

BA is accused of predatory pricing over cut-price subsidiary, report

Nicholas Wood and Arthur Leathley

THE airline price war took off yesterday with the first flight of Go, British Airways' new low-cost airline. About 150 passengers paid £100 return to fly from Stansted, Essex, to Rome.

But BA's entry into the competitive but expanding budget market — which serves up to 10 million passengers a year — was clouded by claims from smaller rivals that its predatory pricing is intended to drive them out of business.

Five airlines have cut profit margins to the bone, or are even prepared to lose money in the short term, to win a share of the "low-fare" market — the fastest-growing sector in British air travel.

Fares as low as £29.99 into Europe are being offered to attract passengers to a "no-frills" sector that has cut out complimentary drinks and food and other traditional extras to slash prices.

Bargain-hunters have never had such a range of destinations available, with more than 30 European cities on offer. Examples include £123 return to Madrid, £68 return to Edinburgh, £129 return to Venice and £92 return to Barcelona.

But many offers are hedged around with restrictions and often few seats are available at the lowest prices. For example, although airlines proclaim return fares to Rome beginning at just under £100, the reality is that many of the bargain seats are rapidly taken, leaving passengers facing supposedly low-fares of up to £229 or having to connect with a second flight.

In some cases, as few as 30 seats on an aircraft seating more than 150 are available at advertised low prices and have to be booked at least 21 days in advance.

In addition, there are drawbacks in the lack of flexibility on some routes compared with full-price scheduled services. Some fares are non-refundable, while additional charges are sometimes made for changes to travel arrangements. EasyJet, for example, charges £10 for making a change to its cheap flights. Another disadvantage is that some low-cost flights are to secondary airports, leading to long and sometimes expensive journeys to city centres.

Although the market is expanding at a huge rate, there are doubts whether there will be enough passengers to support the five airlines offering low-cost fares. Industry speculation suggests that at least one will be forced out of business or into a merger.

The airlines leading the no-frills crusade are Ryanair, the pioneers of the British low-fare market, easyJet, Debonair, Virgin Express and Go, the British Airways subsidiary.

Yesterday, easyJet, which is taking legal action against the national flag carrier on the ground that it is abusing its dominant market position, tried to steal the limelight from Go's first flight.

EasyJet's chairman, Stelios Haji-Ioannou, was among the passengers on the Rome flight. He was accompanied by six easyJet staff dressed in the airline's distinctive orange uniforms.

Mr Haji-Ioannou said: "Go has been given permission by BA to lose £29 million and then close in three years, having put its rivals out of business. You only have to look at BA's track record to see how predatory they are."

But Barbara Cassani, chief executive of Go, denied that the company had been set up merely to drive other no-frills rivals from the field.

Richard Branson, whose Virgin Express group is among the five leading players in the low-cost market, leapt into the fray by accusing BA of subsidising its new no-frills service. He claimed that, for the four airlines already in the market and about to face the might of British Airways, the impending struggle is akin to "a bleeding competition against a blood bank".

Go passengers will get refreshments on flights — but have to pay. All the rival firms have managed to reduce costs heavily through using airports that have much lower charges than Gatwick and Heathrow, although Virgin Express has flights to Brussels from both.

Luton and Stansted airports have become the main battleground of the low-cost carriers, although Ryanair and easyJet also use other regional and Scottish airports.

Business, page 27

EasyJet chairman Stelios Haji-Ioannou with Go's Barbara Cassani yesterday

CUT-PRICE FARES COMPARED

Destinations	Prices	Restrictions
Debonair, from Luton		
Barcelona, Madrid, Dusseldorf, Munich, Nice, Rome.	From £82.90 to Dusseldorf to £123 to Madrid.	Up to 40 seats at the cheapest rates are available on 98-seater aircraft. Some cheap flights require a midweek flight, with a Saturday stopover.
easyJet, from Luton and Liverpool		
Aberdeen, Edinburgh, Glasgow, Inverness, Amsterdam, Nice, Geneva, Barcelona, Palma, Majorca.	From £68 to Aberdeen, Edinburgh and Glasgow to £110.70 to Nice. From Liverpool: Amsterdam £71.20, Nice £112.70	Number of cheapest seats is not disclosed. Bookings are made direct with airline and confirmed with credit card on departure, and can be transferred to another flight for a £10 fee.
Go, from Stansted		
Rome, Milan and, from June 5, Copenhagen.	All seats initially £100 return including taxes, although fares will increase next month, when new destinations will be added.	All bookings are direct and not through travel agencies. Bookings cannot be changed.
Ryanair, from Stansted and Luton		
Cork, Dublin, Kerry, Knock, Glasgow (Prestwick), Carcassonne, St Etienne, Pisa, Rimini, Venice, Kristianstad (Malmo), Oslo, Stockholm.	From £88 to Glasgow to £129 for Pisa, Rimini and Venice. One-way tickets to Dublin from Luton and Stansted on selected flights £29.99 including airport tax.	Half the seats are sold at lowest prices and tickets can be transferred between flights. No seat reservations.
Virgin Express from Gatwick, Heathrow and Stansted		
Nice, Barcelona, Madrid, Milan, Rome, Copenhagen.	From £92 to Barcelona and Madrid, to £101 for Copenhagen. Special offer price of £39 plus airport tax for one-way journeys.	All journeys require aircraft change at Brussels, with one-hour wait. First 30 seats at cheapest fare, have to be booked at least 21 days ahead of travel

1998: easy in GREECE

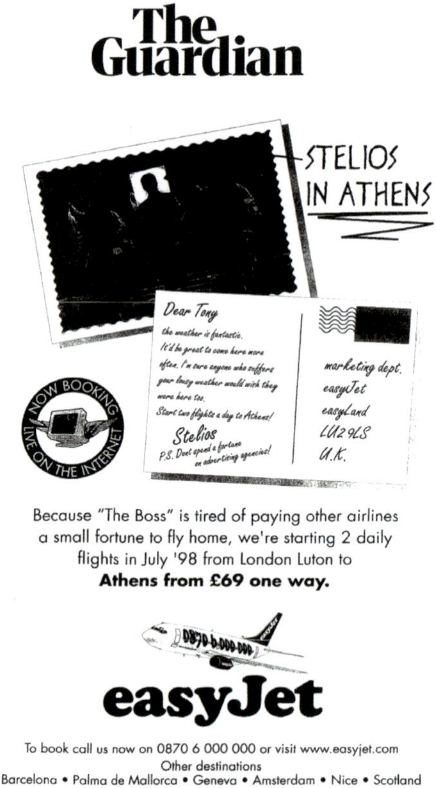

The Guardian ad 16 May 98

For more than two years after easyJet began flying Stelios was consistently asked about flights between London and Athens, the city of his birth.

It used to be said that every airline has a so-called "Chairman's route", a destination chosen for the convenience of the Chairman despite the commercial case for flying the route not being so strong. For the first three years Stelios resisted the temptation to start this service until the airline had reached a point in its growth and brand awareness that it could support a route with high operating costs where high load factors were essential.

easy outside the movie theatre in Athens 2022

Early easyJet web banner ad 2000

The Guardian ad 28 Jan 03

When Stelios decided that the time was right for easyJet to operate to Athens he asked the marketing team to design a press advertisement making a joke on the theme of the Chairman's route.

The first easyJet flight touched down in Athens on 1st July 1998. The plane was full and the new service soon proved to be profitable.

Since then easyJet has become established as the largest scheduled operator between London and Athens.

1998: easy in GREECE

continued

Stelios' Greek-Cypriot heritage meant that the arrival of easyJet on the Athens route was always going to be high profile. Until this point easyJet's strategy had been to pick a fight with the national carrier, however Olympic airlines was in such a bad financial state that it could hardly be described as a David versus Goliath battle. So instead Stelios decided to pick a fight with the Greek Travel Agents Federation.

He ran a series of controversial advertisements in the Greek press encouraging the public to book direct and cut out the middleman. He even arranged for the slogan "cut out your travel agent" to be written on the side of the aircraft flying to Athens.

Greek plane with anti-travel agent message - 1998

The Federation of Greek travel agents accused Stelios of 'commercial hooliganism' and the dispute eventually ended up in the Greek courts.

On the day of the hearing in July 1998 Stelios offered free flights to London for members of the public prepared to turn up and support him. A crowd of several hundred supporters including several travel agents, assembled outside the courts.

The Guardian

Flight wars

EasyJet seeks fare play

Cut-price airline issues court challenge, **Helena Smith** reports from Athens

Airtours makes £81m swoop

Article on Athens court case- 22/07/98

easyLand Greece interior

easyLand, Evripidou 10, Athens 105 59, Greece

easy in GREECE today

In the EU post Brexit

The easy family of brands have had a continuous presence in the Greek market dating back to 1998 when easyJet first started flying to Athens. Awareness of the easy brand had been high since 1995 due to Stelios having been born in Greece. This meant that many Greeks took pride in his achievements.
Today that strong brand awareness is reflected in the presence of many other easy branded companies.

easyJet destinations from Athens 2024

easyJet fly 126 international routes from Greek airports

easyJet destinations from Mykanos 2022

easyJet Destinations from Thessalonika 2022

In 2017, Ferryhopper a startup from Athens won Stelios' Young Greek Entrepreneur Award. Since then, the two parties have collaborated to create easyFerry, trademark number 2359916 at easyferry.com – an innovative platform for booking ferry tickets online to the Greek islands and beyond.

Stelios with easyFerry team 2019

Stelios has never been afraid to try something new, so taking advantage of a recent legalisation of CBD in the EU he partnered with a Greek company to launch an online retailer under the brand easyHemp, trademark number 18126667 at www.easyHemp.gr. This certainly got the media talking in his native Greece.

Stelios and Christos Botsis of easyHemp

MarketingWeek

www.easyStudies.gr: New guide to studying abroad

easyStudies Marketing Weekly July 2020

easyStudies is a more recent venture launched in 2020 providing information on studying abroad to prospective students. Find out more on www.easyStudies.io.

In 2023 a brand licence was signed with the homeware retailer Aithrio that enables Greek customers to purchase products for the home via easyCasa.gr

In 2020 a landmark ruling by the Greek trademark Office recognised easy as a distinctive sign and a famous brand.

Stelios with Giannis Xoxolis of easyCasa.gr

1998: Relentless innovation

Discounts for booking via the web

It is a little-known fact that easyJet offered a facility for customers to book online through Compuserve all the way back to the first flight in 1995 though this was never really developed or promoted in the first three years. In April 1998 easyJet launched a website with an online booking capability, something very novel at the time. The number of bookings made through the website surpassed all expectations. Stelios was initially sceptical about the internet but soon realised the game-changing potential of the new technology. He took the bold decision to incentivise easyJet customers to switch from the telephone to the internet by offering them a discount. Some customers were upset at first because they did not have access to the web which is one of the reasons Stelios got into the internet café business. Advertising efforts were focused on encouraging customers to book online with 'the web's favourite airline' (mocking BA's "The world's

Article on website development easyUpdate 1997

Whats Coming?

The easyJet web site is currently under development and will be launched next month. This will be a huge advertising tool for easyJet and allows our customers to readily access current information about us at all times. With time we are looking to develop the web further to allow our customers to dial in and actually make their own reservations themselves via the internet.

The easyJet Web Site

What's Going?

Those of you who've been with easyJet for a year or more will have noticed that the easyJet cartoon plane has disappeared from our advertising and is becoming an endangered species. Feedback from our customers told us that it was re-inforcing the misconception shared by some people that we fly old aeroplanes when of course the reverse is true. The cartoon aeroplane has been replaced with a line drawing which looks far more professional.

The Cartoon Plane

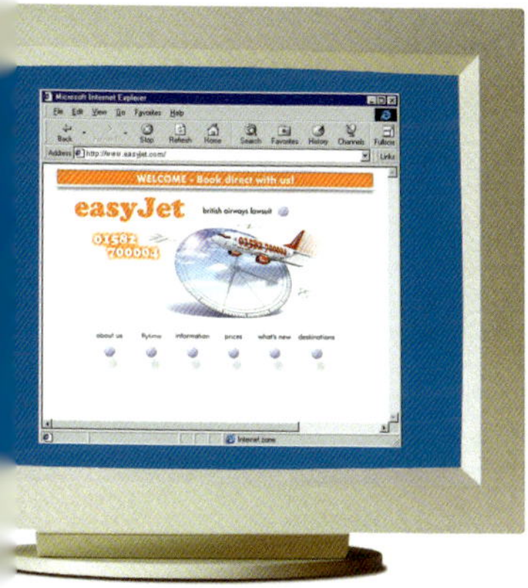

First easyJet website 1998

easyJet tagline – 1999-2001

favourite airline") while the telephone number on the side of the aircraft was replaced with the easyJet.com website address. Some journalists described easyJet as one of many so-called "dot-com" companies that floated during the first internet bubble in 2000. But in easyJet's case but instead of bursting it was able to use the internet to build a strong business model. On the back of his airline's success with online booking Stelios could see the strategic importance of the internet for the easy family of brands. In 1999 Stelios paid $50,000 to an American company to purchase domain name easy.com. It was a bubble era price and he never again paid that sort of money for a domain. Web-based email has been available free-of charge at easy.com continuously since 2000.Today the service is offered in partnership with the California based company Mail2World through easyemail.org.

Fuselage website livery

Economist ad 29/04/00

easyJet website 2019

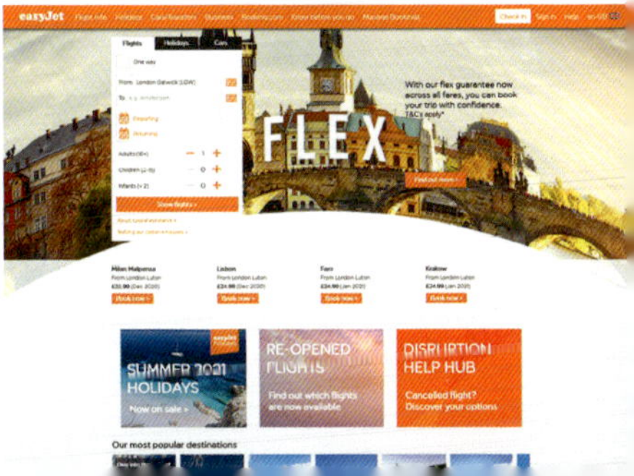

1998: Relentless innovation

easy Internet access for the many

Campaign against AOL 1999

10 million customers per year.

On the 5th of June 1998 Stelios registered "easyWeb" with trademark number 2168668 seen at www.easyweb.mobi. Three months later he revealed to the BBC a plan to bring internet to the masses with the launch of a chain of giant internet cafes to be called easyEverything, trademark number 15591639 seen at easyeverything.com that later rebranded to easyInternetcafe, trademark number 2671097 filed on the 15th April 2002, see easyInternetcafe.com. The brand choice was deliberate: Stelios was making everything easy: easyEverything. In 1999 with the internet boom gathering pace, the first store opened opposite Victoria station, one of five central London locations, offering high speed internet access 24 hours a day.

Stelios outside Victoria easyInternetcafe 1999

Mirror

Bargain buys on easy Net

EXCLUSIVE

CUT-PRICE airline easyJet is about to take the High Street by storm.

Not content with battling British Airways, easyJet boss Stelios Haji-Ioannou will next week announce the launch of easyEverything – Britain's biggest Internet store.

Slicker can reveal that the Greek tycoon will open a massive shop just off London's Oxford Street in the early summer. For around £1 an hour, shoppers can use one of the store's 500 computers linked direct to the Internet.

Buyers can order virtually anything – from books and CDs to TVs and hi-fis – at knockdown prices.

WEB: Haji-Ioannou

The computers are linked by the Internet direct to warehouses, cutting out the overheads of conventional retailers. Goods are paid for by credit card and then delivered to the home.

Stelios told Slicker: "It will be like going to an Argos shop, except you won't just have Argos goods – you can get hold of virtually everything at lower prices."

The London store will be followed by openings later this year in Liverpool and Edinburgh. And there are plans to take the venture into Europe.

Stelios said: "The Internet is the way forward. Once this gets going, people will no longer pop down the shops to go shopping. They'll just pop down to our Internet shop and do it from in there."

Daily Mirror article 09/03/99 (left)

easyEverything ad Daily Mirror 03/12/99

Just a few months later a second store opened in Tottenham Court Road, followed by outlets in Oxford Street, High Street Kensington and the Strand (next to Trafalgar Square). This new retailing concept was initially highly successful attracting large volumes of customers. This led to a major expansion in major cities across Europe that resulted in massive awareness for the easy brand.

In November 2000 easyEverything opened the world's largest internet café at 42nd Street, Times Square, New York with over 1,000 seats and earned a place in the Guinness Book of Records. The store was opened by Carly Fiorina who was then the CEO of Hewlett Packard and later became a Presidential Candidate for the Republican party.

DAILY EXPRESS

Crowds queue to surf Net for £1 an hour

BY MICHAEL HANLON
SCIENCE CORRESPONDENT

THE world's biggest cyber cafe opened in London yesterday and a crowd of more than 100 people were waiting to sign on.

The cafe, called easyEverything, has 400 terminals and users can surf the

easyEverything Express 22/06/99

easyEverything sets World Record

1998: Relentless innovation

easy Internet access for the many .... continued

CBS

World's biggest cyber cafe opens
EasyEverything plans cafes across U.K., Europe

By Gareth Vaughan, CBS MarketWatch
Last Update: 2:24 PM ET Jun 21, 1999
LONDON (CBS.MW) -- It's got Buckingham Palace, Madame Tu
London. Now Britain's biggest city can also boast that it possesses
Internet cafe.

Opening Monday, opposite Victoria Station in central London, is EasyEverything. With 400 computer terminals spread across 10,000 square feet, it is -- according to Ernst Larson of NetCafeGuide.com, which has surveyed 2,300 cyber cafes in 115 countries -- the largest Internet cafe on the planet.

As part of an introductory offer, EasyEverything will charge customers $1.58 (1 British pound) per hour to surf the Net. It will be open 24 hours a day, seven days a week. The British group that's opening the behemoth site claims its economies of scale bring down the price of both shopping and Net access.

"EasyEverything prices will start at 1 pound an hour, undercutting the British Telecommunications (BTY: news, msgs) peak-rate local (phone) call charge and making EasyEverything cheaper than the so-called free Internet access deals," EasyEverything said in a statement.

CBS NewsWatch 21 June 1999

The huge customer numbers visiting easyEverything helped easyJet to become known as the 'web's favourite airline'. By 2000 more customers were visiting the easyEverything stores each month than were flying on the airline. Then Stelios learnt a hard lesson in technical obsolescence. In 2001 he bought his first Blackberry and realised people no longer needed to go to a physical shop to access the internet. He started closing down some of the internet shops that were on expensive leases.

Today the easy family of brands is still selling coffee and refreshments on the high street via the easyCoffee brand. The irony is that the Blackberry devices of the early 2000s themselves were made obsolete by the new generation of smartphones like the iPhone. Clearly this was a very fast changing business. Stelios often mentions signing the property leases for the internet cafes as being his most expensive mistake in business; however the lasting legacy is that...

he introduced millions of people to their first internet experience for just £1.

Evening Standard

It's easy @café

The biggest cybercafé in the world opens in London today offering round-the-clock Internet access through 550 terminals at easyEverything's latest venture in Kensington High Street. The huge scale of the £500,000 project reflects the massive boom in people who would rather go out and socialise online than visit a pub or nightclub. **EMILY SHEFFIELD** reports

Evening Standard 04 Feb 2000

The Guardian 16 May 2000

The Guardian

Stelios takes Easy's brand of net cafe to US and Europe

Mary O'Hara

EasyGroup, the company which runs the no-frills airline EasyJet, has set its sights on expanding its chain of internet cafes into the US and Europe.

The company will use £10m financing secured from investment group, Apax Partners, to part-fund the launch of its EasyEverything stores – which have proved popular in London.

"will roll out in premium, high footfall locations across Europe and the US".

James Rothnie, the director of corporate affairs, confirmed that a flotation of EasyEverything was inevitable at some stage, saying that this was in line with EasyGroup's "masterplan to float individual companies within the group in their own good time".

Mr Rothnie claimed that despite the trend toward cheaper

According to EasyEverthing, its in-store research shows that as many as 25% of all visitors to the five London stores are individuals who not only live in London but also have independent access to the internet at home. Approximately 40% are tourists.

Mr Rothnie predicted that rather than the high levels of internet penetration in the US presenting a threat to the enterprise, it would actually bol-

Queues form outside London easyEverything locations (left & above)

easy in household cleaning products

Taking on the big guys

With a heritage stretching back for 150 years and former owner of the famous Jeyes brand, the company today known as easy Cleaning Solutions has led the development of effective, affordable cleaning solutions in the UK.

easyCleaning product delivery fleet 2021

For fifty years they have operated from one of the largest integrated cleaning product factories in Europe, a 35,000 sq m factory/ warehouse located in Thetford, Norfolk.

easyCleaning now headed by David Pearce and Darren Mosley employs over 300 people and produces 33 million consumer facing units per annum. In December 2020 easyGroup acquired brand rights including prior use for easy cleaning thus providing further diversification for the easy Family of Brands.

Darren Mosley
easy Cleaning
Solutions CEO
darren.mosley@
easycleaningco.com

David Pearce
easy Cleaning
Solutions
Chairman

easyCleaning product line 2022

easy in household cleaning products

Taking on the big guys continued

P&G Unilever

This means that easy branded cleaning products have adopted the distinctive orange get-up under licence from easyGroup.

The terms of its licence agreement with easyGroup allow easyCleaning to use the easy brand in colours other than orange provided the compliant orange version is included in the range.

Stelios with easyCleaning products 26 May 2021

easyCleaning factory in Norfolk, UK

easyCleaning products on shelves next to competitors

Competitors to our easyCleaning products include two of the world's largest companies: P&G that owns Fairy Liquid and Persil and Unilever which owns the famous bleach brand Domestos. This takes easyGroup's brand value of taking on the big guys to a new level.

> **The market cap for Unilever was £95.2 billion and £293 billion for P&G on 15th Apr 2024.**
> **Annual turnover of easyCleaning in 2023/2024 was £64 million, with 130 million units produced by the easyCleaning factory for all brands.**

Today easyCleaning products are available in a wide range of supermarkets and discount stores across the UK. They can also be found on the shelves of Dunnes stores in the Republic of Ireland and other locations in mainland Europe.

easyCleaning products on shelves next to competitors at great value

easy in household cleaning products

Taking on the big guys continued

easyCleaning invests heavily in research and development and has a reputation for innovation in its sector. In 2023 the company added some exciting new products to their range. These include premium coloured bleaches and new Mega Value laundry powders with less packaging and higher concentrate reducing the environmental impact. More new cleaning products are in the pipeline for launch in 2024. Visit www.easyCleaning.biz for details.

As shoppers continue to seek out value, easyCleaning is growing its distribution in the UK and overseas. The number of stockists of the company's continues to rise including new retailers now stocking the company's products. Look out for them in a supermarket near you.

easyCleaning coloured bleach range and assortment of products available in 2024

Buy easy Products in-store at:

- B&M
- Fab Finds
- Farmfoods
- Home Bargains
- Iceland
- Poundland
- Poundstretcher
- Savers
- Tesco
- The Range

1999: Doing battle with

LONDON LUTON AIRPORT & BARCLAYS

Taking on the big guys

Stelios made an important decision back in 1995 when he chose to base his new airline at Luton rather than Stansted. This choice went against the tide because most new airlines chose to base themselves at Stansted. Luton was considered a package holiday airport used by charter carriers rather than a home for an operator of scheduled services.

Stelios signs deal with then CEO Richard Gooding at Luton Airport Aug 95

But Stelios saw the airport had plenty of scope for growth and he managed to secure a great deal from his negotiations with the airport which was owned by Luton Council.

However in 1997 the Council issued a 30 year concession contract to a public-private sector partnership jointly owned by Airports International Group and Barclays private equity. The partnership published plans to construct an expensive and over-elaborate new passenger building designed by award winning architect Sir Norman Foster that Stelios nicknamed the "Taj Mahal".

FT 13 August 1997

Stelios predicted that the new facilities would end up being paid for by easyJet's passengers in the form of higher fares.

In May 2000 the Times reported that Luton intended to raise landing fees from £1.68 per passenger to between £6 and £7. Stelios initiated a high profile campaign against Barclays including a stunt where he cut up a giant Barclaycard outside the bank's Luton branch. These activities further developed the easy brand's reputation for standing up for the rights of the consumer against the big corporate fat cats of which Barclays was a prime example. Stelios subsequently imposed a "Barclay's Fat Cat" charge of £4 for easyJet's departing Luton passengers.

FT FINANCIAL TIMES

EasyJet threatens move after Luton turns down offer

By Charis Gresser

A row has erupted between the local authority which owns London Luton Airport and its most important customer, low-cost airline EasyJet.

Luton Borough Council has rejected EasyJet's proposal to run the airport, which is 30 miles north of London, in return for a capital investment. The airline is now considering shifting some of its operations to Liverpool, blaming capacity constraints at Luton.

The council, which is seeking £170m of development capital in exchange for granting a concession to run the airport, has said it did not think it "appropriate" to select a commercial partner "with links to any airline operating at the airport".

Luton Airport 1996 easyLand top left

FT 19 may 1997 (below)

The battles with Luton led to the accelerated development of a second UK base for easyJet at Liverpool Airport.

FT FINANCIAL TIMES

Easyjet's owner wants to buy Luton airport

By Michael Skapinker, Aerospace Correspondent

The owner of the low-fare airline Easyjet, Mr Stelios Haji-Ioannou, has told Luton Borough Council that he wants to buy Luton airport.

airport to operate as a commercial entity while remaining wholly owned by the council.

One analyst said he thought Luton airport could be sold in spite of the council's reservations. "In the brave new world of Labour, anything is possi-

In [illegible], Luton council, then under Conservative control, was set to sell an [illegible] per cent stake in the airport to Lockheed of the US for [illegible]. But Labour campaigned in the [illegible] local elections on a promise to keep the airport under council

Stelios cuts up his BarclayCard June 1999

1999: easy Co-working & serviced offices

With his experience of disrupting outdated business models, Stelios was among the first people to spot that the traditional office market was not providing the value and flexibility demanded by the entrepreneurial occupiers of the new economy. Alongside this, Stelios has a long-standing interest in the budget office space dating back more than two decades. The development of easyOffice came off the back of the learnings from easyEverything which was established in 1998.

easyOffice Kensington High Street building and Poster from Jan 2008

easyOffice Camden (left) & Hammersmith (above)

Stelios realised that many internet start-ups were using the internet cafes as an office to run their businesses. He applied for the EU trademark easyOffice on October 18th 2002, opening the first easyOffice at High Street Kensington in 2007. Today, the company has evolved into an online broker for office space and operates alongside its sister brand easyHub, trademark number 17929119.

easyOffice.co.uk website & Manchester Brochure 2008

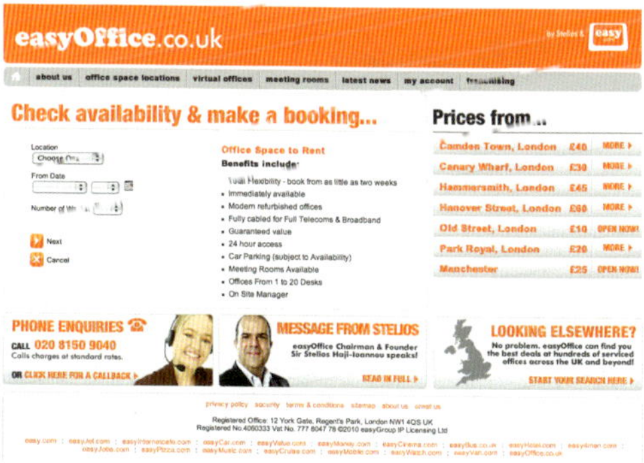

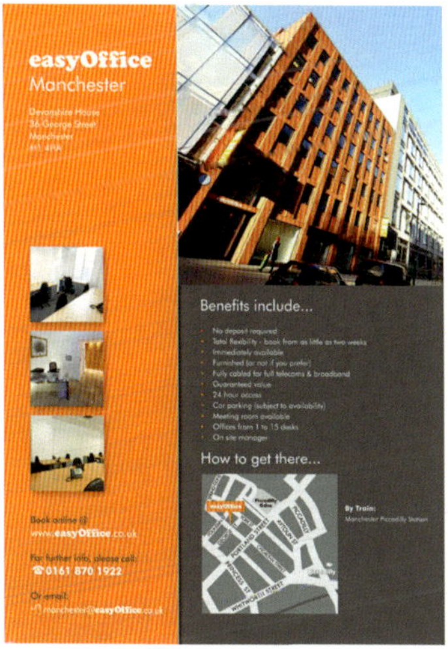

1999: easy Co-working & serviced offices

continued

easyHub is a flexible workspace offering for SMEs and entrepreneurs and has a flagship hub in fashionable Chelsea, Central London, for which Stelios paid £16m for the freehold. The centre itself is home to many of the early stage members of the easy family who benefit from a special deal offering them office space at a fantastic rate of £50 per desk per month, one of the many benefits of membership.

Other easyHub centres can be found at Croydon, Derby, Park Royal, Burgess Hill, Walsall and Horsham and are rapidly expanding across the UK.

Today easyHub manages over 250,000 square feet of office space.

easyHub Croydon

easyHub Chelsea exterior & Interior

Steve Jude - CEO easyHub

The business model for expansion involves selling franchises to building owners and property office entrepreneurs, with Citibase, led by CEO Steve Jude having the master franchise. If you are a property owner and are looking to set up a new office space, check out www.easyHub.com, call us on 0844 499 3433 or email: franchise@easyHub.com.

easyHub Horsham

easyHub Burgess Hill

easyHub office interior

1999: easy in Financial services

On 19th January 1999 Stelios revealed in an interview with Reuters that he was working on a business plan to develop an online financial services business called easyMoney, trademark number 2184834 filed on 18th December 1998.

In August 2001 an easyMoney credit card was set up in partnership with independent credit company Accucard. The card allowed customers to personalise their credit conditions by adjusting the variables of cashback, interest rates and annual fees. Accucard was later acquired by high street banking giant Lloyds TSB. During the banking crisis of 2008 the bank decided to close down that side of the business.

Mirror

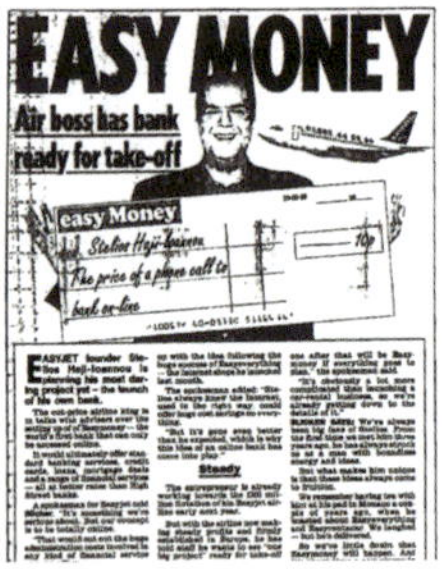

FT FINANCIAL TIMES

EasyJet founder to set up bank on internet

By James Mackintosh

Stelios Haji-Ioannou, founder of EasyJet, is planning to set up his own internet bank next year, after he has taken on the car rental industry.

The bank will continue the move by Mr Haji-Ioannou's Easy group to embrace the internet. EasyJet, which moved into profit last year, sells more than 20,000 tickets a week online. The company recently launched a chain of "Easyeverything" internet cafés and an online car rental operation is under development.

The bank, provisionally titled Easy Money, is designed to take on "an industry that has grown fat", said James Rothnie, director of corporate affairs. However, it is still at the early stages of development and could start as a fund management operation – the route taken by Richard Branson's Virgin Direct – before moving into full-blooded banking.

Daily Mirror article - 12/08/99 (top left)
FT article - 13/08/99 (top right)

easyMoney.com Website 2001

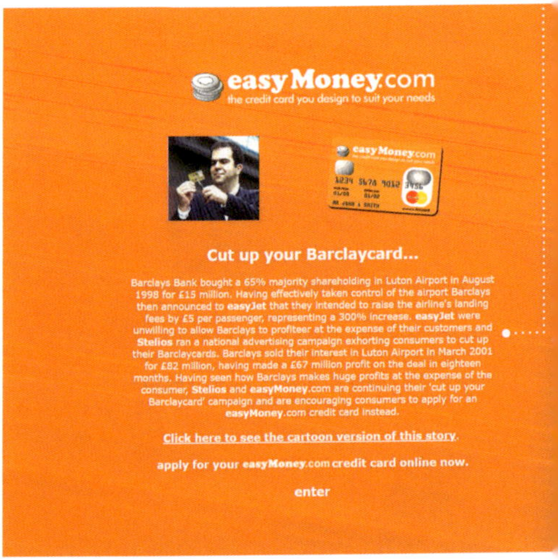

Cut up your Barclaycard...

Barclays Bank bought a 65% majority shareholding in Luton Airport in August 1998 for £15 million. Having effectively taken control of the airport Barclays then announced to easyJet that they intended to raise the airline's landing fees by £5 per passenger, representing a 300% increase. easyJet were unwilling to allow Barclays to profiteer at the expense of their customers and Stelios ran a national advertising campaign exhorting consumers to cut up their Barclaycards. Barclays sold their interest in Luton Airport in March 2001 for £82 million, having made a £67 million profit on the deal in eighteen months. Having seen how Barclays makes huge profits at the expense of the consumer, Stelios and easyMoney.com are continuing their 'cut up your Barclaycard' campaign.

easyJet v Barclays purchase at Luton Airport Cartoon 2001

FT 19 May 2001

FT FINANCIAL TIMES

EasyMoney loans or credit cards on launch

By Jane Croft

EasyMoney.com, the online financial services company to be launched by Stelios Haji-Ioannou, founder of EasyJet, is likely to begin by offering credit cards or personal loans when it launches this summer.

The new service, which does not yet have a banking licence, has no current plans to offer savings or other interest-bearing products.

1999: easy in Financial services .... continued

Stelios as he often does looked to find other business partners to use the easyMoney name which is such a natural brand extension. The brand was also licensed for a period of time to Zurich insurance for selling motor insurance. Today easyMoney is run by entrepreneur Andrew de Candole operating a "fin-tech" business. This is where the financial world meets the tech world to disrupt the legacy banks. easyMoney is offering innovative finance such as peer-to-peer online lending backed by real estate. So if a property developer wants to borrow money against a property and is willing to pay say x% and an investor is willing to lend such funds at say y% income for them, then easyMoney acts as a platform to facilitate this transaction.

The Guardian

Easymoney for airline chief

Easyjet founder Stelios Haji-Ioannou is to go into banking under the name Easymoney, it was reported last night. His first move will be to introduce an online credit card, due in about a month, which will be followed by personal loans. London Scottish is expected to act as a business partner.

The Guardian article 21 Aug 01

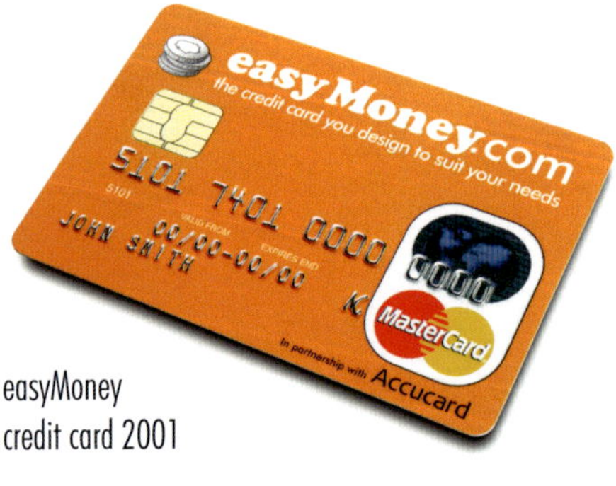

easyMoney credit card 2001

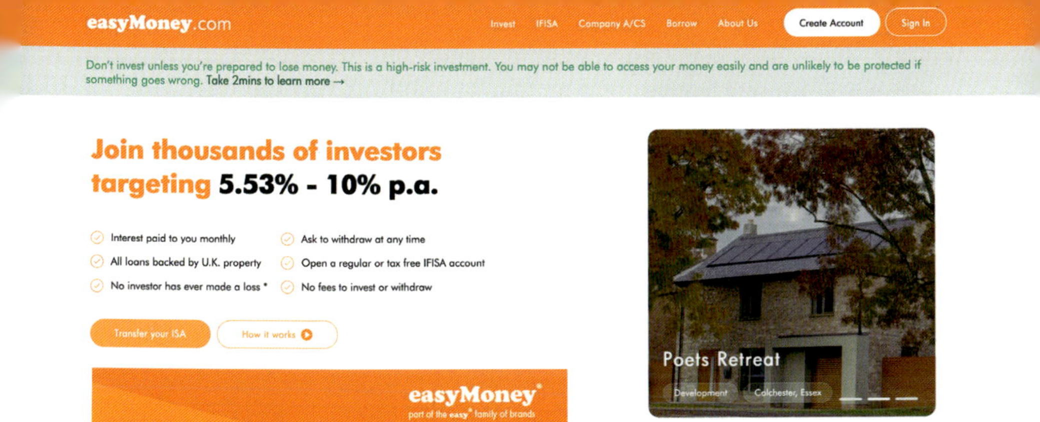

easyMoney Innovative Finance ISA (above)

easyMoney website 2024 & recent awards

easyMoney Financial Times Advert 2010

Andrew de Candole -
CEO easyMoney
andrew@easymoney.com

Jason Ferrando -
easyMoney Head of Lending
jason@easymoney.com

1999: easy in Financial services

continued

The loans provided through easyMoney have been used to finance property developments around the UK. For example, the Rivermead student accommodation located in the South-east of England which was a multi-tranche draw-down facility. Every unit in the development was taken and deposits paid pre-completion. Students have now moved in. The easyMoney brand has also featured in TV advertising on Sky in the UK. A second football match advertising easyMoney was played on 15 Oct 2022 between Watford and Norwich City and broadcast on Sky. Visit www.easyMoney.com for details.

The easyMoney loan book value as of March 2024 was £189.2 million.

Deposits received since inception until March 2024: £305.5 million.

ALTERNATIVE CREDIT INVESTOR

MARCH 15 2024

easyMoney investors earn more than £30m

easyMoney's investors have earned more than £30m in interest payments since the platform launched in 2016.

This comes just months after it was revealed that investors in the property-backed peer-to-peer lending platform were earning in excess of £1m per month.

Jason Ferrando, chief executive of easyMoney, says that this figure has grown since the monthly milestone was reached. He believes that compound interest and tax-free earnings are part of the reason for the platform's growth.

"Our investors can use compound interest to make their money grow faster," says Ferrando.

"Compounding can create a snowball effect, as the original investments plus the income earned from that investment grow together."

easyMoney in alternativecreditinvestor.com 15 Mar 2024

Properties securing the easyMoney loans 2022 - 2024

£366,701,505
Total loans funded

£0.00
Investor losses
*as at 22/04/2024

under 24 hours
Time to invest (last 12 months)

under 24 hours
Time to withdraw (last 12 months)
*as at 22/04/2024

easyMoney numbers 2024

A group of South African investors have signed a licence agreement for the brand easySure offering low-cost insurance initially to customers in Denmark under the easy brand. Visit www.easySure.dk for more.

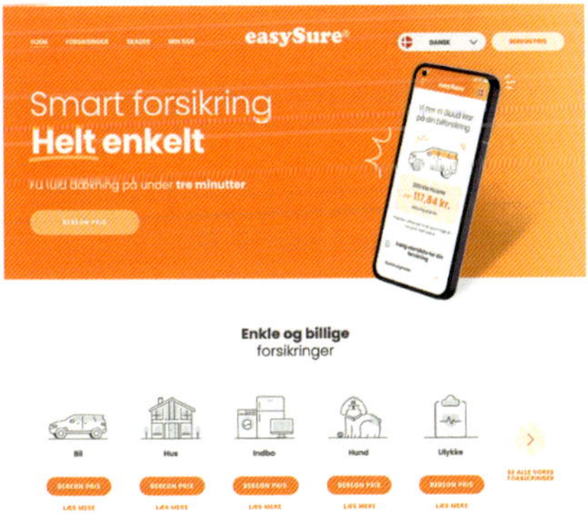

easySure.dk 2024

Søren Pedersen
CEO of easySure

1999:

easy in vehicle rental

Advertising on easyJet confirmation letter 2000

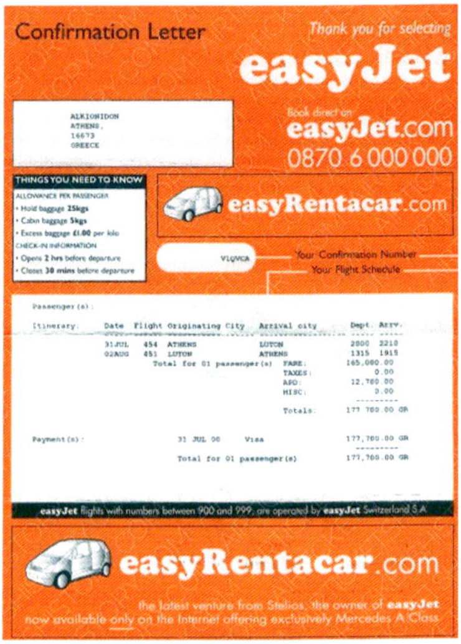

In an interview with 'Reuters' on 10th May 1999 Stelios revealed plans to launch an innovative new vehicle rental concept called easyRentacar, trademark number 2273663 filed on 27th June 2001 seen at easyRentacar.com; (later re-branded as easyCar) offering car rental from £9 per day.

To lower costs the service could only be booked online (considered very novel back then) and there was only a single car type, the Mercedes 'A' Class.

easyRentacar National Post Toronto 01 Mar 2000

NATIONAL POST

EasyRentaCar picks Mercedes for rental fleet

PUSHING LOWER PRICES

BY TIM BURT

GENEVA • Stelios Haji-Ioannou, the entrepreneur behind EasyJet, the low-cost British airline, will announce a tie-up today with DaimlerChrysler AG to launch a European car rental company using the group's Mercedes cars.

easyRentacar ad 2000

The idea was that having a single car type would keep costs down. There was a significant investment in advertising to support the new business, at one point £244,000 was spent in a single day. The easyRentacar business began trading on17 September 1999 from a site near to London Bridge. This was followed by the launch of sites in Glasgow on 24 April 2000 and Barcelona on 26 April 2000. As with the launch of other easy brands there was significant media attention and publicity well before the launch date.

easyRentacar ad Financial Times 13/03/00

easyCar Barcelona 2002 (right)
easyRentacar Snowsfields location

1999: easy in vehicle rental .... continued

EASY'S £9 CAR COUP

Stelios stuns rental market with lowest-ever daily deal

CAPITAL IDEA: Stelios

EXCLUSIVE

EASYJET boss Stelios Haji-Ioannou is to offer car rentals for just £9 a day.

The move, which will stun the British car rental industry, is expected in April with the launch of easyRentaCar, a spin-off from hugely successful low-cost airline easyJet.

Initially, cars will be available at Luton, Glasgow and Madrid.

But Stelios is also planning a London site, targeting thousands of people in the capital who can't afford to run a car but want to run one for a weekend or a few days. The five-day offer, rubber-stamped by Stelios and his top executives last night, will send shivers through top rental firms Avis, Hertz and Europa Car.

The rate will be the only offer from easyRentaCar. The company is in negotiations with Peugeot, Vauxhall and Ford, and plans to offer just one standard car, probably a Peugeot 206, to all customers.

They will also receive a substantial free mileage of several hundred miles, after which a surcharge will be added. This fixed-rate deal will work out up to 40 per cent cheaper than most car-hire companies, and threatens to spark an all-out industry battle similar to that when Stelios first launched his low-cost airline easyJet.

A source close to the company says: "Renting a car is a very expensive business for ordinary people, and there is no reason why it should be.

Cheaper

"In exactly the same way that we made cheaper air travel available to the masses, we aim to do the same with car rentals.

"This price will send a message to the big boys that they can't get away with it any longer."

SLICKER SAYS: Top work, fella. This is a big year for our old pal Stelios – he plans to float easyJet on the stock market and is looking closely at launching an Internet bank.

But car rentals is where the really big money could be. Stelios will face tough competition at overseas sites, as many rival airlines will try to tie in customers to their own car rentals with package deals.

However, in big UK cities, Stelios could really clean up – particularly London and Glasgow, where it often costs more than £5 just to use public transport.

Go for it — we're right behind you on this one.

Daily Mirror 6 Jan 2000

Mirror

Evening Standard 12 July 2017

Evening Standard

EasyCar revs up ride-sharing on a budget

Jamie Nimmo

STUDENTS heading to Glastonbury on a budget will soon be able to hitch a ride with strangers as easyJet founder Sir Stelios Haji-Ioannou jumps on the ride-sharing bandwagon.

His car-rental business is launching easyCar Pool, matching drivers with hitchhikers looking for a spare seat from just £2 a head.

EasyCar already allows users to rent their cars out, but will now operate a model similar to airbnb, where users can rent out seats in their cars.

Today through the easyCar.com and easyRentacar.com websites, customers can compare and book car hire from over 1,700 brands in over 55,000 locations in 153 countries worldwide. Stelios has realised you don't need to own every car in every location to make money out of car rental.

The shareholders of easyCar, TM number 2168714 filed on 3rd April 2001 include VC Fund PROfounders Capital run by Rogan Angelini-Hurll.

Rogan Angelini-Hurll – Chairman easyCar Rogan@profounderscapital.com

CarTrawler's account manager for easyCar.com is Paul O'Brien paulobrien@cartrawler.com

It is a successful company making a profit of about £1m p.a. and distributing it as dividends to all shareholders. The business partner/expert in this venture is world leading broker site CarTrawler who also power the easyJet ancillary revenue stream and cooperate with many brands including:

CarTrawler

Hertz, Thrifty, Europcar, AVIS, Alamo, enterprise, keddy, SIXT, dollar., Firefly, FOX RENT A CAR, National, greenmotion, Payless, Maggiore, FLIZZR

Stelios with his own orange easyCar in Monaco (right)
Stelios with easyVan The orange van man! (bottom)

easy in vehicle charging

In 2022 Monaco-based entrepreneur Frank Scolaro approached Stelios with the idea of setting up a Europe-wide EV charging network under the easy brand. The following year working in partnership with Finnish company Virta the business easyCharging.app was born.

Through an easy-to-use app the user has access to over 100,000 charging points across the UK and Europe suitable for all types of electric vehicle.

easyCharging facilitates access to rapid and cost-effective charging that puts the customer in control.

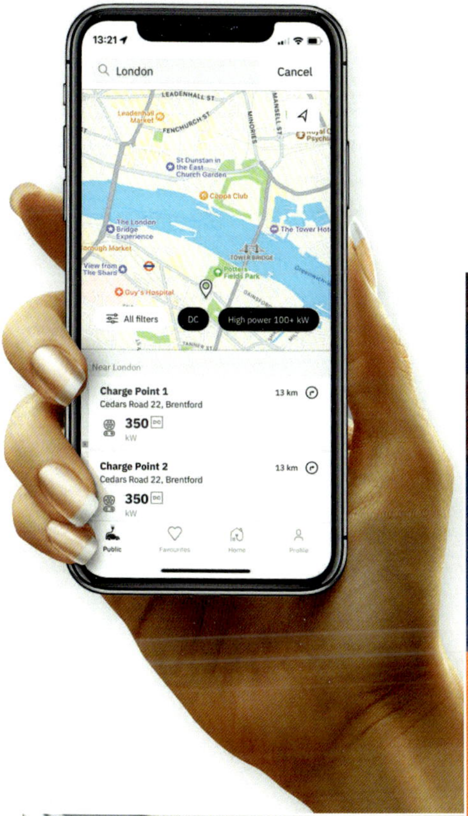

easyCharging App with London Locations (left)

easyCharging Poster 2024 (below)

easyCharging App user account 2024 (bottom)

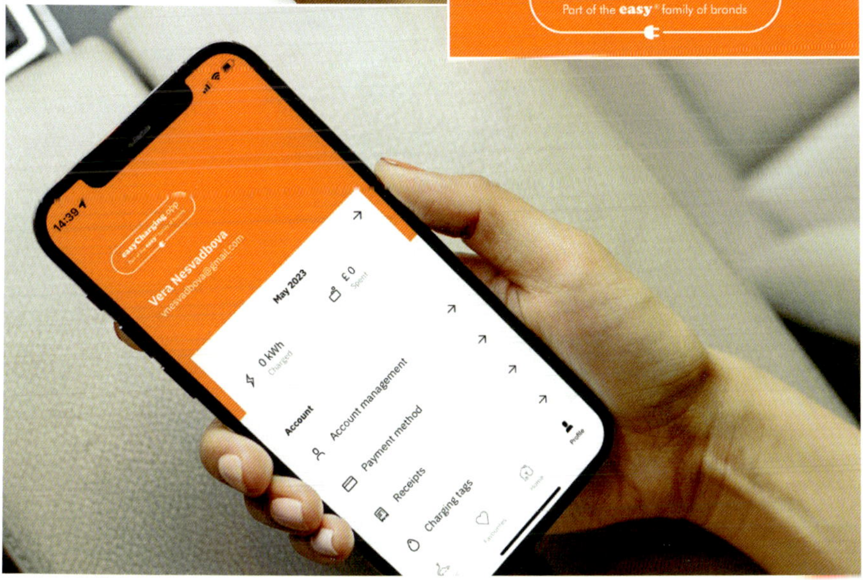

2000: Relentless innovation

easy in Price Comparison

easyValue launched in November 2000, was an online price comparison service that allowed customers to compare the price charged by retailers across a range of products and services. These included photographic goods, financial services, insurance, property, books, music, mobile phones and accessories, games and audio/visual goods.

Within six months of its launch easyValue was attracting over one million visits each month. In December 2001 easyValue was awarded website of the year in its category by the Sunday Times who stated "Another triumph for Britain's on-line trailblazer".

A great benefit of growing the easy family of brands was that each brand could promote others.

easyValue Ryanair spat in Sunday Telegraph 05 May 2002

The Sunday Telegraph

Easyvalue's website data riles Ryanair

By Becky Barrow

RYANAIR, the no-frills airline, is threatening legal action against the empire owned by the Easyjet founder Stelios Haji-Ioannou if its arch-rival continues to publish information about its flights on the Easyvalue comparison website.

Easyvalue, whose slogan is "impartial comparisons for online shopping", uses information from all sources, including Easyjet, to help consumers find the best price available for any flight. It also compares prices on other products, such as books and music players.

easyValue website of the year Sunday Times December 2001 & web banner 2008

THE SUNDAY TIMES

SHOPPER'S FRIEND

www.easyvalue.com
Robot shopping sites of varying quality have multiplied this year, favoured by savvy shoppers for the unique way in which they compare prices across the net. Standing out from the crowd is Stelios's EasyValue.com, which is sensibly limited to checking online prices only, comparing books, DVDs, electrical goods and cameras, but also life-insurance policies. Distinguishing features are transparency — all prices include delivery costs — speed and easily sortable results. Another triumph for Britain's online trailblazer.

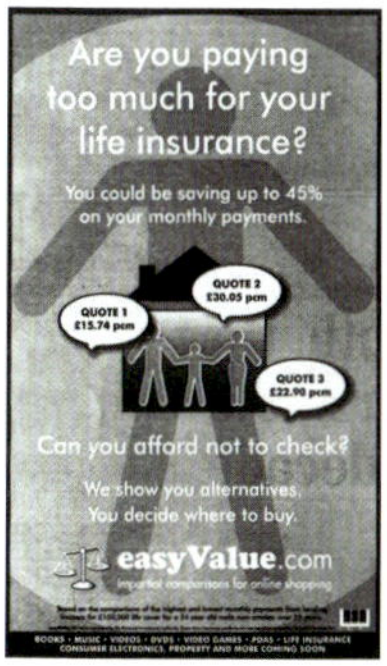

easyValue Ad Daily Mail 10 Dec 2000 (left),
Life Insurance ad Daily Mail 28 Feb 2001 (right)

In 2000 easyValue entered into an agreement with easyEverything to promote and negotiate advertising opportunities of a sponsorship nature in relation to the easyvalue.com website. The easyValue brand remains in use today under a partnership agreement with Booking.com allowing access to hotel rooms around the world at great prices through the website easyValue.com.

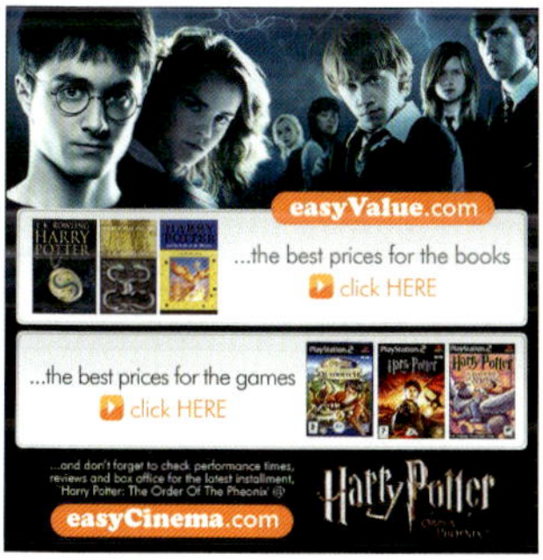

easyValue Web Banners 2001 - 2007 (above)

easyValue Website Homepage 2004 (below)

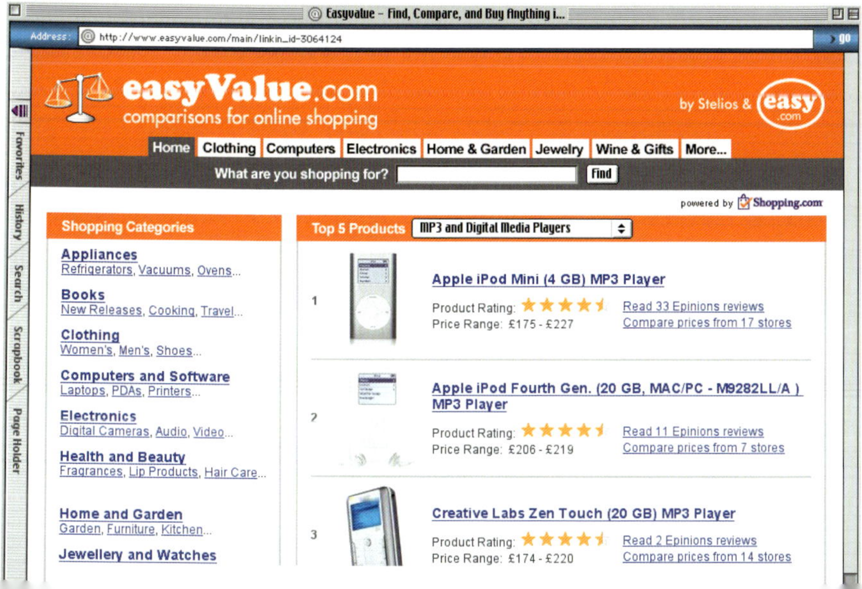

2000: Relentless innovation

easyLife & Online Shopping

The easyLife brand first came to prominence in the summer of 2000 when entrepreneur Gregory Caplan launched his first easylifeonline.com branded catalogue. The catalogue offered a wide range of products with the common theme of solving every day practical problems for its customers, most of whom were in the 65+ age group.
This first catalogue was mailed to a customer database of around 200,000 names. The initial response rate was low, possibly because the internet was still relatively new and the use of a .com suffix in the name may have alienated customers drawn from an older demographic.

The branding was therefore changed to simply easylife (at this point written with a small 'l') and under this brand the business grew significantly. The catalogues were mainly distributed through inserts in national and local newspapers and magazines. Orders were made through printed forms at the back of the catalogues, by telephone or via the easylifeonline.com website. As easylife became more established in the mail order catalogue space it started to develop joint venture relationships with the national newspapers and publishers to produce own branded catalogues.
Newspaper partnerships included UK titles with the largest circulations such as The News of the World, The Sun, The Mirror, The Daily Telegraph, The Guardian and The Radio Times.

easyLife Radio Times Reader offer 2008 (page right)

Greg Caplan
CEO, easyLife
greg@easylife.co.uk

easyLife has printed more paper catalogues than any other business in the UK

easyLife joined the easy family of brands in 2022

Products were mainly sourced from China and in most cases were new to the UK market. The wide range included personal care and cleaning products. All products had easylife branded instructions while some also carried easylife branding on the packaging. Over the course of its trading history (up to 2022) easylife has inserted more than a billion catalogues and mailed out over 100 million catalogues to its customer database and served over 5 million customers with over 10 million orders.

With the rise of the internet, newspaper circulations have gone into decline and a greater emphasis has been placed on internet distribution. Easylife now sends out tens of millions of marketing emails to its base each month. Since 2016 a new marketing channel has been set-up whereby easylife undertakes outbound calls to previous customers who have given permission to be contacted.

In July 2022, easylife Limited joined the easy family of brands. As part of an agreed settlement the company transferred to easyGroup Limited its considerable goodwill, its common law rights in the Easylife brand, the easycare brand, the easygreen brand and the easyclean brand (including the right to sue for passing off) as well as its rights in a large number of easylife related domain names and the Easylife Trademarks.

easyLife Daily Mail White Label ad 2012
easyLife with easy getup, The Mirror 3 Sept 22

easyLife
everyday solutions

Protect your furniture and keep it looking new for longer

Family-proof your furniture and keep it looking new for longer with these reversible protectors. They're made from soft, plush, quilted fabric that's actually a lot tougher than you'd think. Hardwearing and water-repellent, they provide an effective shield against splashes, spills, dirt, stains and pet hair. And as the protectors are reversible, giving your armchairs, two and three-seater sofas a new look only takes seconds. Held securely in place by an adjustable strap, our protectors are machine-washable and come with a zipped storage case.

REVERSIBLE FURNITURE PROTECTOR

	Brown	Sage	Wine	Black	
Armchair	6211	6306	6490	6493	**£14.99**
2-seat Sofa	6212	6307	6491	6494	**£19.99**
3-seat Sofa	6213	6308	6492	6495	**£24.99**
Recliner	3297	3299	3298	3300	**£19.99**

SAVE £20

up to 1500 piece puzzles

Jigsaw organiser gets puzzles sorted

Puzzling where to do your jigsaw? Here's the tailor-made solution. A non-slip surface (large enough for a 1,500-piece puzzle), with 4 reinforced sliding drawers underneath. These are ideal for sorting jigsaw pieces and storing them until needed. Made from MDF and pine for durability and strength, it measures L89xW66xD14.5cm with an L84xW61cm puzzling surface and four L40xW27cm drawers.

Deluxe Wooden Jigsaw Organiser
5272 **£49.99**
WAS ~~£69.99~~ **SAVE £20**

Trustpilot
'We're rated 'Great'!'

Pay in 3.
Interest free
with **Klarna.**
For online orders over £35

Your purchase is Sliced into 3 equal card payments

The first payment is collected when the order is shipped. The remaining two will be automatically collected in 30 and 60 days

No fees, No interest and no credit check. No impact on your Credit Score.

Sound good? Just Select Klarna. at checkout

2000: Relentless innovation

easyLife & Online Shopping continued

Among the thousands of products offered by easyLife is one of their best-selling products the easyHose which saves space and time for gardeners and car washers. Versatile, The easyHose expands to up to three times its length and has a five-year burst proof guarantee, see easyHose.net

easyHose, available for sale on easyLife.co.uk

In 2023 easyLife opened a new warehouse in Sheerness, Kent with over 40,000 square feet of space to support their continued growth and expansion.

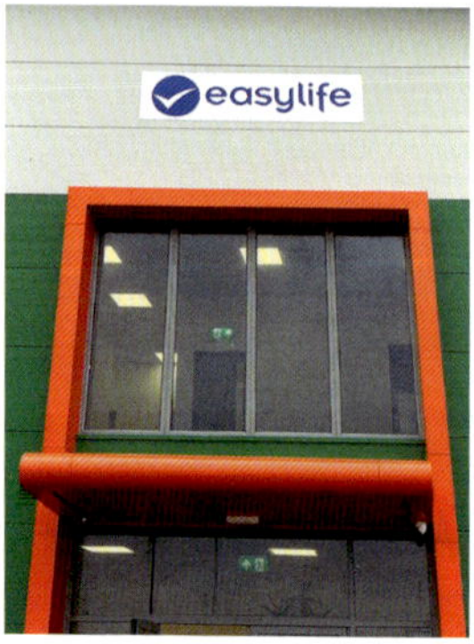

Today easyLife fulfils over one million orders per year and has a large-scale and sophisticated order processing centre.

easyLife warehouse 2024

1999: easy in online travel content and metasearch

In late 1999, a time when the internet was less widely available than today, Mr Jean-Pierre Nadir conceived a website that provided editorial content and allowed comparison of services within travel. In early 2000 the company began trading in France under the name Easyvoyage offering services through easyVoyage.com.

Around 2002/03 as more and more people started to use the internet, traffic to the portal and its usage for flight comparison grew rapidly. The company created a new website dedicated to price comparison for flights, under the trademark easyVols. Activity expanded into other territories in Europe, including to Spain, the UK, Italy and Germany. Visit easyVols.com

easyVoyage.com receives 60 million visits per year

easyVoyage

easyVols

Easyvoyage Websites
2003 (left)

2011 (below)

1999: easy in online travel content and metasearch

continued

The company continued to grow and in 2015 easyVoyage was acquired by Webedia, a leading French internet group focused on the themes of leisure and entertainment. Today it is under the leadership of CEO Herve Lemoine.

With over 60 million visits each year easyVoyage offers customers a powerful search engine that compares hundreds of options in seconds to locate the best deals for flights, hotels, apartments/villa stays as well as car rentals and airport transfers. Camping has become a significant growth area for the business. Over 1m Euros was spent on advertising the brand in 2022

Several other brands incorporating an easy prefix have previously been used by the company including easyViajar and easyViaggio for the Spanish and Italian markets respectively. In December 2020 easyGroup acquired the rights including prior use for all the easy prefixed marks used by Easyvoyage which became a member of the easy family of brands.

rebranded

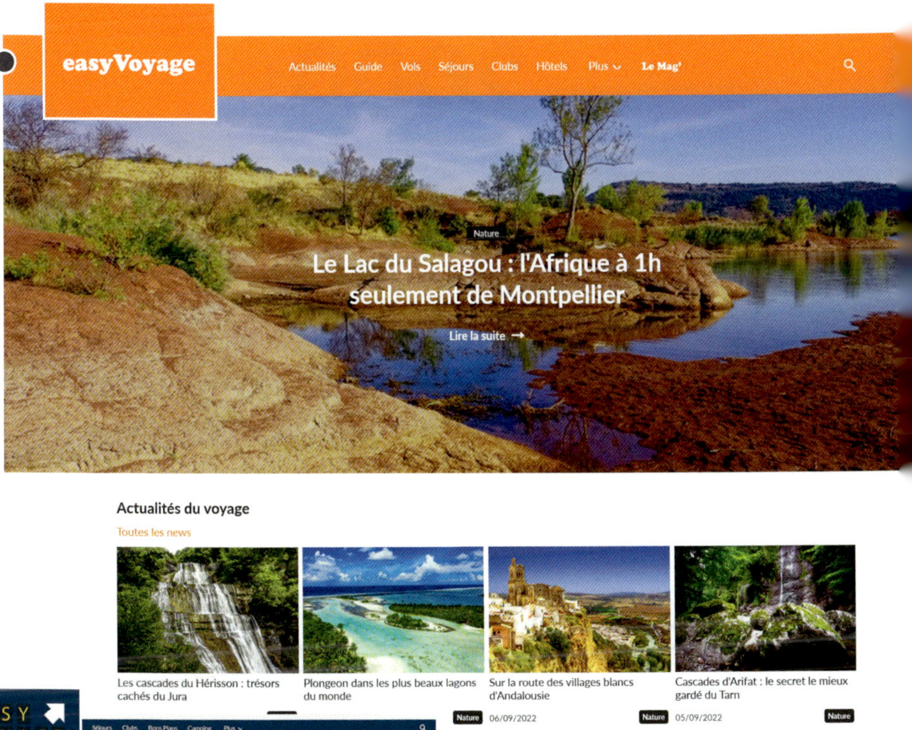

easyCamping website 2022

Herve Lemoine - easyVoyage CEO,
herve.lemoine@webedia-group.com

2000: easy in the USA

The New York Times

Stelios Haji-Ioannou, heir to a Greek shipping fortune, enjoys the good life. As an entrepreneur, however, he has made a career of meeting the needs of consumers who must stick to budgets

Making 'Easy' Stand for 'Budget'

By ANDREW ROSS SORKIN

LONDON

STELIOS HAJI-IOANNOU is the first to admit that he likes the finer things in life. "My ideal hangout would be a gentleman's club," he said, laughing, during a $70 breakfast and handed out free plane tickets for his airline to other passengers.

While Mr Haji-Ioannou may not need to count pennies — or even have his businesses turn a profit — he says EasyJet is profitable; he is planning an initial public offering in London this July. In his latest published financial statements, for the year ended September 19

New York Times 11/06/00

The easy brand is naturally best known in Europe where easyJet was first created back in 1995. But the high profile of Stelios as a recognised entrepreneur and the industry disrupting activities of some of the easy businesses he created, has led to significant awareness of the easy brand in the United States.

In particular there was significant interest in and coverage of the launch of easyJet because it was following in the footsteps of pioneering American low-cost carriers like Southwest and Valujet.

CNN Money 08/07/2001

easyEverything in Times Square New York 2000

www.businessweekeurope.com

BusinessWeek

EUROPEAN EDITION / JUNE 11, 2001

A PUBLICATION OF THE McGRAW-HILL COMPANIES

The STARS of EUROPE

STELIOS HAJI-IOANNOU

Founder and Chairman, EasyGroup

Stelios Haji-Ioannou speaks the language of Silicon Valley, tossing off phrases such as "frictionless Internet" without blinking. But behind the jargon is an entrepreneur who's showing Europe how to combine radically simple business models with the Net to reshape old-line industries.

Haji-Ioannou, 33, is founder and chairman of London's easyGroup. Its holdings include easyJet Airline; easyEverything, a chain of cybercafes; and a rental car company called, naturally, easyRentacar. All rely on the Net to keep costs low: EasyRentacar offers only one type of vehicle and requires reservations be made online. But its prices are 60% below the industry giants.

The granddaddy of the group—and only public company—is easyJet, Europe's second-largest discount carrier after Ireland's Ryanair. easyJet saw sales in the first half climb 42%, to $206.4 million. But first-half losses also grew, to $14.6 million, because of higher fuel prices and slow winter traffic.

ELECTRIC ORANGE. Haji-Ioannou keeps going, though. It's nearly impossible to go anywhere in urban Europe without noticing the Easy brand: Everything he touches, from Boeing engines to billboards, is painted electric orange—Pantone 021C, to be exact. Maybe someday, he jokes, it'll be renamed "Stelios Orange."

Next stop: America. The second son of a Greek shipping tycoon, Haji-Ioannou has already anchored an easyEverything cafe in New York's Times Square. This is one European who's not staying in the Old World.

BusinessWeek 11/06/2001 easyEverything interior New York in 2002

The launch of the easyEverything internet cafes provided another huge boost to awareness and captured the public imagination. On 17th December 2000 Stelios together with former US Presidential candidate and chief executive of Hewlett Packard, Carly Fiorina, opened the world's largest internet café in Times Square New York, earning a place in the Guinness Book of World Records. There was significant coverage of the event in both the New York and national press.

Stelios was also interviewed on US primetime television, appearing on the show "Good Morning, America" which at the time was one of the two most watched morning shows in America.

Over the years millions of American business travellers and tourist visitors to Europe would have been exposed to the easy brands. Many of them have taken flights on easyJet, stayed in easyHotels booked via easyHotel.com or rented an easyCar via the website easyCar.com.

2000: easy going global

easyHotel Dubai 2010

easyJet begins flights to Moscow 11/06/2013

The easy brand has moved even beyond Europe and the United States. This is perhaps unsurprising given that travellers from countries around the world study, visit and work in Europe.

But wherever you live in the world, easy is only a few clicks away. For example today you can fly to & from anywhere in the world by booking with easyFly, UK trademark number 3343002 & EU number 014770697 via the easyFly.com website or book your long-distance flight via worldwide.easyJet.com or easyAir.com. In 2013 easyJet launched a Chinese language site to cater for the many Chinese travellers visiting Europe just one many sites in different languages.

A selection of press coverage that easy has received around the world.

easyEverything, Arizona Daily Star 17 Dec 2000

Arizona Daily Star

Fast-growing chain of Internet cafes is a money-saver

EasyEverything offers computer access for tourists — cheaply

By Arthur Frommer
KING FEATURES SYNDICATE

It began a year and a half ago as a tiny, eight-seater shop in London. Today, it boasts some 2,300 computers in that city alone. In September, some 1.25 million people went online at its shops all over Europe. And last month, its New York City store opened with a staggering 800 PCs — enough to qualify it in the "Guinness Book of World vately owned storefront cafes holding no more than a dozen computers each. No longer. With its day-glo orange awnings and cavernous computing halls, EasyEverything has quickly fashioned itself into the 800-pound gorilla of e-mail. As it becomes a ubiquitous player on the European scene, budget-minded tourists might come to as in the morning, late evening and overnight, that $1 can get you between an hour's access and six hours' access. During peak hours, which are generally midafternoon to midevening, that $1 will get you between 15 minutes and one hour of access. Not only will you probably not have to wait for a machine, but at off-peak hours can make your communications costs nearly negligible. For example, if you're in Paris and pop in after breakfast before your day's touring, you can easily jot messages of "I'm alive" to the whole crew back home and still have plenty of cash leftover for a whole hip's worth of fresh and the company is looking at a second space in Union Square.

In London, you can find them at Tottenham Court Road and Oxford Street, as well as opposite Victoria Station, a few steps off Trafalgar Square and in High Street Kensington. In Paris, it's close to the Pompidou Centre. Berlin's is by the Zoo so that when you're abroad you can dash inside to dash off a note.

Right now, there are more than a dozen EasyEverythings located in Europe (in Amsterdam, Antwerp, Barcelona, Berlin, Brussels, Edinburgh, Glasgow, London, Madrid, Manchester, Munich, Paris, Rome and Rotterdam), plus the one at Times Square in America. But four more Euro pean locations

DAILY NEWS

Internet cafe in Times Sq. promises to connect 800

By NANCY DILLON
DAILY NEWS STAFF WRITER

What promoters promise will be the world's largest Internet cafe is set to open in Times Square this October.

Called easyEverything, the ca- that the preference for Web surfing from home is overstated. New York apartments tend to be cramped, he noted.

And the idea that wireless devices might eat into his business-traveler/tourist clientele is

easyEverything, New York Daily News

Los Angeles Times

European river trips: Easy does it

EASYCRUISE, a London-based budget cruise line run by EasyJet entrepreneur Stelios Haji-Ioannou, will add a second ship, a new look and new river trips in Europe this summer.

Weeklong cruises will start July 14 along rivers and canals of the Netherlands and Belgium, from Amsterdam to Rotterdam. The vessel, a refurbished riverboat with 50 twin cabins, will sail in the

easyCruise Los Angeles Times 30 Apr 2006

The Palm Beach Post

Hitch a ride on easyCruise, for $53 a day

Set itineraries are for fuddy-duddies. And on easyCruise, the ship remains in port late into the night.

tiny, closetlike, double-occupancy cabins and minimalist furnishings (like shelves). The ship, called easyCruise, will emerge from Singapore this coming March, sail several one-week Asian itineraries, and then move to the western Mediterranean for continuous cruising from then on.

Greek businessman Stelios says the one-week pattern of most cruises is passé. On easyCruise, you board the

easyCruise, The Palm Beach Post 28 Nov 2004 (above)

easyHotel & easyCruise, Miami Herald 07 Nov 2005

INTERNATIONAL

EASY **DOES IT**

Miami Herald

EASYJET TYCOON STELIOS HAJI-IOANNOU LAUNCHES INTO NEW VENTURES IN HOTELS AND CRUISES

BY JANE WARDELL
Associated Press

LONDON — In an elegant row of white Georgian town houses, one building stands out — a lurid orange band around its balcony and the backpackers on its doorstep break the stately harmony of the rest of the crescent.

Behind its doors, Stelios Haji-Ioannou chats with patrons of the easyHotel, a venture that replicates the model of his outstandingly successful easyJet airline by offering basic accommodation over the Internet at prices dependent on demand.

One guest complains about the lack of a pay phone. Haji-Ioannou politely explains that most people these days have mobile phones and, as an aside, that a phone in the narrow hall — there is no lobby — wouldn't make enough money to return the investment.

That's a key concern for Haji-Ioannou, who has made serious money out of investing in no-frills services that allow consumers on a budget to stay in London's upmarket Kensington district.

Patrons on the cruise ship don't get a traditional cruise so much as a large boat that takes them from place to place. The rooms are porthole free and activities are limited to a hot tub on deck and a bar.

Visitors to the easyHotel, which recently opened a branch in Switzerland and plans more across Europe, will find that 25 pounds — around $45 — merits them a cubicle just large enough to accommodate a bed, a shower pod and a plasma TV on the wall that costs another $9 a day to watch.

"My criteria for choosing a hotel for a one-night stay is different from a week," Haji-Ioannou said, but he acknowledged that the next easyHotel will have more windows and space.

OTTAWA CITIZEN

Empire building done the 'easy' way

The Internet tycoon behind easyJet, easyRentacar and easyEverything sees no end to his empire, writes **Bryan Brumley.**

London

When a competitor launched a no-frills airline two years ago, the owner of easyJet and its co-workers donned orange jumpsuits, boarded the rival's inaugural flight and passed out free tickets for their own carrier.

That irreverence typifies Stelios Haji-Ioannou, whose growing network of "easy" enterprises use the Internet to build a common brand and cut transaction costs.

"What I do is genetic engineering for businesses," said Mr. Haji-Ioannou, whose other ventures are easyRentacar, an online agency, and easyEverything, a string of cybercafes

Ottawa Citizen (Canada) 9 Nov 2000

easyJet IPO fuelled continued growth

For five years following its inaugural flight easyJet continued to expand and proved its business model worked by moving into profit. But Stelios knew that the airline business is very capital intensive and that the only way to fund further growth was to sell a share of his company to institutional investors while keeping a meaningful minority stake.

The New York Times

Airbus Gets Big Order From Easyjet; Boeing Out

By Edward Wong

Oct. 15, 2002

Airbus announced yesterday that EasyJet, the low-cost airline based near London, had agreed to buy 120 passenger jets from Airbus and had taken an option to buy 120 more at a fixed price over the next decade. That is the largest order placed for commercial aircraft this year, and it comes as a big blow to the Boeing Company, which had also been negotiating with EasyJet.

Airbus executives would not give dollar figures for the order. Industry experts said that at list price, the order for 150-seat A-319 jets would come to more than $6 billion. But they added that Airbus had offered a discount of about 30 percent, raising questions about how profitable the order would prove to be for the manufacturer. It

easyJet move to Airbus 15/10/02

easyJet fleet growth 2000 - 2023

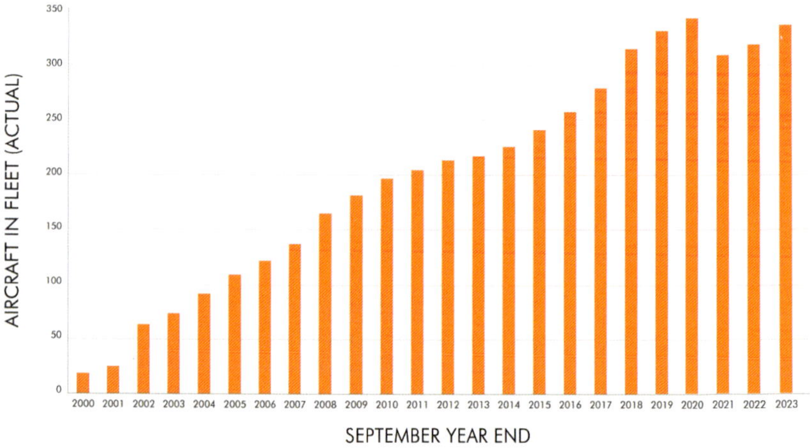

Passenger numbers in 2023: 82.8 million

The Guardian

The Guardian Thursday November 16 2000 3

EasyJet gets £850m shares lift

Low-cost carrier started five years ago with £5m is hit with investors

Julia Finch

Stelios Haji-Ioannou, the founder and chairman of easyJet, yesterday saw the airline he started with a £5m loan from his father valued at more than £850m by the end of its first day as a quoted company.

The 33-year-old easyJet chief, known simply as Stelios to his 1,400 staff, has sold 35% of the airline to outside shareholders. He has retained a 32% stake, worth some £275m at last night's closing share price.

EasyJet's flying start on the stockmarket contrasts sharply with its larger rival British Airways. It announced last week that it was pulling out of the no-frills airline business and putting its loss-making Go subsidiary up for sale.

EasyJet – which BA tried to buy just a year after it started flights from its Luton base – is one of the success stories of the skies. Last year it carried 5.6m passengers and made a profit of £22m. BA's Go carried 1.9m passengers last year and lost more than £21m.

The low cost carrier will use the money it raised from the stock market – about £200m – to buy more jets for its fleet, a move seen as a shot across the bows of its rivals.

With its trademark orange livery, easyJet has helped revolutionise short-haul

Chasing the cheap flight millions

RYANAIR THE LOW FARES AIRLINE

Europe's biggest low-cost airline started flying in 1985 with one daily flight in a 15-seater from Waterford in Ireland to Gatwick. Today it carries some 7m passengers a year on 45 routes to destinations in 11 countries, and its staff number 1,400.

The company – started by the wealthy Ryan family – now is run by Michael O'Leary, an ebullient former accountant. Ryanair is listed on the Dublin stock exchange with a valuation of £2.1bn, about half the current value of British Airways.

The carrier has 35 Boeing 737s on order, to add to its fleet of 31. Last year it made a profit of IR£45.3m (£40.7m) while offering some of the cheapest fares.

www.ryanair.com

buzz

Newest of the no-frills operators, Buzz is part of the Dutch KLM airline. Its first flights were in January this yuear and there have been no published passenger figures.

It operates eight BAe 146 aircraft and two Boeing 737s to 14 European destinations and flies into some

easyJet

Started in 1995 by Stelios Haji-Ioannou with a £5m loan from his shipping magnate father.

The Luton-based carrier operates 18 with Boeing 737 airliners and has a further 32 on order. Last year easyJet's orange planes flew 5.6m passengers on 18 European routes and made a

The Guardian article 16/11/00

On 15th November 2000 easyJet was floated on the London Stock Exchange valuing the airline at £850m and raising £195m to fund aircraft purchases. The proceeds of the IPO were largely invested in funding what was in its day a huge order from Airbus for 120 aircraft plus 120 options that was announced by Stelios to the world's media on the 15th October 2002. A headline in the New York Times said it all: "Airbus in and Boeing out". Later that year Stelios stepped aside from chairing the board of the airline paving the way for the first fully independent Chairman to take over.

The crucial decision made by Stelios during the 2000 IPO of easyJet was to separate the Intellectual property assets from the company that floated on the stock market and keep them in his private company – easyGroup

The Guardian cartoon 2012

easyJet growth

For the first 10 years post flotation easyJet's enjoyed rapid but managed growth. In 2001 when other airlines were cutting back capacity following the 9/11 attacks easyJet announced that Gatwick would be its fifth base. The acquisition of Go in 2002 provided another boost to growth as well as a strong presence at Stansted and Bristol airports.

In 2007 easyJet acquired GB airlines and routes to Southern European and North African destinations. Then in 2008 the airline opened its 19th base at Charles de Gaulles in Paris the stronghold of Air France.

Stelios at easyJet 20th Birthday Event

EasyJet founder calls for higher investor payouts

Sir Stelios presses for dividends to be set at 50% of post-tax profits

Financial Times article 10/02/16

easyJet Innovation day 2017 (below)

A landmark was passed in 2009 when for the first time more than half of easyJet's passengers originated from outside the UK. This proved definitively that easy had become a major pan-European brand, Then, in 2010 figures produced by the CAA showed conclusively that easyJet had overtaken British Airways to become the UK's largest airline.

The Times 22/01/20

Stelios wants more of the same after Easyjet boosts its revenue

easyJet growth .... continued

By early 2020, easyJet was carrying close to 100 million passengers per year on a fleet of 350 all Airbus aircraft. At that time Stelios and his family owned 34% of the shares with the rest widely distributed amongst many institutional investors and pension funds.

In accordance with the agreement reached between Stelios and the board in 2010, half of all profits were distributed as regular dividends to shareholders each year. Stelios and his family earned a dividend of £78m in March 2019 for their shares in the airline.
Of course in an industry like aviation which is vulnerable to external factors shareholders cannot rely on dividends being paid every year. This is when the benefits of royalty income become apparent.
Stelios and easyGroup now earn 0.25% of all easyJet revenues as royalty for the brand. This resulted in royalties of £16m from revenues of £6 billion in 2019. But even when the airline's revenues fell sharply to £3 billion in 2020 and then £1.5 billion in 2021 due to the pandemic, the royalties continued at £8m and £4 million respectively.

easyJet Airbus 321 with new livery - 2015

This clearly shows the value of a royalty-based business model for a brand owner.
The nature of aviation means the industry is a focus of the climate

change debate. In November 2019 easyJet became the first major airline to offset the carbon emissions from the fuel from all its flights. Carbon offsetting is generally regarded as an interim measure while new technologies are developed which is why it will continue to support the development of innovative technology so aviation can be decarbonised over the long-term.

In 2022 easyJet made a new commitment to the environment when it launched what was described as the aviation world's most ambitious plan to achieve net-zero carbon emissions by 2050. The plan which is aligned with the science-based targets initiative (SBTi) is to deliver a 78% reduction in carbon emission reduction with residual emissions addressed through carbon removals.

The ultimate goal is to operate zero carbon emission hydrogen-powered aircraft. In this regard easyJet has committed to being an early adopter in transitioning the fleet and has signed partnership agreements with the likes of Rolls Royce, Airbus, Cranfield Aerospace solutions and GKN Aerospace.

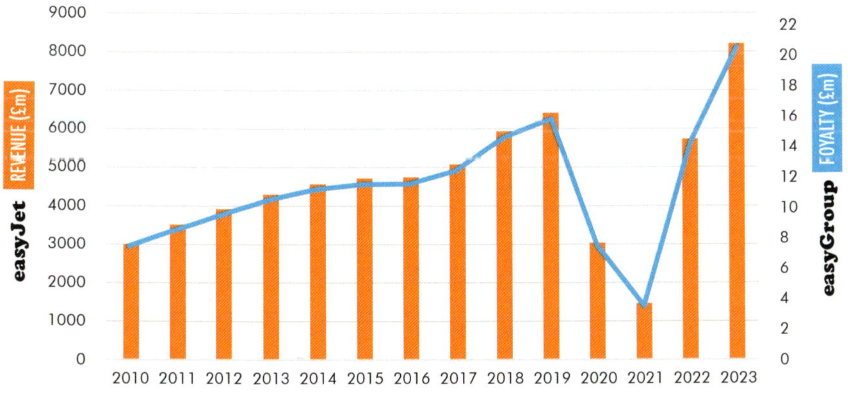

easyJet revenue and easyGroup royalties

2020-2022: COVID-19 survival and recovery

Over the 30 years since the easy family of brands was first created, the travel industry and aviation has experienced many crises. From the terrorist attacks in 2001 using hijacked aircraft, to the Lehman Brothers instigated 2008 global financial crisis, each has driven airlines out of business.

In previous crises easyJet had been relatively fortunate. For example, 9/11 happened in a part of the world where the airline did not operate directly and therefore affected its competitors to a greater degree. Stelios will never forget how surprised he was that the easyEverything internet café on Manhattan's 42nd street was packed with customers after the attacks. Back then for many people it was the only way of emailing home to say they were safe.

Stelios firmly believes that shareholders value the regular income provided by dividends and that they have the right to de-risk their investment by taking some of the profits out of one business and investing elsewhere for diversification.

However, in comparison with previous crises the impact of Covid-19 on the global travel business was truly unprecedented. People simply stopped travelling and one year after the virus struck, 95% of the Airbus aircraft in the easyJet fleet were simply parked up and idle.

2024: easyJet today

Fortunately, easyJet successfully navigated the existential threat of the pandemic. Covid19 provided the ultimate test for a diversified family of brands. The travel businesses were hit particularly badly as were those businesses that depended on retail sales. The majority of licensees experienced reductions in demand but thanks to the brand licensing business model under which the business risk was shared with other business partners the easy brand has demonstrated its resilience.

The airline's recovery has been truly impressive. In 2023 easyJet achieved a record summer performance supported by strong consumer demand and the airline's leading brand position. Overall revenues for 2023 were £8.2 billion up by 42% on the previous year.
For the first time since Covid easyJet declared a dividend for all shareholders including easyGroup which was paid in January 2024.

Stephen Hester
Non-Executive Chair
of easyJet

Johan Lundgren
CEO of easyJet

Kenton Jarvis
CFO of easyJet

easyJet numbers as at 30 Sep 2023

Passenger numbers:
82.8 million p/a

Current fleet size:
336 Airbus Aircraft

Revenue:
£8.2 billion

Profit:
£455 million

At the end of its financial year on 30 September 2023 easyJet had £2.9 billion of cash and money market deposits

Market Capitalisation (22 Apr 2024):
£4.14 billion

The strong financial performance and growing confidence in easyJet's future has been reflected in the airline's share price.

In March 2024 easyJet returned to the ranks of the FTSE index of the UK's most valuable companies.

easyJet holidays

A key driver of easyJet's continued expansion has been the success of the airline's holiday operation.

easyJet holidays was launched in 2019 to offer holiday packages which encourage the 84% of customers travelling for leisure purposes to spend more with the airline rather than booking accommodation elsewhere.

In 2023 easyJet holidays continued its impressive growth becoming a major player within the sector and doubling its UK market share year-on-year. easyJet holidays has recorded 77% customer growth compared to 2022 and made a profit before tax of £122 million. The boss of easyJet holidays Gary Wilson has outlined an ambition for it to overtake Tui and Jet 2 to become the UK's largest tour operator.

easyJet Holidays advertising at Gatwick Airport 2023

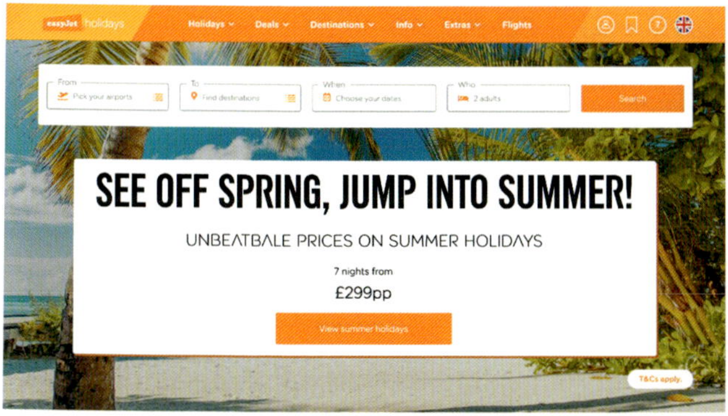

easyJet Holidays Homepage & Search results Apr 2024

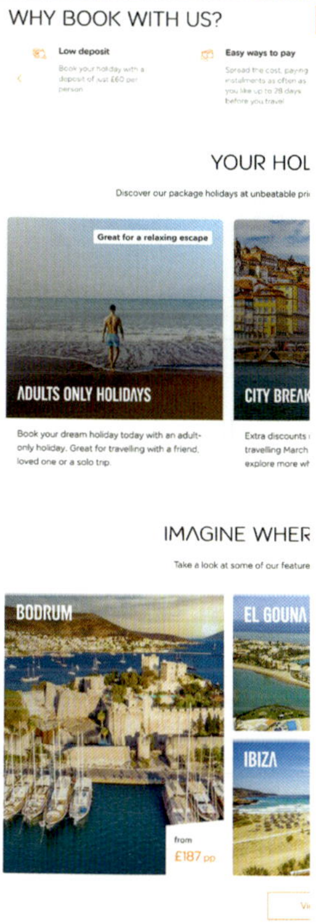

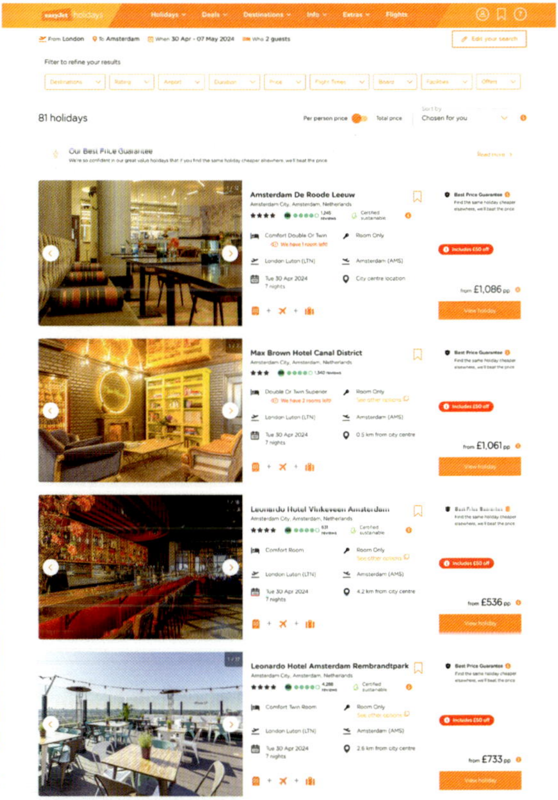

Doing battle with RYANAIR

THE LOW FARES AIRLINE

Taking on the big guys

> **"Stelios flew Ryanair in 1994 for market research purposes and then never again.**

Stelios has always accepted that being a high profile figure in the public eye means you will sometimes be parodied and that people may make jokes at your expense. But in 2010 Michael O'Leary the famously outspoken CEO of Ryanair went too far when he published advertisements in the Daily Telegraph and Guardian that depicted Stelios as Pinocchio and implied he was lying.
The ads referred to Stelios as "Easyjet's Mr Late Again" and called on him to stop "hiding the truth" about easyJet's on-time performance.

Stelios initiated a libel action and O'Leary was forced to back down. He apologised "unreservedly" and paid a settlement of £50,100 that Stelios immediately donated to his philanthropic foundation. The victory was dedicated to "all those who have suffered verbal abuse at the hands of O'Leary".

Michael O'Leary CEO of Ryanair

Mirror

News › UK News

EasyJet founder Stelios wins libel payout from Ryanair over 'Pinocchio' ads

The Guardian

Ryanair ad accusing Stelios of not telling the truth & retraction apology ad

Guardian cartoon

As well as a financial settlement Ryanair committed to not publishing the advertisements again and took out full page apologies in both the Daily Telegraph and the Guardian. Stelios said "It is not very often that someone as arrogant and powerful as O'Leary is forced to apologise to someone else in public and in writing".

Financial Times 15 July 2010

Ryanair's O'Leary apologises to easyJet founder over 'Pinocchio' ads

Ryanair chief pays £50,000 damages after newspaper ads implied Stelios Haji-Ioannou lied about easyJet's punctuality

Michael O'Leary attends confession...

The Guardian

FINANCIAL TIMES

Sir Stelios wins apology from O'Leary

Jane Croft JULY 15 2010

Ryanair and its outspoken chief executive Michael O'Leary have "unreservedly apologised" in the High Court to Sir Stelios Haji-Ioannou, founder of rival low-cost airline EasyJet, over a series of advertisements referring to EasyJet's flight on-time statistics.

Sir Stelios, one of the UK's best known entrepreneurs, issued a claim for libel after a Ryanair advert featured his picture which the High Court heard yesterday was "distorted so his nose was elongated in the style of the character Pinocchio and referred to him as "EasyJet's – Mr Late Again'."

Guardian 15 July 2010

easy & Fitness

Stelios' interest in the fitness sector extends back to 31st December 2001 when in a short piece talking about his plans for the year ahead, he told The Guardian he was considering launching an easyFitness brand, UK trademark number 2318292 & EU number 2981991, today seen at www.easy.fitness.

Paul Lorimer-Wing – co-founder/CEO easyGym (right) with George Taylor, director

On 13th August 2010 Stelios signed a brand licence agreement and in May 2011 easyGroup announced the launch of a chain of no-frills gyms targeting cost-conscious fitness enthusiasts who were seeking to avoid expensive monthly contracts.

easyGym.co.uk homepage 2011

The Daily Telegraph

Sir Stelios offers an easy way to keep fit

JAMES QUINN

SIR Stelios Haji-Ioannou has signed a deal to roll out a chain of easyGyms across the UK.

The Greek-Cypriot billionaire – best known as founder of airline easyJet – is working with private equity firm Fore Fitness on the project. Fore has signed a licensing deal which gives it brand rights.

The first two gyms will open in the summer, with plans for others later in the year and then a roll-out of 10 sites a year from 2012.

The first two will be in Slough, Berkshire, and Wood Green, north London.

Like all of the "easy" concepts, the gym business will focus on providing a value-for-money offering in what can be an expensive marketplace.

Prices will begin at £15 a month, with no fixed annual contracts and the potential to pay as you exercise.

The decor may be a drawback, however, incorporating Sir Stelios' beloved bright orange.

ONLINE

easyJet boss defends new route to Jordan

telegraph.co.uk/finance

INDEPENDENT

FITNESS

EasyGym sites to open in summer

EASYJET'S FOUNDER Sir Stelios Haji-Ioannou is to launch a no-frills fitness club chain, easyGym, this summer after the venture secured its first two sites. The entrepreneur's foray into the fitness sector comes after he teamed up with the private equity-backed Fore Fitness last year.

EasyGym will offer basic gym facilities – without pools or saunas – with membership costing from £15 a month. It will open two sites, in Slough and Wood Green, London, this summer.

easyGym Sunday Telegraph 03 Apr 2011

easyGym The Independent 05 Apr 2011

easy & Fitness continued

The business was owned by a group of four financiers who signed an original 10-year brand licence agreement. The first easyGym, UK trademark number 2310603 & EU number 2866150 filed 13 September 2002 opened in Slough in June 2011 closely followed by a second site in Wood Green and the business expanded steadily over the following years. The gym industry was hit particularly hard by the pandemic but a new licensee has driven significant growth in France with a business model that focuses on larger gyms in high traffic areas with easyGym.fr.

easyGym Locations in France 2024

Evening Standard

New regime set to revive easyGym after buy-out

THE easyGym budget fitness chain is set to be resurrected a year after most branches were sold, with plans for 50 new sites in London and hundreds overseas after a management buy-out.

The firm's IT systems and brand name, launched by easyJet founder Sir Stelios Haji-Ioannou in 2011, have been sold for an undisclosed sum to a consortium led by chief executive Paul Lorimer-Wing.

Backed by other directors and private investors, the purchase is from private equity firm Argosy Capital which sold 13 sites, the bulk of the estate, to rival The Gym Group in June 2018.

Lorimer-Wing said: "I believe there is so much growth potential for easyGym. We can offer membership from £20 per month, and customers can pay as they go for extras such as classes and health foods." The first new gym will open in Camberwell in October and there are plans to franchise easyGym in Ireland, India, Saudi Arabia and France.

Joanna Bourke

easyGym Evening Standard 22 Aug 2019

easyGym France Paris Republique 2022 (top)

easyGym Denmark Hill (left, right)

Inside a French easyGym

easy in art, watches and cosmetics

easyArt.com is an online retailer offering inspiring art for your home at great prices. The business has been trading since 2001. According to a deal struck with Stelios in 2017 the brand joined the easy family and it is now run in partnership with King & McGaw who work with brilliant printers, framers, designers, customer service, accounts and admin teams. They continue to make everything by hand and focus on creating beautiful products for many of the world's greatest museums, galleries and artists as well as through the retail web site easyArt.com.

easyArt website 2024

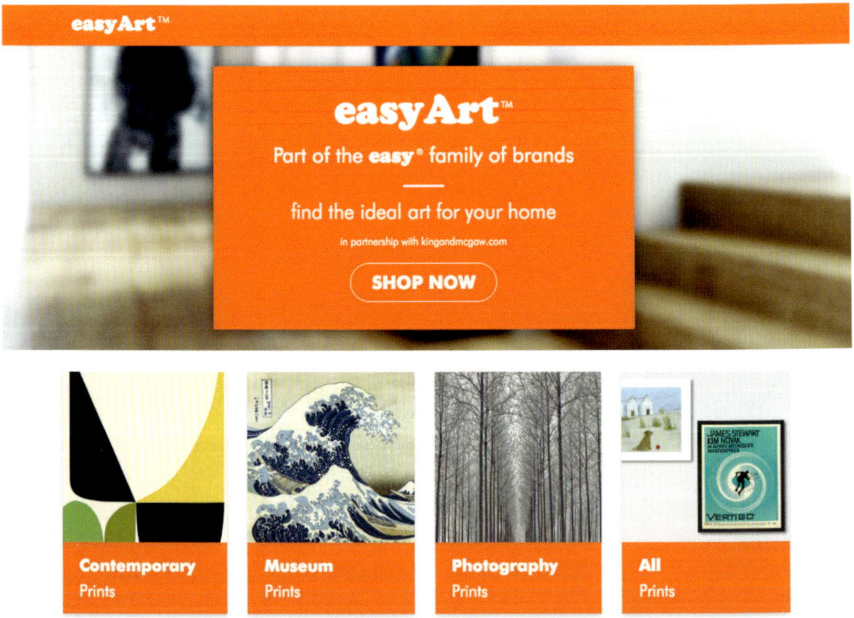

easy4Men products

In 2004 Stelios announced he had signed a deal with High Street retailer Boots for them to manufacture under licence and distribute a range of men's grooming products in over one thousand of their UK high street stores under the brand easy4men, trademark number 3763489 seen at easy4men.com.

easyWatch in Campaign 12 Jul 2005 (below)
easyWatch Website 24 Nov 2005 (bottom)

campaign

Wind up, wind up for Stelios' newest brand extension

LONDON - Watches are following pizzas, cinemas and cruises as the latest product to be made 'easy' by Stelios Haji-Ioannou, who says he is filling the void left by Swatch's move upmarket.

The range of 16 watches starts at £9.95 and will only be available online, at EasyWatch.com, to cut out retailers' overheads. The range is manufactured by volume watchmaker Zeon.

In June 2005 Stelios awarded a licence to UK-based manufacturer Xeon limited and launched a range of low-cost easy branded watches priced at between £15 and £30, taking on industry giant Swatch. The watches were available from the website easyWatch.com

easy in music

In September 2004 Stelios announced that he was launching a music download service called easyMusic. Working with a licensee called Wippit the new service, accessed via easyMusic.com contained both copyleft and Copyright music. Copyleft music some of it free was sourced largely from unsigned artists, allowing them to showcase their music for free. The copyright service involved re-selling the Wippit catalogue at prices from 25p per song. Stelios was taking on the market leader Apple iTunes who he accused of ripping of UK consumers by charging them more for their music than other European countries.

Today via easyMusic.com visitors can access the latest music news and concert information. Through a partnership with Amazon easyMusic sells subscriptions to Amazon's music streaming service.

easyMusic Web Banner 2005
easyMusic.com 2005

Mirror

Easy on the ears

AN online music download service is the latest venture planned by the tycoon behind easyJet.

Stelios Haji-Ioannou's easyGroup will launch easyMusic.com by linking with London-based subscription service Wippit.

It will feature current hits, back-catalogue numbers and tracks from unsigned artists.

Mr Haji-Ioannou said the service will offer "free or best-value music down-

Launch Daily Mirror 18 Sep 2004

The Daily Telegraph

From easyJet to easy listening

Stelios Haji-Iouannou, the founder of easyJet, is starting a music download service, he said yesterday.

Mr Haji-Iouannou's easyGroup has teamed up with London-based music subscription service Wippit to create easyMusic.com.

The service will consist of two sections, Copyleft – with music, some of it free, from unsigned artists, and Copyright – with paid-for current chart and back catalogue music. Both services should be running by Christmas.

The business joins easyJet, easyInternetcafe, easyCinema, easyBus, easyPizza, easyCar and easy4Men in the no-frills group. Mr Haji-Iouannou said: "Music is a market which will grow if the price is lowered."

Lanuch Daily Telegraph 18 Sep 2004

INDEPENDENT

Stelios goes online with easyMusic

▶ EASYJET'S FOUNDER, Stelios Haji-Ioannou, plans to launch a music download service in the coming weeks, a year after he lost a music copyright infringement lawsuit to the British music industry. The service, which is dubbed www.easyMusic.com, will re-sell the catalogue of the download company Wippit with songs starting at 25p each.

The Independent 18 Sep 2004
easyMusic A5 Flyer (right)
easyMusic.com 2022 (bottom)

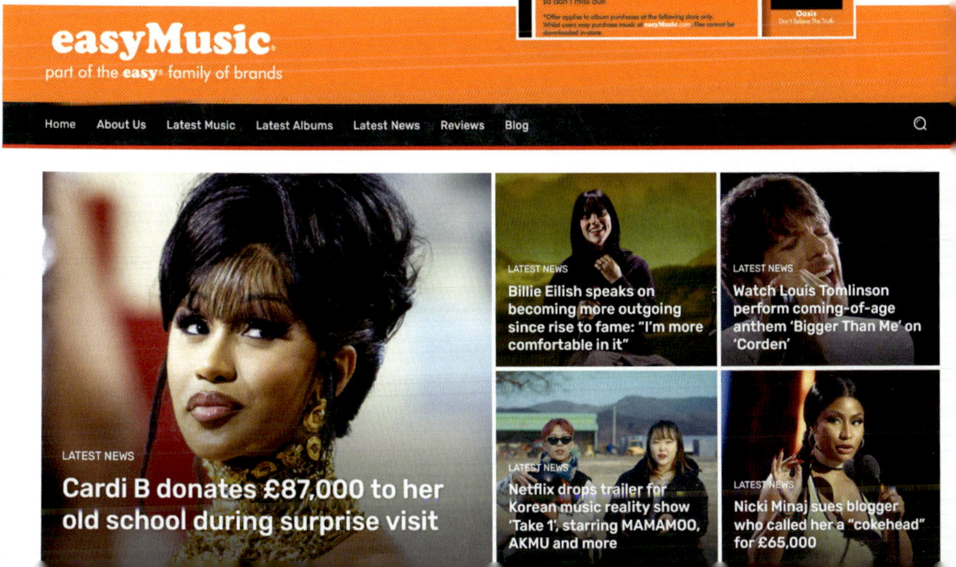

easy in food & takeaways

The easy brand has an association with food dating back to 1995 when Stelios first had the idea of selling snacks on board easyJet flights through an easyKiosk. Another food brand easyPizza, (UK trademark number 2324372 & EU number 3069861) was first used in 2003. Stelios had the idea of applying variable pricing to the pizza business with customers paying less when demand was lower. easyPizza remains in use today with fulfilment now provided by easyFood.

THE SUNDAY TIMES

Sir Stelios orders a takeaway — to challenge Just Eat

When the easyJet tycoon came across food delivery service easyFood, he sent in his lawyers. But he liked the business so much he bought a stake

'It was just like a real-life Dragons' Den pitch," said Gurpreet Sidhu of his first encounter with the founder of easyJet. He and his business partner, Jeewan Sagu, were summoned to a meeting in Kensington, west London, after unwittingly becoming embroiled in a legal skirmish with Sir Stelios Haji-Ioannou.

The Sunday Times 29 April 2018

The brand easyFood (trademark number 17808098) was registered by two Midlands based entrepreneurs, Jeewan Sagu and Gurpreet Sindu in 2006. They developed a food ordering app which is simple for customers to use and offers restaurants a more attractive proposition than competitors. They later assigned all IP rights to easyGroup and joined the easy family of brands. The model has been successfully piloted in the Midlands and will soon be available on a UK wide basis. Visit easyFood.co.uk to find out more.

A different kind of food business called easyFoodstore (trademark number 11949716) was trading in North London between 2016 and 2023 offering a range of low-cost non-perishable food items to the public. In 2024 the site of the physical store in Park Royal was converted to an easyStorage location where customers will have access to easyContainers for storage.

Following the sale of the site the easyFoodstore.com domain has been integrated into the easyFood.com operations.

Evening Standard 05 Aug 2013 (top right)
easyFoodstore open 2016 (above)
easyFoodstore article BBC 04/08/13
Guardian cartoon 10/02/16 (left)

In December 2020 easyGroup entered into an agreement with Zahra publishing regarding the use of the brand easyFood in relation to a widely read printed food magazine.

As part of an agreement dated 24th November 2022 all brand rights including those for prior use were purchased by easyGroup and Zahra joined the easy family of brands using the easyFood brand under licence.

easyFood is Ireland's number one food magazine. Average 20,100 copies per issue (ABC Audits 2022). Readership: 80,364 per issue.

John Mullins CEO of Zahra Publishing
jmullins@zahramediagroup.com
easyFood Magazine May 2023 (above)

easy in the maritime sector

Stelios always wanted to maintain strong links with his heritage industry: the maritime sector. On 31st December 2002 he first revealed plans to launch a new type of cruise experience to In March 2003 he announced in an interview with the Daily Mirror that prices would start at £29 per cabin night, significantly undercutting other cruise operators.

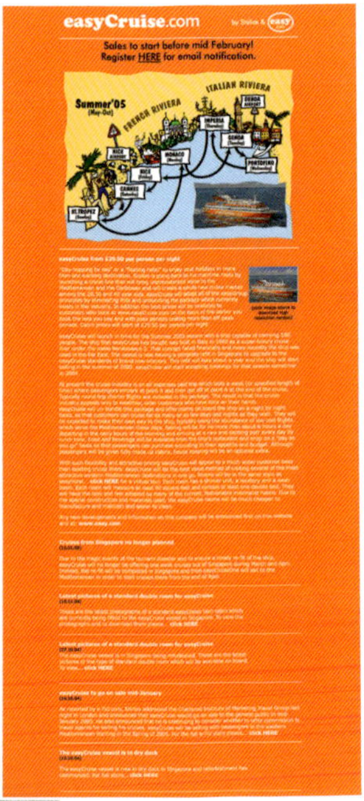

easyCruise.com Website Feb 2005 (right)
and how it appears today (left)
Variety Cruises ships today (right)

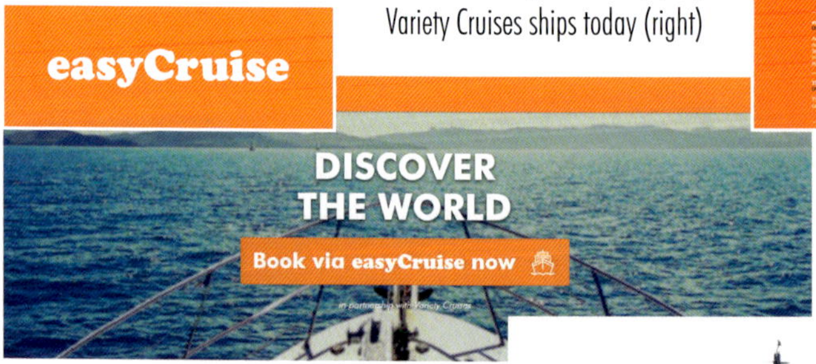

Variety Cruises

WORLDWIDE CRUISE DESTINATIONS

Visit places you always wanted to see or explore somewhere new, our small ships currently serve selected cruise destinations worldwide including Greece, Italy, Turkey, the Canary Islands, the Adriatic Sea, Cape Verde, the Seychelles, Costa Rica, Panama & Cuba, with Madagascar & Iceland coming soon!
We look forward to welcoming you aboard one of our ships soon and discover the world the **easyCruise** way

OVERVIEW

easyCruise offers a great yacht cruise experience with its 11 fully owned vessels with capacity ranging from 5 to 36 cabins. The cruise itineraries are carefully selected and curated showcasing the best of each destination by visiting loving and unfrequented ports

CABINS	GUESTS	CREW	DRAFT	DESTINATIONS
36 Ocean View	72	32	3.5m/10ft	Italy & Malta

easyCruise ad 2003 (below)

Cruise with Stelios on Sky One, Sky Mix & Sky Travel 2005

The idea was to take the frills out of the cruise business and reduce prices which meant customers would have more money to spend during their ashore at the stops on their journey.

FT FINANCIAL TIMES

Haji-Ioannou considers a no-frills cruise line

Financial Times 24 Feb 2003

easy in the continued maritime sector

In 2005 the orange painted 'easyCruise One' departed Nice on its maiden voyage around the Italian and French Rivieras. Additional ships followed in the Caribbean and Greece until Stelios decided it was more profitable to dispose of the physical ships while continuing to sell cruises online.The brand's high profile came not just from advertising and PR but also through the broadcast of a Sky TV series called 'Cruise with Stelios' which attracted millions of viewers over the years not just in the UK but in the US and elsewhere on the Travel Channel. See easyCruise.com for more.

easyCruise One and Cabin 2006

The easyCruise brand, (TM number 2475549 filed 20th November 2001) remains in active use today in partnership with the speciality cruise company Variety Cruises who operate 11 fully owned vessels with capacity to carry up to 72 passengers. The smaller sized cruise ships allow access to the heart of destinations that larger cruise ships cannot reach. Through easyCruise.com you can book a small ship cruise on many different itineraries worldwide although the company's speciality is the Greek islands.

FT FINANCIAL TIMES

EasyGroup poised to go cruising down the river

By Ian Limbach
in Washington

EasyGroup, wholly-owned by entrepreneur Stelios Haji-Ioannou, is to add European riverboat cruises to its list of Easy-branded businesses, alongside the low-cost airline and mobile phone reseller.

The UK-based company will this week announce an agreement to license the EasyCruise brand to Boonstra River Line, a private Dutch riverboat operator, which is converting one of its 10 boats to the orange-coloured Easy-brand and will offer multi-day cruises between Amsterdam and Brussels. The service is scheduled to begin in June.

"They should appeal to a younger market, especially to American travellers," Mr Haji-Ioannou said, at the World Travel and Tourism Council conference in Washington DC.

Cruises on the 50-cabin boat will cost about €30 to €40 (£21 to £28) per person, per night.

Mr Haji-Ioannou gave no financial details about the the franchising agreement.

He said that the company will not cross-sell the cruises with other Easy travel products, such as flights on EasyJet. "I have never believed in bundling. I like the idea of each of my businesses competing on their own."

EasyCruise was created last year and operates just one ship so far, offering low-cost cruises in the Caribbean and Western Mediterranean. Like EasyJet, the service is no-frills and the cruises target younger holiday goers. It is hoping to capitalise in particular on this summer's World Cup in Germany and is also in talks to extend its business to Greece.

easyCruise FT 18 Apr 2006

The Guardian

Stelios planning EasyCruise line

Richard Adams

EasyJet founder Stelios Haji-Ioannou is to return to his roots as a shipping magnate, outlining details of his planned low-cost cruise line.

Named EasyCruise, the service could be shuttling to popular tourist destinations in the Mediterranean from next summer at the earliest, with passengers paying as little as £29 a night for a spartan cabin.

can have room rates starting at £29, then if you want to have a meal you go to a restaurant and buy one."

The company has unveiled architects' plans for a prototype cabin, measuring 8.4 sq m (90 sq ft), with a simple fold-up futon bed that doubles as a couch.

Passengers could bring their own bedding and clean their cabins, or pay an additional fee for the service. Passengers would be free to get on and off

easyCruise Plans Guardian 20 Jun 2003

easyCruise USA internet ad 2006

Evening Standard

EasyCruise launch marks change of course for Stelios

By Nick Goodway

MR EASY, Stelios Haji-Ioannou, is set to abandon the principles behind all his ventures ranging from easyJet to easyCinema with the launch early next year of easyCruise.

For the first time, he will use and pay intermediaries — in the shape of travel agents — rather than relying solely on customers booking directly through the internet.

Launching his first six test cruises, each a week long, out of Singapore next March and April, Iannou said that travel agents will be able to book with an extra 5% discount over members of the public. This effectively means that they receive 5¼% commission to encourage them to book up and create packages for punters including flights to and from Singapore and extra nights' accommodation before or after the cruise.

He said: "I think this will be win-win and travel agents will be making money for both themselves and for easyCruise. Punters are more likely to want to use travel agents the more complex their holiday plans are. I also think that they are likely to be going along to their normal travel agents and saying they want to book an easyCruise."

The cruises, which will be based on the Mediterranean from next May, are aimed at 20- to 40-year-olds with prices starting at £29 a night. Sailing for a short while early each morning, the easyCruiser will arrive at a new port before lunch each day. The bright orange cabins with basic beds and washing facilities are designed for "self-cleaning".

easyCruise Launch Evening Standard 01 Nov 2004

easy in the maritime sector

continued

The presence of the easy brand in the maritime sector has been further boosted by the launch of easyBoat which joined the easy family of brands in 2022. Founded by two Greek entrepreneurs Alex Nastos and Simos Lalagos the venture is an online comparison site for those looking to charter a yacht for their holiday – anywhere in the world.

easyBoat.com provides transparency to the customer as to the yacht owner/operator allowing them to compare charter prices for the same class of boat (typically up to 100ft in length) offered via multiple operators at the same embarkation port. This direct transparent comparison, similar to Skyscanner for flights or Booking.com for hotels, saves both time and money for clients.

easyBoat.com
website articles 2022

easyBoat crowdfunding video 2022

Alex Nastos promotes easyBoat
alex.nastos@easyboat.com

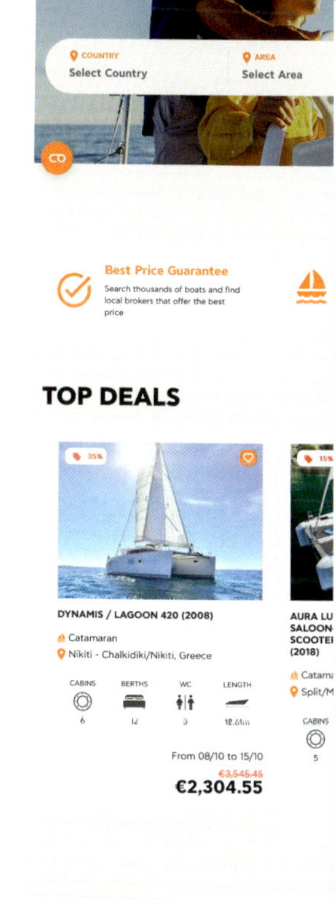

easyBoat.com 20 Sep 2022

easyBoat in Startup Magazine 17 sep 2022

ΣΥΝΕΝΤΕΥΞΗ

easyBoat

easyBoat.com

ΣΤΟΧΟΣ ΝΑ ΑΠΟΤΕΛΕΙ ΤΗΝ ΠΡΩΤΗ ΕΠΙΛΟΓΗ ΤΩΝ ΠΕΛΑΤΩΝ ΩΣ ΠΡΟΤΑΣΗ ΝΑΥΛΩΣΗΣ ΣΚΑΦΩΝ ΑΝΑΨΥΧΗΣ!

ΖΗΤΟΥΜΕΝΟ Η ΕΝΙΣΧΥΣΗ ΤΟΥ ΠΛΗΘΟΥΣ ΤΩΝ ΣΥΝΕΡΓΑΤΩΝ ΣΤΗΝ ΠΛΑΤΦΟΡΜΑ ΚΑΙ ΤΟΥ ΑΡΙΘΜΟΥ ΤΩΝ ΔΙΑΘΕΣΙΜΩΝ ΣΚΑΦΩΝ ΜΕΣΩ ΑΥΤΗΣ - ΕΜΦΑΣΗ ΣΤΗ ΔΙΕΘΝΗ ΑΝΑΓΝΩΡΙΣΙΜΟΤΗΤΑ ΤΟΥ BRAND

Αντλώντας έμπνευση από την επαγγελματική ενασχόληση με τον χώρο του yachting και τα εμπόδια που είχε να αντιμετωπίσει εν μέσω της πανδημικής κρίσης, προέκυψε η ιδέα της δημιουργίας της πρώτης ηλεκτρονικής πλατφόρμας σύγκρισης τιμών για ναύλωση σκαφών αναψυχής. Ιδέα που υιοθετήθηκε από τον Sir Στέλιο Χατζηιωάννου και αυτομάτως εντάχθηκε στον όμιλο easy. Σήμερα, έχοντας διανύσει το πρώτο καλοκαίρι της λειτουργίας της, η easyBoat.com αποσκοπεί να αποτελέσει συνώνυμο και πρώτη επιλογή συνάμα στο μυαλό όσων αναζητούν μια πρόταση ναύλωσης σκάφους αναψυχής, σύμφωνα με τον Αλέξανδρο Νάστο, διευθύνοντα σύμβουλο και συνιδρυτή της easyBoat.com.

Του Παναγιώτη Μαρκέτου

PAGE 10

STARTUPPER MAG

Simon Lalagos promotes easyBoat

Storing your stuff with easy

When easyStorage was conceived in 2017 by co-founders Tim Slesinger, Nigel Dawson, and Halim Boumadani, their mission was more than just to start a business; it was to revolutionise the self-storage industry. Frustrated by the high costs and inflexibility of traditional storage solutions, they saw an opportunity to make storage accessible, affordable, and convenient, thereby making it a viable lifestyle option for a broader demographic.

Tim Slesinger - timslesinger @easystorage.com

Hailm Boumadani

Nigel Dawson

Stelios visits easyStorage Park Royal

easyStorage Van livery 2020 (background image)

Stelios signs brand licence agreement with Tim Slesinger 2018

Local easyStorage advertising at Brent Cross

easyStorage Franchisee Manchester

Storing your stuff with easy .... continued

The Evolution of easyStorage

In the six years since its inception, easyStorage has not only met its initial goals but has far exceeded them, achieving an impressive coverage of 85% of the UK. This remarkable journey from a disruptive startup to a market leader is a testament to the synergy between the company's own operations and the contributions of its highly motivated and capable franchisees. Operating in tandem, easyStorage's direct management and franchisee network, combined with the power of the easy brand, form a dynamic ecosystem. The franchisees, handpicked for their drive and expertise, have not only spread the easyStorage brand far and wide but have also infused the business with local insights and entrepreneurial vigour. This powerful combination has been pivotal in their ability to scale swiftly and sustainably, positioning easyStorage for continued growth and innovation on a European scale.

The easyStorage team at Elite Franchise Awards, Top 50 Franchisee 2022

Franchisees undertake training at the new easyStorage Academy in Uxbridge

easyStorage flagship storage centre in Uxbridge

Trustpilot
Excellent

James Butler
5 reviews GB

A day ago

Had a very positive experience using...

Had a very positive experience using easyStorage recently. From the initial booking experience and speaking with the team to the actual collection on the day, everything was seamless and stress free. Many thanks and regards to Gavin, Darnell and Vermell for their friendly professionalism and help with my move yesterday. It was a pleasure Gentlemen! My very best, James from SE10

Date of experience: 06 April 2024

Celebrating Customer Success Stories

Part of what makes easyStorage's journey so compelling are the stories of customers who have found value and convenience in its services. From families decluttering their homes to make space for home offices or growing families, to businesses using easyPods to manage inventory during peak seasons, the impact of easyStorage's solutions on people's lives and livelihoods is profound. Each customer story underscores the brand's mission to provide storage solutions that are not just spaces to store belongings but enablers of lifestyle changes and business growth.

The Advent of easyPod : A Modular Marvel

The introduction of easyPod represented a significant milestone in easyStorage's journey. These portable storage units, designed with the customer in mind, offered a novel way to manage space. The easyPod system's modularity, combined with VAULT, the company's bespoke easy-to-use online booking and management system, revolutionised the customer experience by offering flexibility, security and most importantly, affordability. Visit www.easyPod.uk for details.

easyStorage Oxford retrieval

easyStorage Warehouse Uxbridge 2022

Scaling New Heights with easyContainer

Building on the success of easyPod, easyStorage expanded its offerings with easyContainer, catering to those with larger storage needs with 'drive up' access. Whether for commercial inventory, equipment, or personal belongings, easyContainer provided a secure, scalable solution. This expansion demonstrated easyStorage's commitment to offering diverse storage solutions that cater to the unique needs of its varied customer base. Visit www.easyContainer.biz for details.

easyContainer promotion on easyStorage.com 2024

Steventon branch storage containers 2022

Steventon branch storage containers 2022

easyVan : Seamless Storage Mobility

The introduction of easyVan was a natural progression in easyStorage's quest to provide end-to-end storage solutions. This service ensured the smooth transportation of customers' belongings to and from storage facilities, encapsulating the hassle-free experience that easyStorage stands for. With easyVan, the company not only offered space but also the convenience of moving, further solidifying its position as a comprehensive storage solutions provider. Visit www.easyVan.com for details.

easyStorage van being unloaded at depo (left)

easyStorage vans showcased at franchise exhibitions

easyStorage vans and pods at Park Royal Depot

Vans helping frontline workers during the covid lockdowns

Technology:
Enhancing every aspect

easyStorage digital dashboards in action

While technology has been a cornerstone of easyStorage's operations, its application has always been with the aim of enhancing customer service and operational efficiency. From the bespoke VAULT platform that streamlines franchisee operations to the digital dashboards that optimise marketing efforts, technology at easyStorage is always a means to an end – better service.

Storing your stuff with easy .... continued

Looking Forward

As easyStorage looks to the future, the company is poised for even greater achievements. The brand's commitment to innovation, customer satisfaction, and strategic expansion will continue to drive its success. With plans for European growth and continuous improvements to service offerings, easyStorage is well on its way to becoming the go-to brand for storage solutions.

easyStorage, together with its innovative sub-brands easyPod, easyContainer, and easyVan, remains dedicated to its mission of making storage a practical, affordable lifestyle option. By staying true to its founding principles and continually adapting to meet the changing needs of its customers, easyStorage is set to redefine the storage industry for years to come. Visit www.easyStorage.com for details.

easyPod Locations 2024

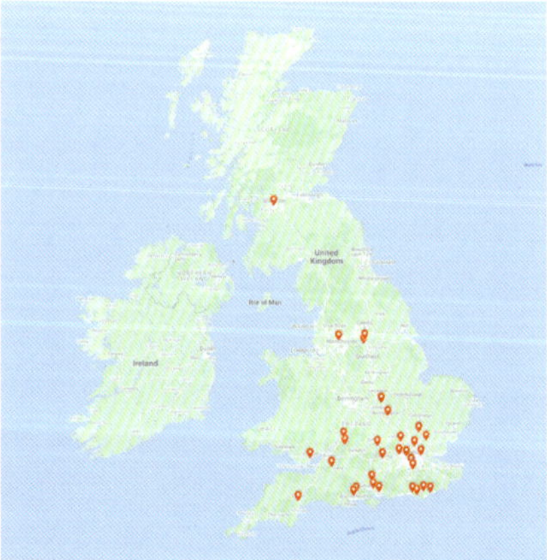

easyContainer Locations 2024

easyPod has 33 locations nationwide, with easyContainer boasting 14 locations in April 2024.

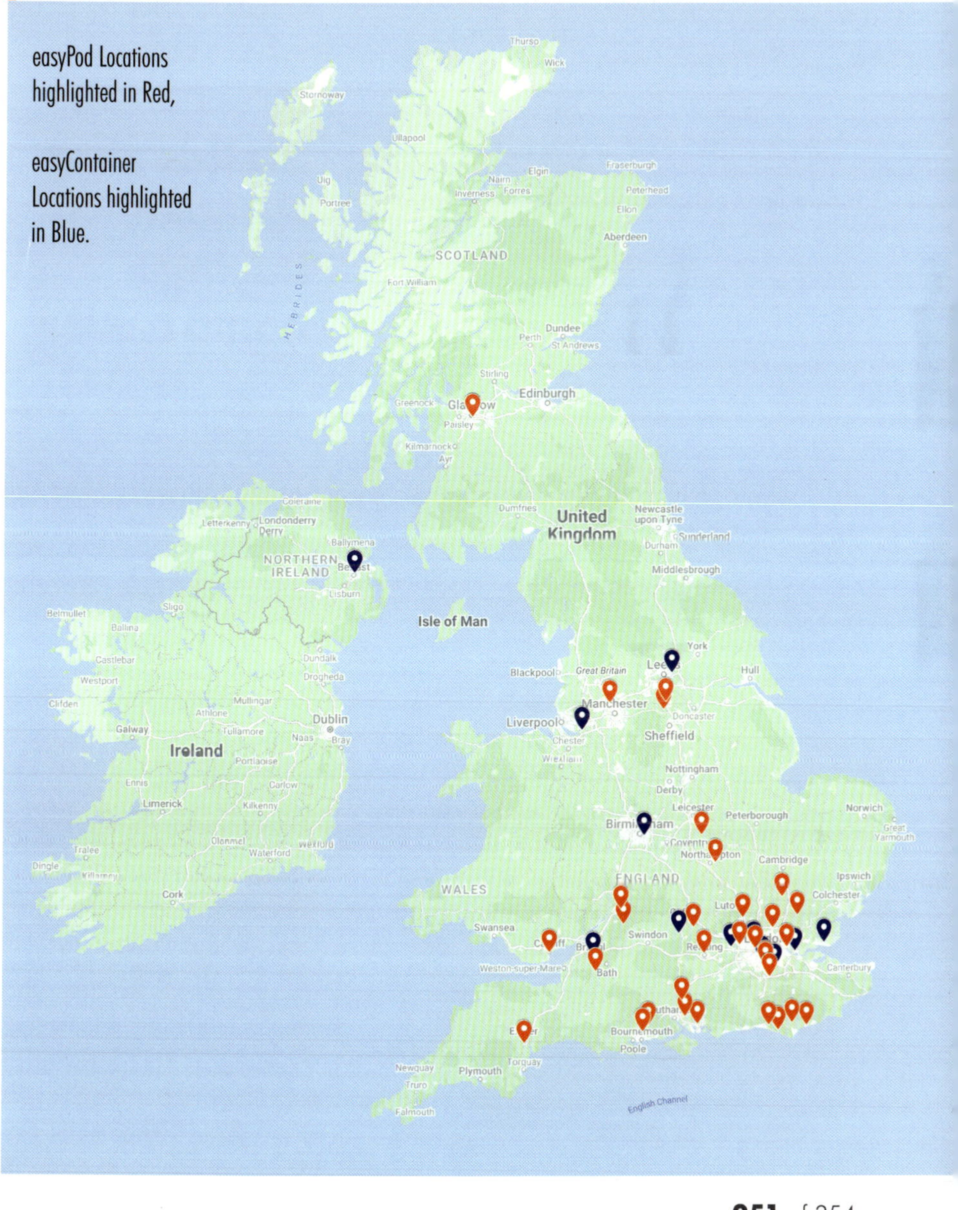

easyProperty

The EU trademark for easyProperty was applied for in May 2004 and granted on 27/09/05, trademark number 3838414.

Today the company offers a cost-effective way for customers to sell their property through an easy-to-use technology platform. See easyProperty.com for more or email Charles Hancock - chancock@easyproperty.com.

Another property related brand is easyConveyance.com which allows people involved in property transaction the chance to compare prices from over 200 UK conveyancing and solicitor's firms.

Independent 19 Apr 2014

INDEPENDENT

Stelios aims to make buying a home easier

The entrepreneur behind budget airline easyJet has entered the competitive world of online estate agents. ROB GRIFFIN *looks at what he, and others, have to offer house hunters*

Financial Times 28 Sep 2015

FT FINANCIAL TIMES

EasyProperty has estate agents in its sights

EasyProperty, a venture backed by Sir Stelios Haji-Ioannou, is trying to bring digital disruption to the task of selling and renting homes. This week, Sir Stelios and Rob Ellice, easyProperty chief, are adding sales to the lettings website they launched last year.

Evening Standard 09 Mar 2015

Evening Standard

Easy does it! Online letting agent has big plans with backing from Stelios

Russell Lynch

GROWTH CAPITAL

Doing battle with STARBUCKS & COSTA COFFEE

Taking on the big guys

Although the easy brand has been serving coffee since the 1990s under the easyKiosk, easyInternetcafe & easyEverything banner, the actual "easyCoffee", trademark number 12715892 filed on 21st March 2014 when plans were hatched to take on the coffee giants head on based on a decent cup of coffee honestly priced. In January 2016 easyCoffee was launched from a small orange kiosk at Earls Court Station offering coffee for £1, a third of the price charged by some of the big High Street brands such as Starbucks or Costa Coffee. The easyCoffee brand is available for franchising and they actively take part in franchise exhibitions in London and Birmingham to find new franchisees. If you are interested in a franchise see www.easy.coffee or email franchisee@easy.coffee. The brand is also available in a vending machine format for smaller sites.

easyCoffee Dartford

easyCoffee promoting franchise opportunities

easy in equipment rental

The idea for the business behind easyHire and the related brands came after co-founders Andrea Guzzoni and Dennis Helderman identified an opportunity to make Europe's £20 billion+ equipment hire easy and accessible for all. After all, you can rent a car online, you can book a flight ticket online, why can't you book your local plant and tool hire end-to-end online?

Andrea Guzzoni & Dennis Helderman
of easyHire and Rentuu 2022
andrea@easyhire.biz

Items available for hire (below)

In July 2019 the business they created called Rentuu, welcomed Sir Stelios Haji-Ioannou and easyGroup on board as shareholders. easyHire was born, offering tool hire and event businesses the opportunity to operate under the easyEventhire or easyToolhire brand, trademark number 18123568.

easyHire's franchise model focuses on technology, partnerships, together with marketing and branding support in protected territories - under the brands easyToolhire & easyEventhire including country localisations such as easyNoleggio (Italy), easyAlquiler (Spain), easyLocation (France), and easyMieten (Germany).

easyHire's cloud-based platform provides private individuals and businesses with an easier way to hire and rent products to encourage continual use of equipment and discourage waste.

easyHire has raised more than £4 million in investment from institutional investors, Angel investors such as London Business School's Enterprise 100, and completed two oversubscribed equity crowdfunding campaigns on Seedrs that welcomed over 1000 investors on board.

easyHire, UK trademark number 2349891 & EU number 3763497 has the exclusive franchise rights to easyEventhire and easyToolhire and is actively looking to work with businesses in the EU and the UK to emulate the success of franchise agreements already in place in the UK, Italy, and Spain.

easyToolhire.com 2024

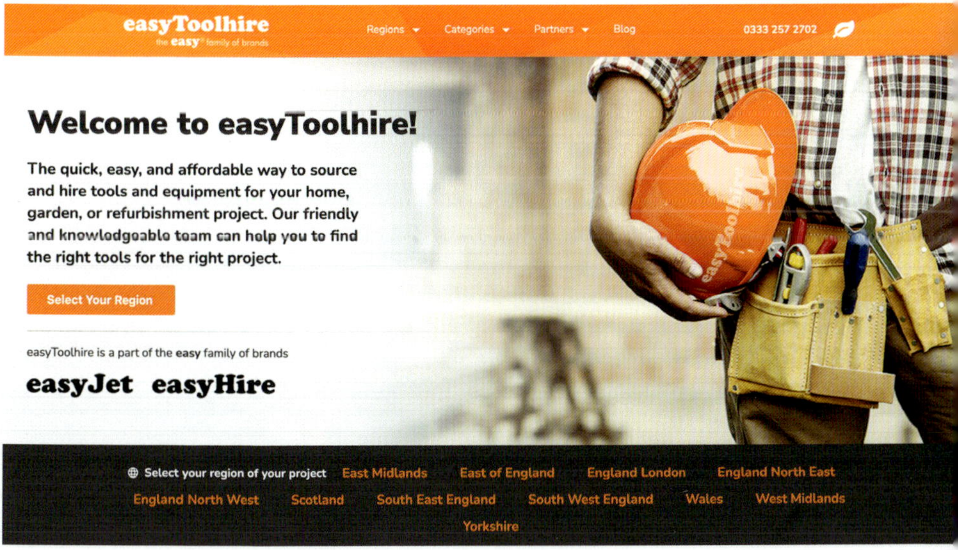

easy in .... continued

equipment rental

easyToolhire powering Wilko Hire 2024

In April 2024 easyHire announced a new partnership with UK discount retailer Wilko.com to bring low-cost toolhire to Wilko customers.

Get in touch now to paint the tool hire and equipment rental market orange, transforming the tool and equipment rental market and giving contractors and consumers the opportunity to hire tools and equipment easily!

Visit:
www.easytoolhire.com,
www.easyeventhireuk.com,
www.easynoleggio.net,
www.easylocation.fr,
www.easyalquiler.com,
www.easymieten.net &
www.easyaluguel.com

easyAlquiler warehouse 05 Jul 2022

easyAlquiler equipment inspection 2022 (right)

Pitch it easy

Another route to join the easy family of brands is by winning the Pitch it easy competition.

First launched in 2019 Pitch it easy is an entrepreneurial competition backed by Bayes Business School (formerly Cass) City, University of London from which Stelios graduated and easyGroup. The contest allows students and graduates the opportunity to pitch their early-stage businesses to Sir Stelios.

In addition to cash prizes, the winners are invited to join the easy family of brands after the signing of a royalty licence agreement. The 2023 competion was won by Alexis Murat an alumunus of Bayes Business School who set-up a business called easyVirtual.tours (profiled on the next page).

Following the success of the 2023 event, Stelios has decided to give more former students the chance to pitch their business ideas and has allowed applications from many more universities.

We are in the final stages of agreeing terms with the 2024 pitchiteasy.com winner who will be using the domain www.easyDigital.tech.

Full details of the competition can be found on the website pitchiteasy.com

Pitchiteasy 2024 promotion from Bayes Business School

easyVirtual.tours

easyVirtual.tours is a start-up developed by a young entrepreneur called Alexis Murat an alumunus of Bayes business school who won the 2023 Pitchiteasy competition and joined the easy family of brands.

Stelios, Alexis & Léo

easyVirtual.tours, founded in 2021, has quickly become a leader in immersive virtual tours, leveraging VR and AR technologies to transform digital exploration in Europe. With a foundation built on innovation and a commitment to accessibility, easyVirtual.tours serves a diverse clientele, including major corporations and cultural institutions. With the backing of Sir Stelios Haji-Ioannou and integration into the easy family of brands, the company is expanding its innovative franchise model throughout Europe. As the company continues expanding its global reach, it is redefining the boundaries between the physical and digital worlds, making it easier than ever to access and explore spaces from anywhere.

Location capture and camera operator

The idea behind easyVirtual.tours is to provide a service to businesses to create 3D/360 virtual tours of buildings and other physical assets. The tours are filmed using state-of-the art cameras to different industries such as real estate, museums, hotels, etc. The company was initially launched in the UK and France and is working to sign up franchisees that sell services within an agreed geographic territory. If you are interested in becoming a franchisee, please contact paul.smith@easyVirtual.tours

easyVirtualtours Team 2024

Empowering entrepreneurs to realise their dreams

New members have continued to join the easy family of brands, covering a wide range of sectors both in the UK and internationally. A tried and tested licence arrangement allows entrepreneurs seeking to set-up or grow their businesses, to bring low prices and great value to customers through access to one of Europe's best-known overarching value brands. Some entrepreneurs join the family through becoming a franchisee.

The National Franchise Exhibition stand London Olympia March 2018 (below) & marketing material (above)

This is a great way for an individual with limited capital to benefit from the strength of the brand.

In 2018 easyGroup made its first appearance at The British & National Franchise Exhibitions in London & Birmingham. The stands have previously featured members of the easy family of brands that offer franchise opportunities including easyStorage, easyGym & easyHotel.

easy presence at the National Franchise Exhibition London 12th April 2024

easy presence at the National Franchise Exhibition Birmingham 2019 (right)

easy

Relentless innovation

Empowering entrepreneurs to realise their dreams

This is MONEY.co.uk
FINANCIAL WEBSITE OF THE YEAR

Money Home | Business | Saving & banking | Investing | Bills | Cars | Holidays | Cards & loans |

From easyJet to Easy Power: Airline pioneer Stelios in talks to turn household rubbish into energy

- Easy Power International was set up last month by a group of businessmen
- Stelios Haji-Ioannou is in talks about licensing his 'easy' brand to the company
- Easy Power turns household rubbish into 'clean' power

By BEN HARRINGTON FOR THE MAIL ON SUNDAY
PUBLISHED: 22:25, 25 July 2020 | **UPDATED:** 10:06, 26 July 2020

easyPower article 26/07/20

The Dutch energy company NieuweStroom has pioneered the launch of real-time energy pricing to consumers in the Netherlands using the brand easyEnergy.com. In simple terms the customer's energy price is directly linked to the current market price which varies by hour for electricity and daily for gas. This allows customers the flexibility to manage their energy consumption using energy when it is most cost effective. As of March 2024, easyEnergy.com had nearly 10,000 customers and over 16,000 gas and electricity connections across the Netherlands.

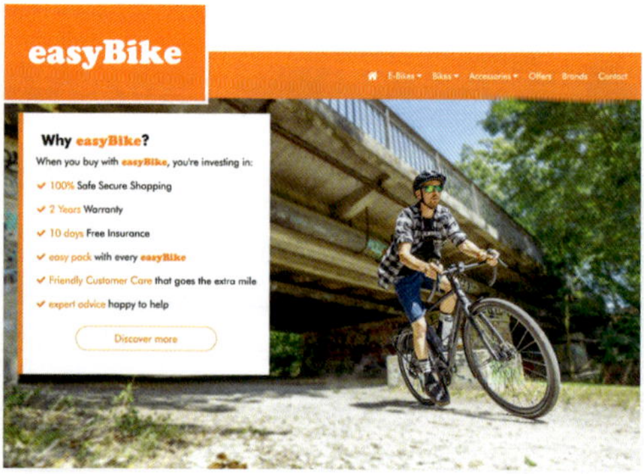

easyBike.com website 08/04/2024

Another start up is easyBike.com founded in 2022 by a young entrepreneur called Mandish Sawan from the West Midlands. easyBike retails electric bicycles online ranging from hybrids and mountain bikes to e-mopeds.

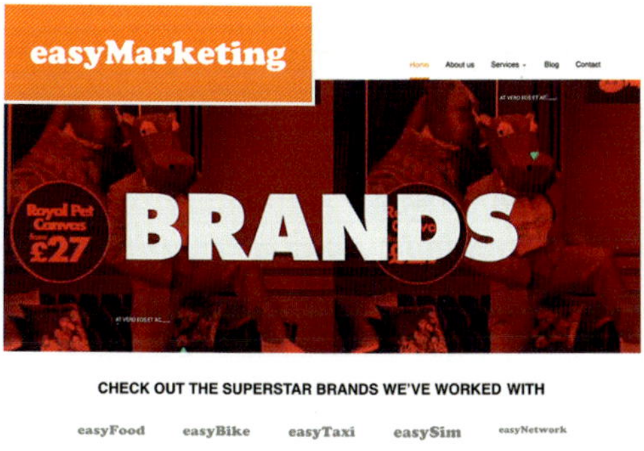

easyMarketing.co.uk website 2024

Launched in 2022 easyMarketing is an innovative low-cost marketing agency based in Birmingham, England led by entrepreneur Amit Sagu. Visit easyMarketing.co.uk for details.

How to join the easy Family of Brands:

There are many different routes by which members have joined the easy family of brands. Some entrepreneurs submit their ideas directly to Stelios, such as Frank Scolaro who in 2020 together with Stelios conceived an idea for easyParking an app allowing users to earn money by making parking spaces available to drivers while also identifying electric vehicle charging points. easyParking now has the TM number 17986555 and can be found on our website www.easyParking.biz

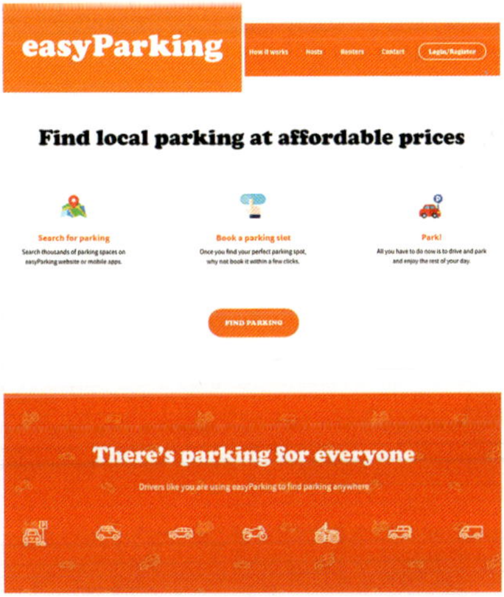

easyParking.biz website 2021

Josh Wintersgill - with easyTravelseat

Another route is the event run by the Stelios Philanthropic Foundation and Leonard Cheshire for supporting disabled entrepreneurs. This award was won in 2018 by Josh Wintersgill. When he was just 18 months old Josh was diagnosed with spinal muscular atrophy, a progressive muscle wasting condition, but he has not allowed disability to get in the way of his achievements.

He came up with an idea to provide wheelchair users with a safer, more dignified and comfortable means of transferring onto an aircraft seat. His invention called easyTravelseat is highly versatile and can be used in a variety of different circumstances including boats, cars, beaches and kayaks. Josh is well known as a champion of disability rights and has achieved significant recognition for his achievements. In 2019 Josh was crowned first South West Great British Entrepreneur as well as Young Entrepreneur of the Year at the Natwest Great British Entrepreneur Awards. easyTravelseat now has the TM number 17986557 and details can be found at easytravelseat.com.or email Joshua Wintersgill - joshwintersgill@easytravelseat.com.

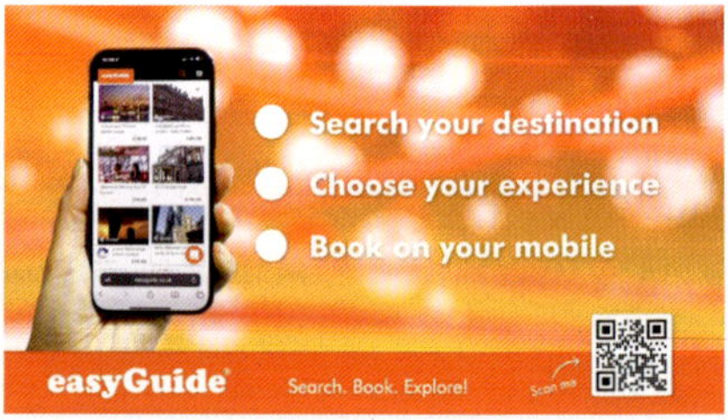

easyGuide.biz website 2024 & easyGuide TV ad 2022

In 2023 easyGroup signed a licence agreement with Musement (part of the Tui Group) allowing customers to access a range of worldwide activities, experiences and excursions through easyGuide.biz

Another idea is easyAccessibility.co.uk which joined the easy family of brands in January 2020. Through the use of Audio Descriptive Information, the goal of the business is to develop and manufacture products that enable visually impaired people and those who also benefit from audio information, to live their lives with dignity and independence. The company provides a device called the RoomMate which makes disabled WCs properly accessible for those with visual impairment. Visit easyaccessibility.co.uk or email info@easyaccessibility.co.uk

easyAccessibility Room Mate device

easyPet.net joins in 2018, vehicle with happy customer!

Empowering entrepreneurs to realise their dreams

The future of the easy family of brands depends not just on the continued growth and success of existing family members but also on new licensees who see the value of operating under a widely known and trusted brand. New members of the easy family in 2022 include:

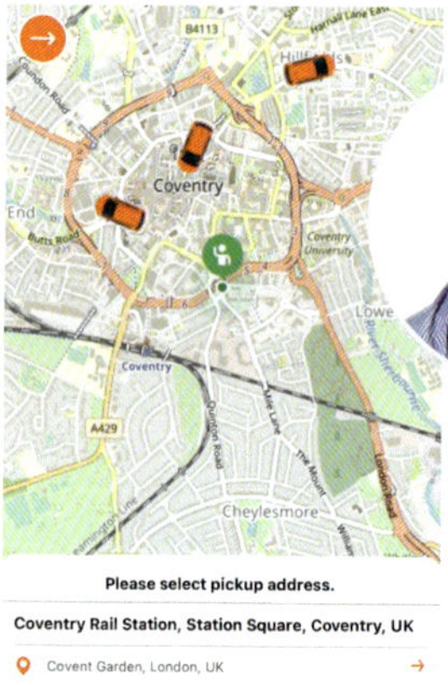

Eugene Mullins eugene.mullins@easytaxi.app

easyTaxi: A technology platform piloted in 2021 that includes a national passenger app and website enabling the public to securely book a safe ride to their required destination with vetted drivers provided by local taxi and private hire companies. The service is now being further tested in Dublin and Cork prior to a wider roll-out
Visit: www.easyTaxi.app & easyTaxi.ie

easyTravel: A centralised B to C travel marketplace incorporating travel agency services such as flights, accommodation, transfers, tours and activities. Available at www.easyTravel.tech.

Stelios with easyTravel Team 22 Aug 2022 - darryl@easytravel.tech, CEO of easyTravel.tech

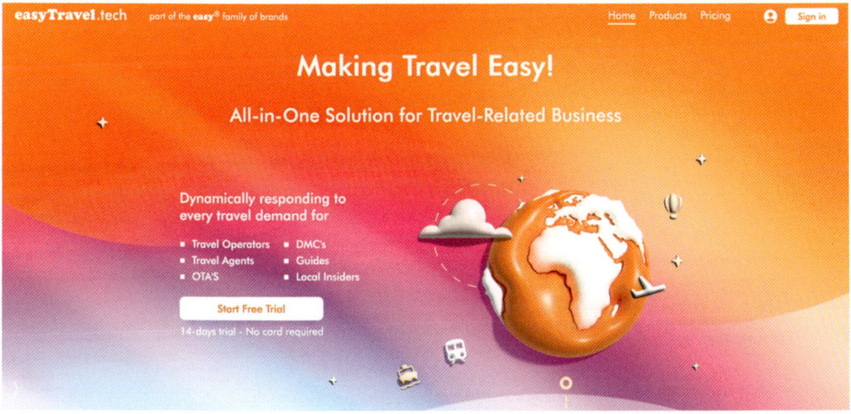

easyTravel.tech website Apr 2024

Other internet brands that have been trading for many years but have now been purchased by easyGroup include easyRoommate (TM 2492498) which has been trading since the 1990s, easyArt.com trading since 2001 and easyFood (TM 17808098) trading since 2006 at easyFood.co.uk.

easyFood customer delivery 2019

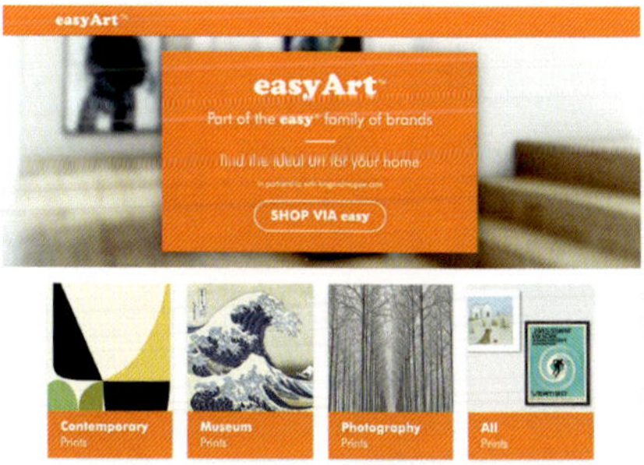

easyArt website 2024

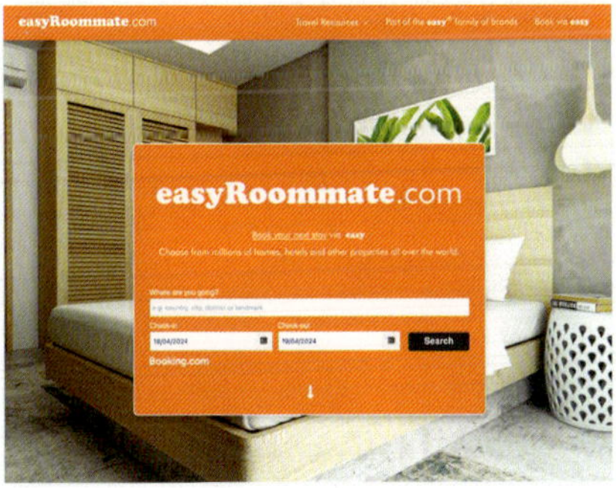

easyRoommate website 2024

easyWoo.com

In October of 2022 a psychologist and entrepreneur named Ester Siakkas and her business partner George Economides launched an innovative relationship support service called easyWoo.

easyWoo Website 2022

Developed by a team of experienced psychologists, psychotherapists and computer programmers, easyWoo adopts a different model from most dating sites that present users with countless of individuals to match with and require users to take out a monthly subscription.

George Economides

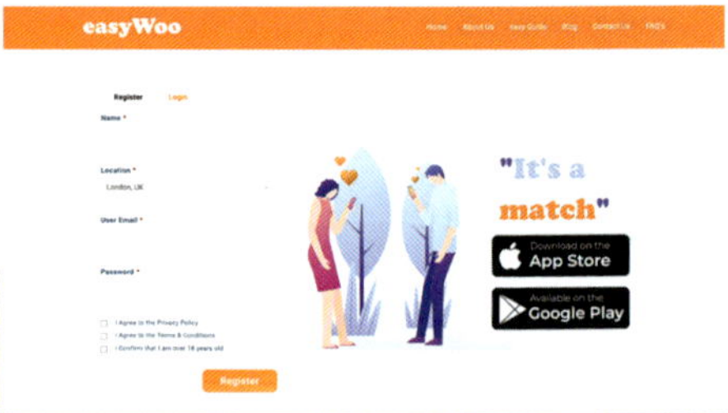

easyWoo website 09/04/2024

Stelios with the easyWoo team in Monaco 2023

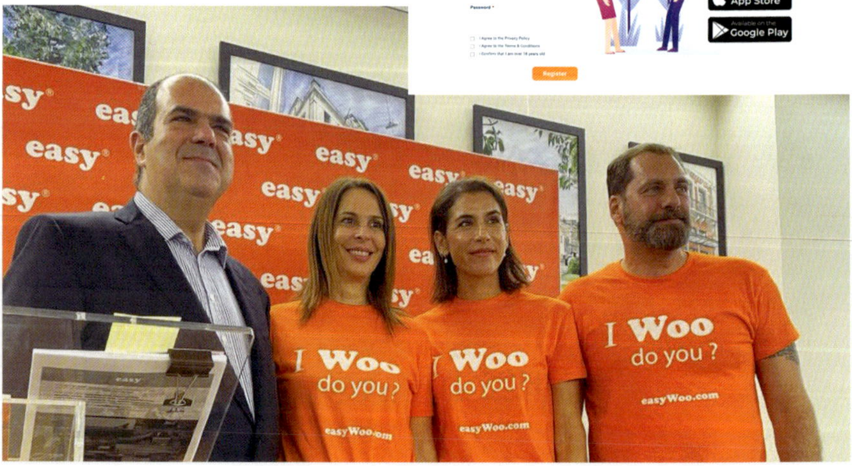

A section of the easyWoo online quiz April 2024

You have taken the first step to discover your Personality and Relationship profile.
Answer all questions as truthfully as possible to enable our algorithms to give you the best advice on how to improve your dating chances.
Our experts will provide their feedback in your Personalised Report and a list of resources that will help you reach your goal.

Gender

○ Male ○ Female ○ Non binary

Sexual orientation

○ Straight ○ Gay ○ Bisexual ○ Other

Ethnicity

○ White ○ Black ○ Asian ○ Mixed ○ Other

Your body type

○ Heavy set ○ Athletic ○ Slim ○ Skinny ○ A few extra kilos ○ Overweight ○ Prefer not to say

easyWoo analyses the relationship persona of each one of its members, presenting them with a free report and guides them towards improving their persona, prior to engaging in dating.
The business model relies on revenue from advertising within the platform, from service providers.
The algorithm's starting point is an easy-to-use online quiz, leading to a free report and extends to online matching.
The service was originally launched in Cyprus and then the UK.

easyWoo in The Sun 16 Sep 2022

Protecting the easy family of brands against brand theft

Taking on the big guys

You can't expect people to pay to use a brand if you allow others to use it for free without permission. It is therefore an important aspect of the easy family of brands business model to pursue and stop unauthorised use of the easy brand. However, despite what is often reported, easyGroup does not claim that it owns a monopoly in the word 'easy'. Third parties are free to use 'easy' descriptively ("our product is easy to use"). What easyGroup objects to is when third parties use 'easy' in a branding sense (especially if it is with a lower case 'e' and conjoined with another word that describes the goods and services being offered). The closer the use is to easyGroup's brand style the more concerning it is.

THE FTSE 100 ROSE 26.95 TO 7,371.22
Sun CITY
Edited by TRACEY BOLES
A WIN THE EASY WAY

Easyway by Air China
Sun - 14/09/19

AIR CHINA
中国国际航空公司

Carrefour outlet before and after rebranding

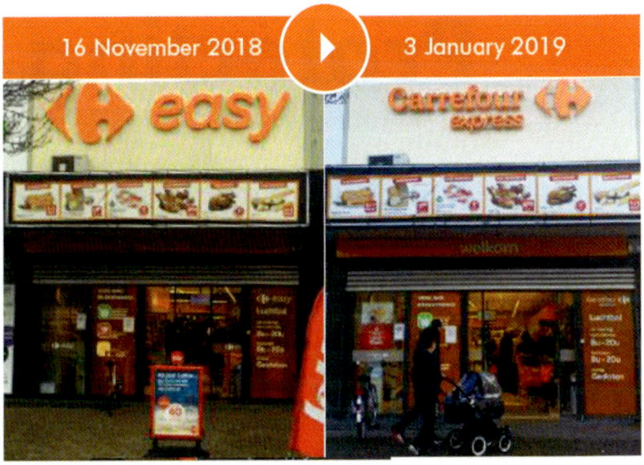

Sigmalive Network | Sigmalive Simerini Sportime Economy Today

CITY ΤΩΡΑ ΕΧΩ ΘΕΜΑ ΜΙΛΑ ΜΟΥ SEX

#Λιβύη #Τρόοδος #Megxit #Σεξομολογής

ΠΕΡΙΕΡΓΑ

Σερ Στέλιος Χατζηιωάννου – Carrefour 1 – 0

Ο Κύπριος επιχειρηματίας κέρδισε τη δικαστική διαμάχη έναντι στον γαλλικό κολοσσό.

#EASY #CARREFOUR #ΔΙΚΑΣΤΙΚΗ ΔΙΑΜΑΧΗ #ΣΕΡ ΣΤΕΛΙΟΣ ΧΑΤΖΗΙΩΑΝΝΟΥ #ΠΕΡΙΕΡΓΑ

Τετάρτη 09 Ιανουαρίου 2019

2 λεπτά

Η easyGroup του Sir Στέλιου Χατζηιωάννου, στον οποίο ανήκουν και όλα τα εμπορικά σήματα easy (easy family of brands), είχε σήμερα μια ιστορική νίκη στη μακρόχρονη δικαστική διαμάχη με τον γαλλικό κολοσσό σούπερ μάρκετ Carrefour.

Κατά την περίοδο 2014 – 2016, ο γαλλικός όμιλος Carrefour έθεσε σε λειτουργία σειρά καταστημάτων τύπου «metro» στο Βέλγιο, χρησιμοποιώντας τη λέξη easy με το χαρακτηριστικό πορτοκαλί χρώμα αλλά και γραμματοσειρά που

https://city.sigmalive.com/article/2019/1/9/ser-stelios-hatziioannoy-carrefour-1-0/

Stelios 1 Carrefour 0

Stelios calls these people affectionately "brand thieves". Their legal "sin" is twofold: by calling themselves "easy something" they are "infringing" one of easyGroup's thousand plus trademarks.

The other brand "sin" in legal terms is called "passing off". It occurs when a non-licensed business pretends to be a legitimate member of the easy family of brands. To prove passing off easyGroup relies on the un-registered rights it has built up from when it started in 1994. easyGroup's legal claim becomes much stronger if the brand thief uses its colours and logos.

Retail Detail (Belgium) 04 Dec 2018

Retail Detail

retailnews retailtv retailevents retailhub

Carrefour stopt Easy-formule

Foto Pat Verbruggen

Carrefour Belgium zet zijn buurtwinkelformule Easy stop. De ondernemers maken de overstap naar het uithangbord Express. Een budgettaire oefening, zegt de retailer: de winkels behouden wel hun specifieke DNA.

Boodschappen in de buurt

De twaalf Easy-winkels van Carrefour vervangen momenteel één na één hun uithangbord: op de gevel komt een oranje Express logo. "We waren al eerder gestopt met de expansie van Easy", reageert woordvoerder Baptiste Van Outryve. "Na de aankondiging van ons transformatieplan in januari hebben we besloten om ons te concentreren op het merk Carrefour met drie uithangborden. We wensen geen bijkomende budgetten te besteden aan andere merknamen."

De naam Easy verdwijnt dus, maar de verkooppunten (die allemaal worden uitgebaat door franchisenemers) behouden wel dezelfde propositie: het zijn winkels voor de dagelijkse boodschappen in de buurt, met elke dag één promotie, de focus op vers en een depannage-assortiment in food. Met hun oranje Express-logo onderscheiden ze zich van de groene Express-winkels, die meestal kleiner zijn dan 400 m^2 en mikken op passanten, met de nadruk op gemak en on-the-go. In de verdere expansieplannen van Express zullen zowel de groene als de oranje formulevariant hun rol blijven spelen.

De wortels van Carrefour Easy gaan terug tot het najaar van 2013, toen de retailer in Moerbeke-Waas een eerste testwinkel opende onder het uithangbord Easy Caddy. De bedoeling was om een lacune te vullen tussen de kleinere Express gemakswinkels en de grotere Market supermarkten. De winkel voerde geen folderpromoties, maar werkte met vaste dagacties. Na de opening van een tweede testwinkel in Melsele werd de formule Easy officieel gelanceerd in 2016, met als motto "vers, snel en eenvoudig". Destijds klonk het nog dat er op de langere termijn potentieel was voor een honderdtal vestigingen.

Protecting the easy family of brands against brand theft

continued

Stelios considers It a huge compliment to the easy family of brands that there are so many people out there who are willing to imitate the brand to profit without paying their dues to easyGroup. For Stelios it is a good indication that there is a sustainable business model in a business sector if there are brand thieves operating in it.

On 19th December 2019 easyGroup won a UK court injunction against an Italian law firm using the brand EasyRimborso and was awarded damages and costs.

Brand thief: EasyRimborso – now out of business - 19/12/19

Brand thief: Easyexport
Defeated in Greek trademark courts 2020

In September 2019 Air China which is a large corporation had to stop using the easyway brand that was used to promote flights. In July 2021 easyGroup was granted an injunction preventing a French Caribbean travel agent, Stephane Roche from using the "easyway" brand to promote his tourist services to customers in the UK. The defendant was also required to pay legal costs of £75,000 plus damages. In his final judgement the judge found that the easy family of brands sufficiently pre-dated Stephane Roche's use of easyway.

Daily Mail 09 Jan 2019

■ **EASY WIN** Sir Stelios Haji-Ioannou, founder of **Easyjet**, has won a battle with French supermarket Carrefour over use of the 'Easy' brand name. The tycoon, 51, took issue with Carrefour's chain of 'easy market' shops, which had logos with an orange 'easy' in them – the signature style of his empire. The supermarket is to rebrand the stores as Carrefour Express.

Belfast Telegraph

EasyGroup claims victory as Air China agrees to ditch 'Easy Way' branding

Sir Stelios Haji-Ioannou has revealed the national flag carrier will drop the name after lawyers got involved.

EasyJet founder Stelios Haji-Ioannou has forced Air China to drop its use of 'Easy Way', claiming a trademark breach (Chris Radburn/PA)

By Simon Neville, PA City Editor
September 13 2019 09:14 AM

EasyJet founder Sir Stelios Haji-Ioannou has claimed victory in a legal battle with China's national airline over the use of the word "easy" in its advertising.

Air China launched a Beijing-Frankfurt service in May 2017, described as the "Easy Way" to visit Europe for millions of Chinese tourists.

But Sir Stelios took issue with its use, claiming it was a breach of copyright for his EasyGroup of brands.

His company said: "Following a brief exchange of solicitors' letters, Air China has agreed to stop use of the wording."

Air China has agreed to drop its 'Easy Way' branding for its Beijing to Frankfurt flight after Sir Stelios got involved (Chris Radburn/PA)

Sir Stelios added: "We have a long-standing and well-publicised policy of pursuing brand thieves in courts in UK, EU courts and beyond. Some brand thieves are small companies that simply fold instead of fighting it out in court.

"So it is reassuring to see a company with the size and standing of Air China accepting the logic and fairness of not using another travel company's brand."

Columbian airline Easyfly and Honduran airline Easy Sky have both been hit with similar legal demands last year, and earlier this year Bangladesh-based cargo carrier easyFly agreed to change its name.

Previous litigation over the word "easy" by Sir Stelios has also seen Netflix come under the tycoon's radar for its TV series Easy, with it facing similar legal action.

Netflix said at the time that it thinks "viewers can tell the difference between a show they watch and a plane they fly (in)."

Sir Stelios launched easyJet in 1995, kickstarting the rise of low-cost air travel. He floated the company five years later, although remains as the largest shareholder with a 34% stake

He subsequently launched several different companies all with the prefix "easy", including easyEnergy, easyCar and easyFood.

The easyHotel chain, which is also listed, is currently in the midst of a takeover battle, with Sir Stelios clashing with the board, claiming the £138.7 million bid by Ivanhoe Cambridge and Icamap undervalues the business.

easyGroup v Air China Belfast Telegraph 13 Sep 2019

Protecting the easy family of brands against brand theft

continued

In November 2019 a Swiss court issued an order to take down the website easyBet.com which was offering online gaming. In September 2020 the Greek TM Administrative Commission ruled that easyGroup owns a "series of marks" all distinguished by the word "easy" as their distinctive element; that the word "easy" is a sign that has acquired exceptional notoriety making it a famous mark (this is art. 124(1)(c) of Greek TM law 4072/2012); and that the choice of the TM applicant of filing Easyexport was strategic in that they aimed at exploiting parasitically (bad faith filing, art. 123 (3)(b) of Greek TM law 4072/2012) the exceptional recognition power of the element "easy" of easyGroup, which is a distinctive sign (other than a TM) "known in the relevant market" and enjoying protection also as a company name of easyGroup (art. 124 (1)(c) of Greek TM law 4072/2012

In September 2021 in a landmark agreement, the Colombian regional airline that had been using the name easyFly without a licence from easyGroup, agreed to rebrand as Clic. Similarly, an airline in Curacao that had been using the name EZ Air without a licence from easyGroup, agreed to rebrand as Z Air.

Bangladeshi brand thief: Saber Chowdry (easyFly) – now out of business.

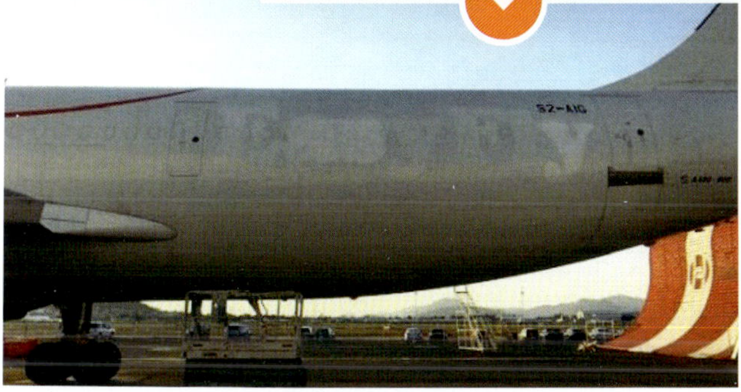

Plane before and after court action by easyGroup

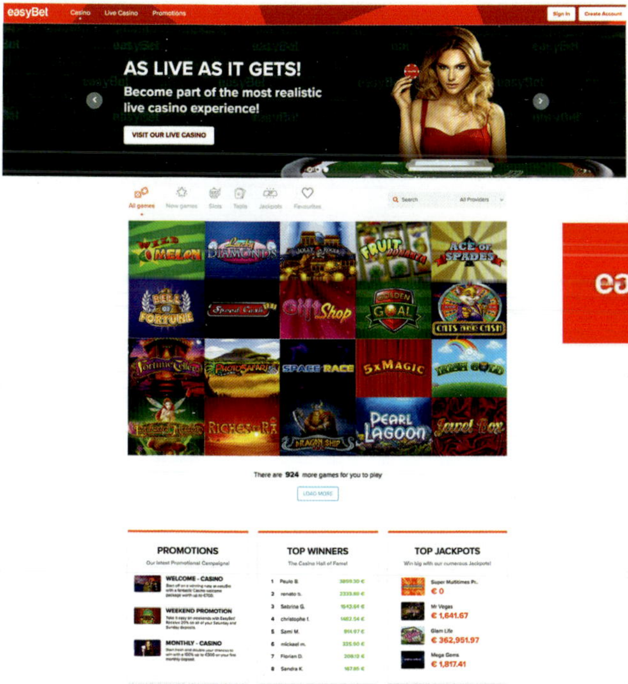

Brand thief: hosting website (Exoscale) facilitating brand thief using www.easybet.com - now out of business

easyBet

Protecting the easy family of brands against brand theft

continued

Since the last edition of easyHistory was published at the start of 2023 there have been positive outcomes for easyGroup in a number of legal actions:

Mr Saleem using easyCarcredit247.co.uk

One of the most egregious examples of using the easy brand without permission was a Mr Mohammed Saleem who set up a company called easycarcredit Ltd selling cars and car finance. Mr Saleem not only used the easy name without a licence, he also adopted the easy get-up including white out of orange lettering using the Cooper Black Font.
easyGroup took legal action and the UK High Court ordered Mr Saleem's company to rebrand.

Easycarcredit247 location interior, exterior and online branding 2023

Mr Matravers using easyLifemusic.com

The music industry is similar to the airline business in that it is high profile and attracts media attention. So when Stelios took action against a band using the name easylife without permission the story received significant coverage. Some people accused Stelios and easyGroup of bullying, not realising that the band were backed by industry giant Universal Music.

As well as using the easyLife brand for the name of their band Mr Matravers and his fellow musicians featured the easy branding on their merchandise including t-shirts:

In early 2024 Stelios reached a settlement with Mr Matravers. The band has already announced that it will be changing its name and it will pass all of its rights in the EASY LIFE name, along with the easylifemusic domain name, to easyGroup Ltd.

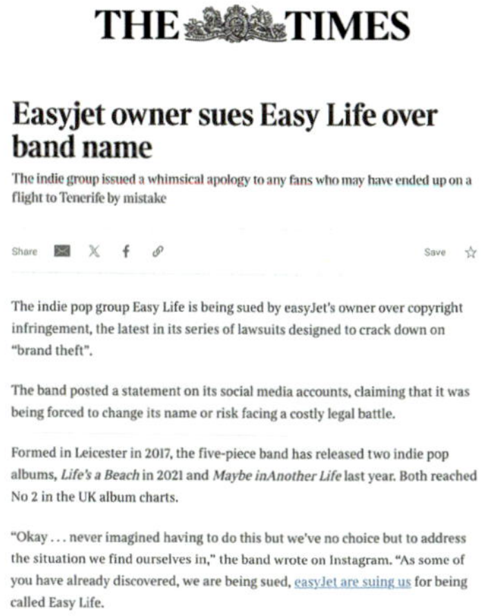

THE TIMES

Easyjet owner sues Easy Life over band name

The indie group issued a whimsical apology to any fans who may have ended up on a flight to Tenerife by mistake

Share Save

The indie pop group Easy Life is being sued by easyJet's owner over copyright infringement, the latest in its series of lawsuits designed to crack down on "brand theft".

The band posted a statement on its social media accounts, claiming that it was being forced to change its name or risk facing a costly legal battle.

Formed in Leicester in 2017, the five-piece band has released two indie pop albums, *Life's a Beach* in 2021 and *Maybe inAnother Life* last year. Both reached No 2 in the UK album charts.

"Okay . . . never imagined having to do this but we've no choice but to address the situation we find ourselves in," the band wrote on Instagram. "As some of you have already discovered, we are being sued, easyJet are suing us for being called Easy Life.

Easylife Music T-shirts & merchandise (above)

TheTimes.co.uk 03 Oct 2023

Dailymail.co.uk 11 Oct 2023

Wednesday, Oct 11th 2023

MailOnline News

Indie band named 'Easy Life' say they will change their name after brand owners of easyJet start legal action against them

- **Band climbs down from fighting lawsuit filed by Sir Stelios' business empire**

By JON BRADY
PUBLISHED: 01:21, 11 October 2023 | **UPDATED:** 01:22, 11 October 2023

A band called Easy Life says it will change its name - after being threatened with legal action by the parent company of no-frills airline easyJet.

Protecting the easy family of brands against brand theft

continued

Mr Bachani and Mr Nanji using easyHotelwifi.com

One of the business sectors most prone to brand theft is hotel accommodation. Over the years various individuals and companies have tried to make use of the easyHotel brand without paying for the privilege. These included Mr Bachani and Mr Nanji who set up a company called EASY hotel wifi limited using the domain easyhotelwifi.com. In March 2024 following legal action by easyGroup (in which the UK High Court confirmed infringement) the company was put into involuntary liquidation.

Easyhotelwifi.com 10 Jul 2023

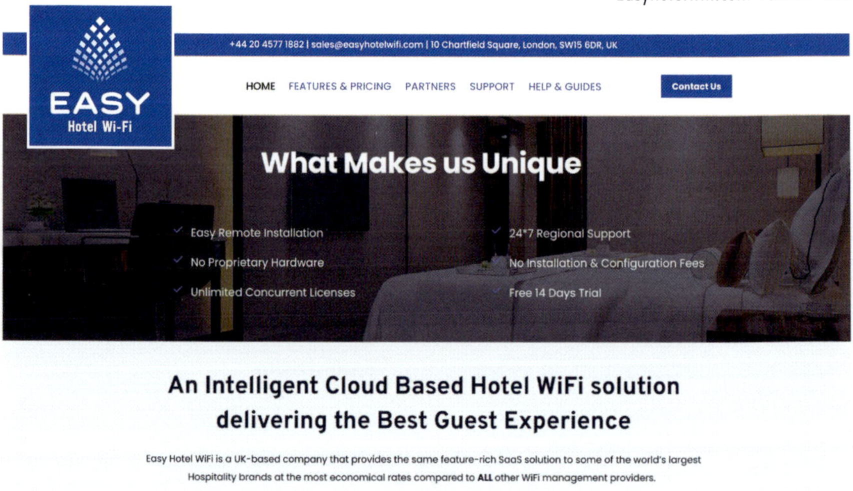

Achilleas Achilleous using easyliveauction.com

Also in 2023 a High Court ruling found Achilleas Achilleous trading as www.easyliveauction.com was "riding on the coat tails' of easyGroup's trade marks and was passing off his business as that of easyGroup or as being connected with easyGroup. In 2024 Achilleous was ordered to pay easyGroup its legal costs (which amount to around £180,000) after losing the appeal stage of an easyGroup claim against him.

The final court judgment 20 Dec 2023
easyliveauction.com website 2018

Neutral Citation Number: [2023] EWCA Civ 1508

Case No: CA-2023-000350

IN THE COURT OF APPEAL (CIVIL DIVISION)
ON APPEAL FROM THE HIGH COURT OF JUSTICE, BUSINESS AND PROPERTY COURTS OF ENGLAND AND WALES, INTELLECTUAL PROPERTY LIST (ChD)
Sir Anthony Mann
[2022] EWHC 3327 (Ch)

Royal Courts of Justice
Strand, London, WC2A 2LL

Date: 20 December 2023

Before :

LORD JUSTICE LEWISON
LORD JUSTICE ARNOLD
and
LADY JUSTICE FALK

Between :

EASYGROUP LIMITED — Claimant/Appellant

- and -

(1) EASY LIVE (SERVICES) LIMITED
(2) ACHILLEAS PAVLOU ACHILLEOUS
(3) JONATHAN RICHARD DEAN BURNSIDE — Defendants/Respondents

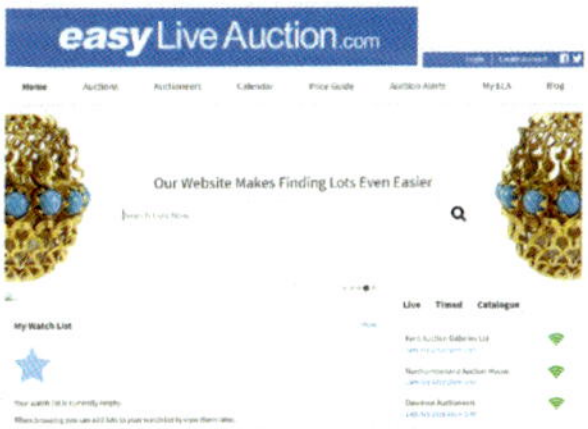

In response to the judgment, Stelios says:

It is a fact of life that brand theft is profitable for brand thieves. There will always be opportunists who want to trade off the back of the reputation of another business rather than invest to build their own...
Our court victory proves that all we want is to uphold the rule of law. We must protect consumers and the legitimate members of the easy family like easyJet.com, easyHotel.com, easyStorage.com and easyLife.co.uk and many others who use the 'easy' logo, under licence from easyGroup.
It is the collective and exceptional efforts of the easy family members that have turned the easy brand into such a trusted institution. We don't want them being mistakenly associated with people who like the Judge said, free ride on our coat tails.
- 20 December 2023

2006: Stelios becomes Sir Stelios

In 2006 at the age of 39 Stelios was knighted by Her Majesty Queen Elizabeth II for services to Entrepreneurship. The knighthood was bestowed within the Queen's birthday honours list. The ceremony took place at Buckingham Palace on 29th November.

Stelios receives his knighthood from Britain's Queen Elizabeth II 2006

BBC

Easyjet founder Stelios knighted

Easyjet founder Stelios Haji-Ioannou has been knighted for services to entrepreneurship.

Sir Stelios says he is surprised but thrilled

Sir Stelios, who has both British and Greek passports, said the honour added to the joy he gets when people stop him in the street to say thanks.

He is joined by fashion billionaire Philip Green, who has been knighted for services to the retail industry.

Sir Philip, the boss of the Arcadia Group and Bhs department stores said it was a "nice honour".

'Great reward'

Sir Stelios said he humbly accepted the honour, which is bestowed within the Queen's birthday honours list.

BBC News 16 June 2006

THE TIMES

y's sections Past six days Explore Times Radio

Founder of easyJet joins the nation's top flight

Two flamboyant tycoons join stars from the worlds of entertainment and sport on the Queen's 80th Birthday Honours list

THE man who brought cheap air travel to millions with his easyJet empire, Sir Stelios Haji-Ioannou, has been knighted in the Queen's Birthday Honours.

He is joined by Sir Philip Green, another flamboyant entrepreneur, who turned round Top Shop and BhS and is behind several other high street successes, and Charles Sir Wheeler, the doyen of foreign correspondents.

The Times 17 June 2006

Stelios says:

On reflection, I am always pleasantly surprised when ordinary members of the public stop me in the street to say 'thank you', I guess for making travel and other goods and services affordable to them."

"To get the same endorsement now from the top echelons of British society is a joy to me and a great reward for the efforts that I have made.

The Daily Telegraph

'They'd laugh if I began calling myself Sir…'

*As easyJet boss Stelios Haji-Ioannou prepares to be honoured by the Queen, **Cassandra Jardine***

Daily Telegraph 29 Nov 2006

Evening Standard

Now it's Sir Stelios, easyKnight

EASYJET founder Stelios Haji-Ioannou, ever the businessman, couldn't resist a chance for a free plug today at Buckingham Palace when receiving a knighthood. He wore a vivid orange tie, the colour of his business empire. Sir Stelios, 39, said: "I don't wear a tie but I thought for the Queen I would… It had to be this one."

Evening Standard 29 Nov 2006

Our reputation

Stelios has also been fortunate enough to meet a number of influential individuals, heads of state and celebrity personalities during the creation of the easy family of brands and numerous charitable events.

Stelios with US President Bill Clinton

HRH Princess Anne and Stelios, Airline of the year lifetime achievement Award 2007

Stelios with HSH Prince Albert II of Monaco & Kirsten Schuijt WWF Director General 2023

David Cameron, former UK Prime Minister at Downing Street

Stelios with Queen Elizabeth II Leonard Cheshire 60th Anniversary Event 27 Oct 2008

Sir Stelios hosted a fundraising dinner for the two charities WWF and the Prince Albert II Foundation (FPA2) on 27 September 2023 in Monaco with all proceeds going to environmental projects. The event raised 864k euro to be split equally between the two charities. The amount raised was an increase of 154% on the 2022 event Since 2013 the Foundation has hosted eleven joint events and raised cumulatively nearly 2.5 million euro for the environment.

King Charles III 12 Jun 2019

Our reputation

continued

In 2015 the National Portrait Gallery's board of trustees voted to include a painting of Sir Stelios in their Primary Collection, alongside HRH The Duchess of Cambridge, Admiral Lord Nelson and Sir Elton John. This work (oil on aluminium panel) was commissioned from the acclaimed artist, Mary Jane Ansell; see maryjaneansell.com.

Stelios portrait,
National Portrait Gallery 2015

Stelios in Forbes Magazine
Monaco Feb 2019

Stelios has also been awarded 4 honorary doctorate degrees from the following educational institutions: City University, Liverpool John Moore, Northumbria (Newcastle) University & Cranfield.

Stelios wearing graduation gown of Liverpool John Moores University

GQ entrepreneur of the year award Sep 2001

CITY UNIVERSITY LONDON

LIVERPOOL JOHN MOORES UNIVERSITY

Northumbria University NEWCASTLE

Cranfield University

Piers Morgan Jul 2009

Stelios and Michael Dell of Dell Inc. 22 Jan 2004

easy awards

Since the 1990s the success of easy branded businesses has been recognised in countless awards ceremonies. Over the years there have been too many awards to list them all individually, but they include:

easyJet – Business Traveller Magazine – Best low-cost airline for 14 consecutive years

easyJet – Conde Nast Traveller Award – Best low-cost airline for 7 consecutive years

easyJet – World Airline Awards – Best low-cost airline in Europe

easyJet – World Aviation Festival - Best Airline App in the World

easyJet – Marketing Society – Special Award for Long Term Marketing Excellence

easyEverything – Future Publishing – e-company of the year

easyEverything – Retail Week – Retail Launch of the year

easyEverything – MAPIC – International Property – Design Innovation and Concept

easyJet Best Low-Cost Airline Award Telegraph with Ray Webster CEO of easyJet 2000 & Jonathan Ross 21 Oct 2000

The Daily Telegraph

2001 Stelios was recognised as the Ernst and Young UK Entrepreneur of the Year.

2005 At the Telegraph Travel Awards Stelios received a special award for services to British Travellers.

2007 Stelios received a lifetime achievement award from the travel industry at the 25th anniversary OAG awards. Previous winners included Lord Marshall the former CEO and chairman of British Airways and Emirates CEO Maurice Flanagan. The award was presented by Her Royal Highness Princess Anne.

2019 More recently, Stelios received another lifetime award for Strategic Philanthropy from the Global Family Office Investment Summit.

Alan Sugar, Tony Blair and Richard Branson

Stelios with Gordon Brown & officials

The 10 Most talked-about brands

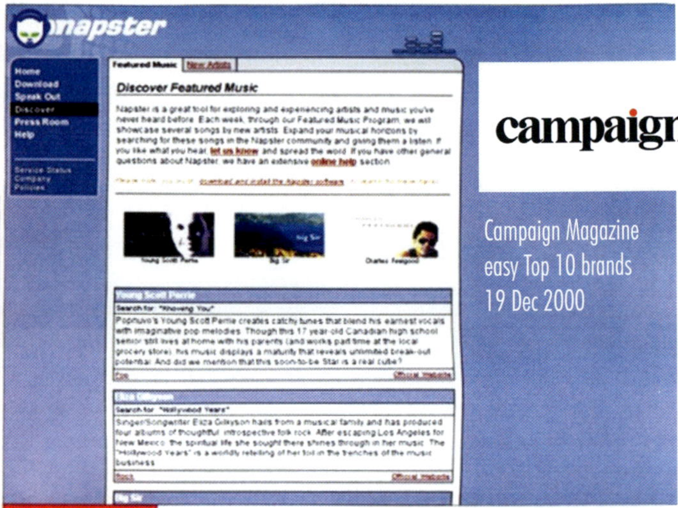

campaign

Campaign Magazine
easy Top 10 brands
19 Dec 2000

1 Napster
Napster launched as a free song-swapping service on the internet. At the last count, it had 38 million users. It has faced multiple lawsuits from the music industry but in November Napster signed a $50 million deal with the German media conglomerate Bertelsmann amid promises that the site would soon compensate copyright holders. This deal was described in a recent report by Morgan Stanley Dean Witter as "a crucial step for both the internet and the music industry".

2 Palm Pilot
The Palm V was the corporate must-have gadget of the year in 2000. Meanwhile, Palm Computer stock became the must-have share of the spring following and initial public offering in March.

3 Easy
What a year for the brand formerly known as EasyJet. In March, its founder, Stelios Haji-Ionnou, launched easyrentacar.com, the world's first online car rental service. Meanwhile easyeverything.com continues to expand its portfolio of internet cafés around the world and the Easy Group has also recently launched easyvalue, an online price comparison service. But don't forget the airline which having survived competition from the mighty BA in the form of Go, floated on the stock market in November.

4 Burberry
Hard to imagine, even a year ago, that one of the UK's more historic brands, (formerly found only on accountants) could become quite so hip. All credit to the veteran US retailer Rose Marie Bravo, who took the helm three years ago, and some great advertising featuring Kate Moss in a tiny Burberry bikini. In 2000, profits doubled and the Burberry look became a celebrity must-have.

5 The Olympics
Sydney 2000 reinjected some much-needed zest into the Olympic brand. Good news for athletes as the event produced positive media coverage, for media owners as the world tuned in, and good news for sponsors who, having forked out multimillion-pound payments, seemed to have got value for money.

6 Audi
At the beginning of the year, Audi (*above*) zoomed into the international car buying public's consciousness in the form of the TT. As the year progressed, it has capitalised on the buzz with more great launches, including the aluminium "supercar" the A2 and the All Road Quattro.

7 Apple
The launch of the iMac (*below, left*) in 1998 is widely crediting with saving the company. It was a textbook example of how design can be at the forefront of revolutionary products. In 2000, Apple has proved it still has more tricks up its sleeve, upgrading the iMac and unveiling the G4 Cube, described as a "super computer in an 8-inch cube".

8 Gucci
Under the guiding hand of Tom Ford, Gucci has evolved from a luggage brand to a worldwide luxury goods retailer. This achievement was ratified in 2000 by the acquisition of the Yves Saint Laurent companies.

9 The Micro Scooter
This polished aluminium, collapsible version of the 60s toy became *the* way to move around for both the young and the young at heart across the globe in 2000. The original was launched by the Swiss inventor Wim Ouboter. Unfortunately, he failed to patent the design so the extent of its massive popularity is impossible to quantify.

10 Tate Modern
Who could have anticipated the hype which would be generated by the launch of Britain's new modern art gallery? Following huge media exposure, the gallery in Bankside became a London landmark attracting 35,000 visitors per day in the first week.

easy awards continued

On 19 December 2000 Campaign Magazine published a list of the Top 10 most talked-about brands of the year.

Twenty-two years later, three of the brands are no longer in existence. One of the brands that has disappeared is Napster which laid the foundations for the music-streaming industry of today. Another was Palm Pilot which was highly innovative at the time but fell victim to the increased capabilities and wide-spread adoption of the mobile phone.

But seven of the brands are still in use and thriving today, including Apple, Gucci, Burberry and The Olympics.

Stelios is very proud that "easy" the brand he created back in 1994 made it into the Top 10 most-talked about list and that we are now in more industries and more geographies than at any time in our history.

Our reputation

easy in the MUSEUM *of* BRANDS London

Established as a charity in 2002, The Museum of Brands examines the history of consumer culture from Victorian Times to the present day. The museum features over 12,000 original items and shows how the brands around us have evolved over the last 200 years. Alongside other famous and established names such as Johnnie Walker, Coca-Cola & Cadburys.

easy® | JOHNNIE WALKER | Coca-Cola | Kellogg's | Cadbury | DIAGEO | vodafone | DS Smith

Sponsors & brands that feature within the museum.

111 – 117 Lancaster Road
Notting Hill, London,
W11 1QT

The objectives of the charity are to educate the public on design and in particular to the subjects of advertising and packaging and their history by establishing and maintaining a museum to be open to the public for displaying exhibitions. The easy family of brands is honoured to have a permanent display presence at the museum. The display has recently been updated to reflect continued expansion of the easy family. The Museum of Brands is located just a short walk from London's Ladbroke Grove Underground station. Why not pay a visit and see the easyHistory display for yourself?

easy exhibition stand at the museum of brands updated in May 2023

Magazine advert for original display in 2021

Original museum display

Contact us:

easyGroup

Directors

easyGroup and its family of brands is owned by easyGroup Ltd, a wholly-owned UK subsidiary of easyGroup Holdings Ltd, based in Monaco. easyGroup Holdings Ltd owns these business assets of which Stelios is the main beneficiary via the Sir Stelios Haji-Ioannou trust.
The Directors are as shown here:

Sir STELIOS HAJI-IOANNOU
stelios@easy.com
President & Founder

Non-executive Directors

PETER BARTON | peter.barton@sydenhams.net
Former lawyer and investment banker, has held appointments in Alliance & Leicester, the Guinness Partnership, Howard de Walden Estates and Oxford University. A former High Sheriff and Deputy Lieutenant of Greater London.

JEAN-CLAUDE EUDE | jean-claude-eude@libello.com
Started with the IMF and later served in the Inter-American Development Bank and the European Commission. More recently was a private banker in the Principality of Monaco where he resides.

DAVID WATSON | dwwatson@hotmail.com
A former international banker. His career spanned more than 25 years including time with Citibank in Europe, Asia and the Middle East and extensive experience with local banks in Greece.

The global HQ of Stelios' family office and easyGroup Holdings Ltd in Monaco where he has been living since 1989. It has a large terrace overlooking Monaco port suitable for events
14 Quai Antoine 1er, Monaco , mc98000 | Tel : +377-9880-1010

easyGroup Ltd UK headquarters, 168 Fulham Road (left)
easyGroup Holdings Ltd in Monaco (below)

Our team and easy family gatherings

In May 2018 we brought together the easy family of brands for some team building. We took over the classic Monaco Grand Prix and invited the easy teams to enjoy two days of fun and learning about the brand while networking. (Photo below.)

easy Family of Brands with advertising at the Monaco Historic Grand Prix, May 2018

Advertising at Monaco Historic Grand Prix 2018

easy Family Reunion Stelios Speaking 7 May 2022

We believe that members of the easy family benefit from meeting in person to share ideas and learn from one another. It also provides an opportunity to update on recent developments. Here are some photographs of previous events.

Monaco Yacht Club Speakers, Jean Claude-Eude, Peter Barton & Stelios 7 May 2022 (above)

easyGroup Family of Brands Monaco 14 Nov 2021

Our team and easy family gatherings .... continued

Stelios & easyGroup staff 13 Nov 2021

Twice a year Stelios hosts a gathering of representatives of the easy family for two days of business and social activity.

easy Family Monaco Event 22 Oct 2022

easy Family Monaco Event 20 Oct 2023

Our Team

richard.shackleton@easy.com
for media enquiries
andrew.lowe@easy.com
for accounts
vikas.kotecha@easy.com
for accounts
holly.mottershead@easy.com
for legal
jonathan.wright@easy.com
for branding and design
mathieu.diop@easy.com
for properties
trudie.porter@easy.com
for easyPet
tony.anderson@easy.com
for easyHistory

Our help desk for easy family of brands members

Email:
easyfamilyofbrands@easy.com

Our advisors

Stelios looks forward to welcoming more entrepreneurs to the easy family in the years ahead. In order to help the nascent members of the easy family of brands to grow faster Stelios has hand picked a number of advisors in key areas who are available to help at preferential rates:

Media relations

Laurie Stone
laurie@easypr.biz

Raising equity capital

Charles Hancock
charles.hancock@easycapital.financial

easy brand index

Our **top 100 most active** easy brands in alphabetical order with their main domains and the first page in the easyHistory 6th edition book that they are mentioned.

easy brand index

The long list of active easy brands with their main domains in alphabetical order.

easy.com
easy.com.pr
easy-usa.us
easyAccessibility.co.uk
easyAgents.info
easyAir.co.uk
easyAir.co.za
easyAir.com
easyAir.eu
easyAir.travel
easyAirporttransfers.com
easyAir-tours.com
easyAlquilar.com
easyArt.com
easyAtlantic.co.uk
easy-Apartments-to-rent.com
easyBags.com
easyBase.biz
easyBet.net
easyBet.ie
easyBike.com
easyBizjet.com
easyBlackcab.com
easyBlackcabs.com
easyBoat.com
easyBooking.holiday
easyBus.com
easyCafes.co.uk
easyCamera.biz
easyCapital.financial
easyCar.com
easyCasa.gr
easyCashback.com
easyCharging.app
easyCinema.com
easyCinema.com.cy
easyCinema.gr
easyCleaning.biz
easyClickit.biz
easyClickit.net
easyClothing.co.uk
easyCoach.com
easy.coffee
easyCome-easyGo.biz
easyContainer.biz
easyConveyance.com
easyCredit.co.uk
easyCruise.com
easyCurrency.com
easyDogwalker.co.uk

easyDorm.com
easyDriver.online
easyDrivingschool.co.uk
easyEmail.org
easyEnergy.com
easyEntertainment.net
easyEsport.fr
easyEspresso.co.uk
easyEventhireuk.com
easyEverything.com
easyExtras.biz
easyFamily.net
easyFarmer.gr
easyFerry.com
easy.fitness
easyFitnessclub.com
easyFlights.co.uk
easyFly.co.uk
easyFly.com
easyFly.travel
easyFood.com
easyFood.ie
easyFoodstore.com
easyFootball.info
easyGaming.com
easyGifts.co

easyGood.co.uk
easyGreece.tours
easyGreek.gr
easyGroup.co.uk
easyGuide.biz
easyGym.co.uk
easyGym.fr
easyHemp.gr
easyHire.biz
easyHire.mobi
easyHistory.info
easyHoliday.com
easyHoliday.us
easyHolidays.co.uk
easyHose.net
easyHostel.com
easyHotel.com
easyHub.com
easyInnovator.com
easyInsurance.co.uk
easyInternetcafe.com
easyISA.com
easyJeans.co.uk
easyJet.com
easyJobs.com
easyKiosk.biz

easy brand index

The long list of active easy brands with their main domains in alphabetical order. .... **continued**

- **easyKiosk**.co.uk
- **easyKiosk**.travel
- **easyLagern**.com
- **easyLand**.biz
- **easyLand**.travel
- **easyLand**.us
- **easyLet**.com
- **easyLife**.co.uk
- **easyLife**.shop
- **easyLimousines**.com
- **easyLocation**.fr
- **easyMarketing**.co.uk
- **easyMieten**.net
- **easy-Mind**.org
- **easyMobile**.com
- **easyMoney**.com
- **easyMOT**.com
- **easyMusic**.com
- **easyNet**.tech
- **easyNetworks**.co.uk
- **easyNoleggio**.net
- **easyOffice**.co.uk
- **easyOffice**.live
- **easyOfficespace**.com
- **easyParking**.biz
- **easyParking**.tv
- **easyPay**.money
- **easyPet**.mc
- **easyPet**.net
- **easyPet**.org
- **easyPetfood**.gr
- **easyPics**.co.uk
- **easyPizza**.com
- **easyPod**.uk
- **easyPoints**.net
- **easyPower**.global
- **easyPR**.biz
- **easyProducts**.co.uk
- **easyProperty**.com
- **easyRailways**.com
- **easyRamp**.biz
- **easyRamp**.co.uk
- **easyRealestate**.net
- **easyRefill**.com
- **easyRentacar**.com
- **easyResort**.co.uk
- **easyRider**.biz
- **easyRider**.company
- **easyRider**.online
- **easyRideshare**.co.uk

easyRoommate.com
easySEO.digital
easyServices.co.uk
easyShipfinance.com
easy.shop
easySim.global
easySky.co.uk
easySky.travel
easySky.us
easyStay.com
easyStorage.com
easyStudies.co.uk
easyStudies.gr
easyStudies.io
easySuperapp.io
easySure.co.uk
easySure.dk
easyTag.app
easyTax.co.uk
easyTaxi.app
easyTaxi.ie
easyTech.info
easyTech.travel
easyTelecom.com
easyTennis.co.uk
easyToolhire.com
easyTours.info
easyTrain.com
easyTransfers.biz
easyTransport.com
easyTrapeza.com
easyTravel.club
easyTravel.tech
easyTravelseat.com
easyTribe.net
easyTruck.com
easyUpdate.net
easyVan.com
easyValeting.com
easyValue.com
easyVentures.com
easyVet.tech
easyVirtual.tours
easyVols.fr
easyVoyage.com
easyWallet.app
easyWatch.com
easyWay.guide
easyWay.holiday
easyWay-sbh.com
easyWeb.mobi
easyWoo.com
easyWorkrooms.com
easy4men.com
easi.co.uk
eaziGroup.com
eazy.biz
ezy.group
Pitchiteasy.com
RestEasyApartments.net

easyHistory

Sixth Edition

All proceeds from any sales of **easyHistory** are donated to the Stelios Philanthropic Foundation.

Design
Jonathan Wright

All enquiries to
easyfamilyofbrands
@easy.com

6th edition published
23 April 2024

First edition published
January 2020

Notes

Since 2010 Sir Stelios Haji-Ioannou and his private company

easyGroup®

have donated more than €84,000,000 to the charity

STELIOS PHILANTHROPIC FOUNDATION

WWW.STELIOS.ORG

- **Some highlights of the charitable work:**
- **36million free snacks given through our *Food from the Heart* programme to those in need in Greece and Cyprus with a retail value of €36million (since 2013).**
- **€8.8million towards 300 Scholarships at LSE & City Universities.**
- **€7.2million in cash prizes to entrepreneurs to encourage job creation in UK, Greece & Cyprus.**
- **€2.5million for the environment working with WWF and Prince Albert II of Monaco Foundation.**

STELIOS PHILANTHROPIC
FOUNDATION

WWW.STELIOS.ORG

ANNUAL REPORT AND ACCOUNTS

for the Financial Year ended 30 September 2023

UK Registered Charity: 1141206

23 April 2024

Dear friends

As you may know I have been "giving back" to society for the last 19 years in my own name and via the Stelios Philanthropic Foundation (www.stelios.org).

The main source of the funds that my Foundation donates to good causes annually is the recurring donation from easyGroup, my private investment company and creator and owner of the easy family of brands (see www.easy.com and the video at www.easyHistory.info).

This printed annual report contains a summary of all the good work undertaken in the financial year that ended on 30th September 2023 all in the interest of transparency and accountability. Happy reading!

Stelios

Sir Stelios Haji-Ioannou
Founder and President
Stelios Philanthropic Foundation

The Giving Pledge

On 30 May 2017, Stelios joined an international group of philanthropists led by Bill and Melinda Gates as well as Warren Buffett see www.givingpledge.org. They have all pledged to give the majority of their wealth to charity. Stelios was the first Greek/Cypriot (and Monaco resident) to join the group.

Stelios' personal giving pledge is to give 50% of his estate as an endowment to his UK Foundation as the perpetual vehicle of his legacy to continue the giving back to society in perpetuity. The other half of his estate will be for his family who will also be involved in the foundation.

This concept of a perpetual legacy is best encapsulated by the Greek word "hysterophemia" (Υστεροφημία), which literally means the reputation that remains after one's passing.

"This is about building on a wonderful tradition of philanthropy that will ultimately help the world become a much better place." Bill Gates

Stelios with his partner Ms Orla Murphy and Bill Gates at a charity lunch in Monaco 29 June 2018.

Our Mission:

The Stelios Philanthropic Foundation's mission is to support a diverse range of good causes in our local communities that we call close to home: the UK & Ireland, Monaco & France, Greece & Cyprus, where the Founder and his family has lived and worked.

President of the Trustees:

SIR STELIOS HAJI-IOANNOU

President & Founder

stelios@stelios.com

+377-9880-1010

The Associate Members:

Orla Murphy (partner of Sir Stelios) murphy.orla@icloud.com

Aria Haji-Ioannou (daughter of Sir Stelios and Orla DOB 29 May 2018)

Tracy Ghori tracy.ghori@stelios.com

Alan Marsh alanrwmarsh@outlook.com

Ken Griggs ken.griggs33@gmail.com

Panicos Hassapis panicos@hassapis.com

Marios Missirlis Marios.Missirlis@stelios.com

Hugo Modderman hugo@dolfinance.mc

Lora Galitzine Lora.Galitzine@Coutts.com

Mary Telemachou mary@half-note.com

Biographies of Trustees: https://stelios-uk.foundation/trustees/

Biographies of Associate Members: https://stelios-uk.foundation/associate-members/

The Trustees:

The Stelios Philanthropic Foundation of the UK is organized under the UK legal form of a company "limited by guarantee" which in effect is owned by its members. These members are the equivalent of the shareholders while the trustees are the equivalent of Directors of the company. The seven trustees and ten associate members, when combined, are the 17 members that in effect "own" the charitable Foundation.

stelios

STELIOS PHILANTHROPIC FOUNDATION

WWW.STELIOS-UK.FOUNDATION

Head office in UK:
34 Thurloe Square, South Kensington London SW7 2SR

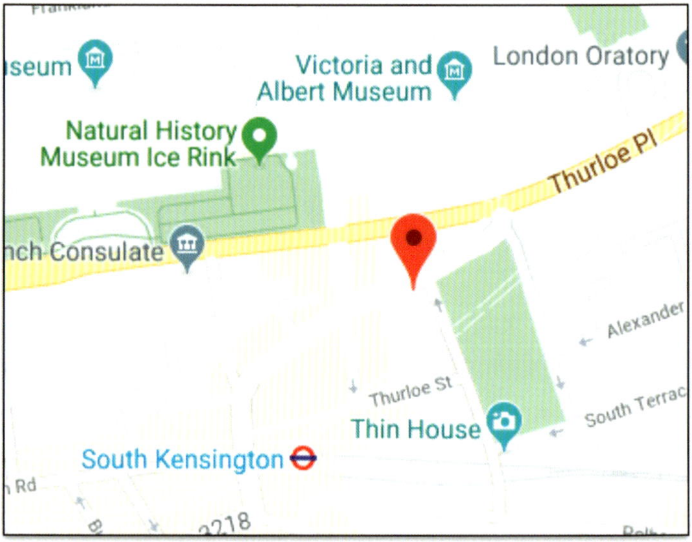

For more info contact tracy.ghori@stelios.com.

Our UK headquarters is available for use by other local charities for their fundraising events.

STELIOS PHILANTHROPIC FOUNDATION

WWW.STELIOS-UK.FOUNDATION

Our work in the UK:

Prince's Trust

www.princes-trust.org.uk The charity was founded in 1976 by King Charles III (the then HRH The Prince of Wales). Sir Stelios is a Prince's Trust Enterprise Fellow who collectively have supported the Trust to help over 90,000 entrepreneurs turn their business idea into a reality.

THE KING'S FOUNDATION

www.kings-foundation.org

London's Air Ambulance Charity

www.londonsairambulance.org.uk

aerobility

www.aerobility.com

BritishRedCross

www.redcross.org.uk

UNHCR
The UN Refugee Agency

www.unhcr.org/uk/

wetwheels
FOUNDATION

https://wetwheelsfoundation.org/

GLASSDOOR
A route out of homelessness

www.glassdoor.org.uk

ROYAL
MUSEUMS
GREENWICH

www.rmg.co.uk

SEA
CADETS

www.sea-cadets.org

THE AIR LEAGUE

https://airleague.co.uk/

Tall Ships
YOUTH TRUST

www.tallships.org

www.lns.org.uk

Stelios Awards for Young Entrepreneurs in the UK:

In Jan 2024 Stelios launched young entrepreneur awards in the UK www.stelios.foundation with £300k in cash prizes supporting the best young UK start-up founders on their growth journey to encourage job creation in the UK economy. £150k 1st prize, £100k 2nd prize & £50k 3rd prize for entrepreneurs aged 35 years or younger running a start-up company registered at Companies House (UK) in the last 5 years, own more than 50% of the company and show revenues of at least £200k per annum. The new awards follow the success of his other UK awards for disabled entrepreneurs run in partnership with www.leonardcheshire.org now in its 16th year and will run in parallel.

Hybrid awards ceremony 16 April 2024 12 noon at the Foundation's London HQ at 34 Thurloe Square:

1st prize winner of £150k
Amelia Christie-Miller
www.boldbeanco.com

2nd prize winner of £100k
Tom Ushakov
www.londonpregnancy.com

3rd prize winner of £50k
Charlotte Stavrou (née Williams)
www.sevensixagency.com

stelios

STELIOS PHILANTHROPIC FOUNDATION

WWW.STELIOS-UK.FOUNDATION

Scholarships in the UK:

LSE THE LONDON SCHOOL OF ECONOMICS AND POLITICAL SCIENCE

Sir Stelios graduated in 1987, BSc in Economics

300 scholars have benefited from the Stelios Scholarships programme since 2005 at LSE and City University where Sir Stelios studied himself.

Sir Stelios with then LSE Director Baroness Minouche Shafik and Professor Kevin Featherstone (left) and Sir Stelios with then current Scholars (above) 13 October 2020.

BAYES
BUSINESS SCHOOL
CITY, UNIVERSITY OF LONDON

Sir Stelios graduated in 1988, MSc in Shipping, Trade & Finance

Sir Stelios with City University Business school Professors Paolo Volpin and Costas Grammenos (right).

Stelios Scholars hybrid reunion 29th November 2023 (left and below).

Stelios Awards for Disabled Entrepreneurs in the UK:

The Foundation's Stelios Awards for Disabled entrepreneurs have been running since 2007 in partnership with www.leonardcheshire.org We support disabled entrepreneurs with cash prizes to stimulate economic growth and job creation. **£1.2m has been given to disabled entrepreneurs and the charity since the awards began.** On 18 May 2023 £100k in cash prizes were awarded to 1st prize winner Cristian Brownlee www.myadaptability.co.uk (£50k), 2nd prize Jon Hill www.wearejackryan.com (£30k)and 3rd prize Miles Nicholas www.morgansbutchery.co.uk (£20k).

Our work in Ireland:

Crois Dhearg na hÉireann
Irish Red Cross

www.redcross.ie

THE KING'S FOUNDATION

www.kings-foundation.org

ATLANTIC YOUTH TRUST

www.atlanticyouthtrust.org

Irish Cancer Society

www.cancer.ie

LauraLynn
IRELAND'S CHILDREN'S HOSPICE

www.lauralynn.ie

Cliona's
For families with a seriously sick child

https://clionas.ie

THE IRISH BLUE CROSS
ANIMAL WELFARE CHARITY

www.bluecross.ie

STELIOS PHILANTHROPIC FOUNDATION

WWW.STELIOSFOUNDATION.GR

Head office in Greece

5 Alopekis Street, Kolonaki, Athens 10675

Our properties in Greece are available for use by other local charities for their fundraising events free of charge . For more info contact Panagiotis.Kostarakis@stelios.com Margarita.Profyri@stelios.com Constantina.Karameri@stelios.com

"Food From The Heart" Programme in Greece & Cyprus:

STELIOS PHILANTHROPIC FOUNDATION

Food from the heart

Φαγητό από καρδιάς

Operating since 2013 from 12 distribution points in Greece and Cyprus. The Foundation has handed out more than 35 million snacks to date to people in need in Greece and Cyprus (spent 35 million euro).

Tottis,Serenata wafer chocolate bars

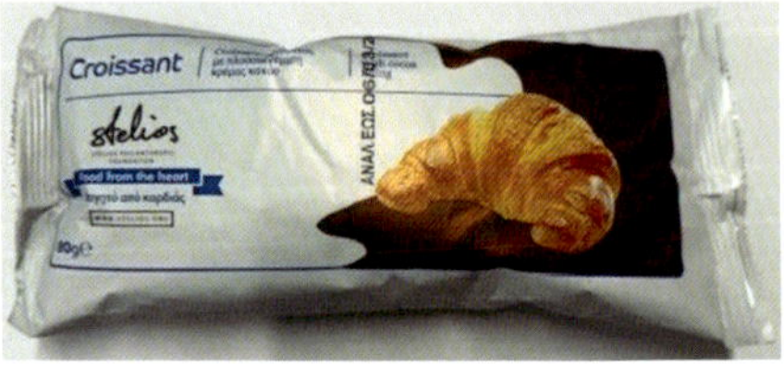

Croissant from Panini

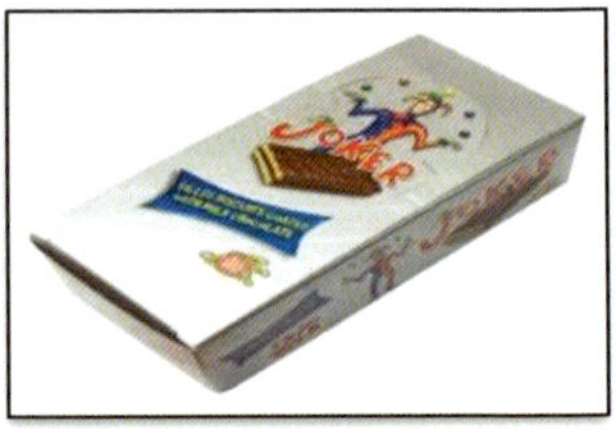

Frou Frou, Joker chocolate biscuits

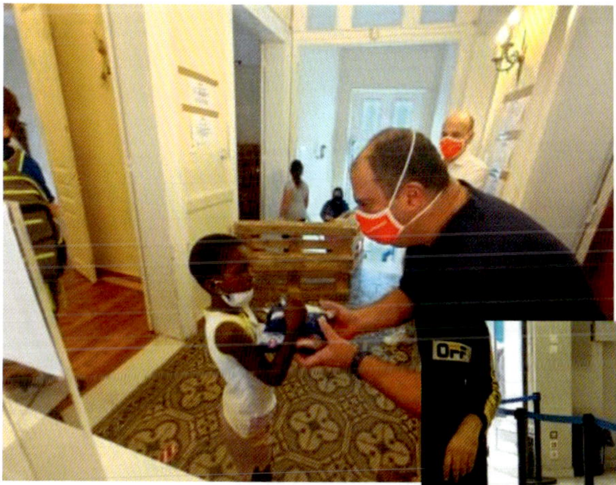

Sir Stelios at the Charilaou Trikoupi distribution point in Athens

stelios
STELIOS PHILANTHROPIC FOUNDATION
Food from the heart
Φαγητό από καρδιάς

Properties in Athens used by our "*Food from the heart*" programme:

Charilaou Trikoupi 118, Athens 11472

Centre of Athens distribution points open now back to peak times with 3 snacks given out per person.

Evripidou 10, Athens 10559

Germanikou 17A, Keramikos
Athens 10436

Depicted in the drawings are the Foundation's three distribution points in Athens by www.liamwales.com, accompanied by real-life photos.

stelios
STELIOS PHILANTHROPIC FOUNDATION
WWW.STELIOSFOUNDATION.GR

stelios
STELIOS PHILANTHROPIC FOUNDATION
Food from the heart
Φαγητό από καρδιάς

Food from the Heart 7 distribution points in total in Greece (four below outside Athens):

FOOD FROM THE HEART 6

26 Psarron, Piraeus, 185 46

FOOD FROM THE HEART 16

21 Marias Chatzikyriakou, Piraeus, 185 38

FOOD FROM THE HEART 17

40 Poseidon Avenue, Alimos, 174 55

FOOD FROM THE HEART 18

6 Shaktouri, Korydallos, 181 22

STELIOS PHILANTHROPIC FOUNDATION

WWW.STELIOSFOUNDATION.COM.CY

STELIOS PHILANTHROPIC FOUNDATION

Food from the heart

Φαγητό από καρδιάς

Food from the Heart 5 distribution points in Cyprus:

FFTH 3 Lysis Street 9 Limassol

FFTH 1 Argirou Drousioti 8 Limassol

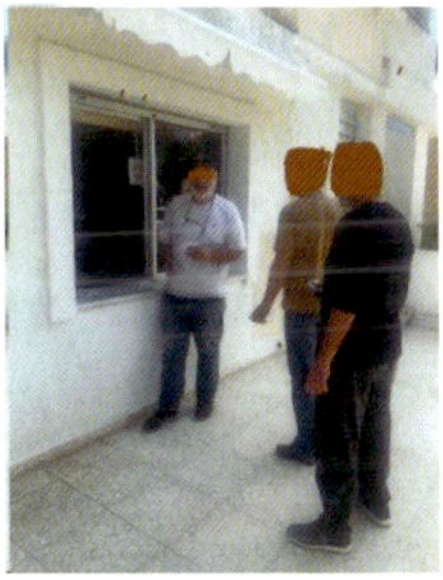

FFTH 5 Florinis Street Kapsolos Limassol

FFTH 4 Corner of Palais ilektrikis, Eptanisou 57 Nicosia

FFTH 20 Markou Drakou 5

STELIOS PHILANTHROPIC FOUNDATION

WWW.STELIOSFOUNDATION.GR

Awards for Young Entrepreneurs in Greece:

stelios AWARDS FOR YOUNG ENTREPRENEURS IN GREECE 2023

In its 14th year the Stelios Awards for Young Entrepreneurs in Greece were hosted by Sir Stelios in person on 4 September 2023 at newly opened Stelios Foundation Conference Hall, housed in the iconic building owned by the Foundation, 22 Kydathinaion Street in Plaka, Athens. Sir Stelios Haji-Ioannou awarded three prizes of €100,000 to young entrepreneurs under 40 years of age all receiving a cheque in person.

Sir Stelios and award winners 2023 in Stelios Foundation Conference Hall, Plaka, Athens 4 September 2023. Full details at www.steliosfoundation.gr

First prize €50,000 to Dafni Bechtsi, for the film streaming platform www.cinobo.com

CINOBO

Second prize €30,000, to youtuber Christos Tsounis and the channel financialgreeks.gr

FG

Third prize of €20,000 to Yiannis Chocholis, for the e-shop www.aithrio.com

Aithrio.com

stelios

STELIOS PHILANTHROPIC FOUNDATION

WWW.STELIOSFOUNDATION.GR

Scholarships in Greece:

Doukas High School Scholarships: https://doukas.edu.gr/

Since 2015 the Foundation has awarded Scholarships at Doukas High School where Sir Stelios himself graduated in 1984. The Foundation is currently funding two Greek scholars per year to study for the International Baccalaureate at Doukas High School.

ΕΚΠΑΙΔΕΥΤΗΡΙΑ ΔΟΥΚΑ 1917

Scholarships on Klelia 1:

A classic motor yacht built in 1957 which belonged to Sir Stelios's late father Loukas Haji-Ioannou berthed in Marina Zeas Piraeus.

- **Omega Academy Scholarships** for Yacht Captain certification. Seven scholarships 7,200 euro, 2 year course starting Autumn 2024. www.omega.gr

- **BCA College in Athens Scholarships** for chefs who are pursuing a career on superyachts. Seven Scholarships 6,500 euro each per year started in 2023.
- https://www.bca.edu.gr/

Other Greek charities the Foundation supports:

MEDECINS SANS FRONTIERES

ΜΑΖΙ για το ΠΑΙΔΙ
Together for Childr

ΕΛΕΠΑΠ
Βήματα ζωής για το παιδί με αναπηρία

φλόγα
FLOGA PARENTS ASSOCIATION OF CHILDREN WITH CANCER

ΑΡΚΤΟΥΡΟΣ
www.arcturos.gr

AURORA
ΜΑΖΙ ΕΝΑΝΤΙΑ ΣΤΑ ΑΙΜΑΤΟΛΟΓΙΚΑ ΝΟΣΗΜΑΤΑ

Our charitable work in Spetses:

We support the local community projects on the Greek island of Spetses including £30k to Koinoniko Pantoleio a supermarket supporting most vulnerable groups. Donation for repair works to Agia Triada church. Also support the Spetses Yacht Club for a sailing dingy Rhodes-19, the Spetses Country Club and the Armata Festival.

Stelios Foundation Conference Hall, 22 Kydathinaion Street in Plaka, Athens. Opened 4 September 2023. The Foundation is offering its hall free of charge to charities. Contact Constantina.Karameri@stelios.com

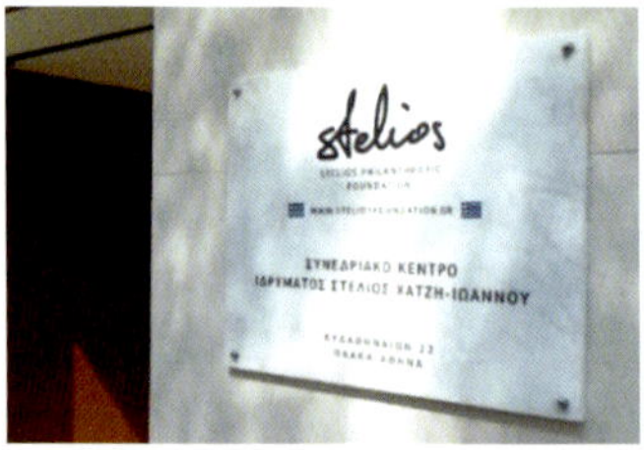

Aerial image of open-air cinema CineParis.gr at 22 Kydathinaion Street, Plaka Athens at the footsteps of the Acropolis taken by www.athensdronestudio.gr.

Charities and partners that are using the Stelios Foundation Conference Hall in Plaka :

MEDECINS SANS FRONTIERES

Make-A-Wish
Κάνε-Μια-Ευχή Ελλάδος

LSE THE LONDON SCHOOL OF ECONOMICS AND POLITICAL SCIENCE

MÉDECINS DU MONDE

ELEPAP
steps forward for the child with disability

BAYES BUSINESS SCHOOL
CITY UNIVERSITY OF LONDON

THE COSTAS GRAMMENOS CENTRE FOR SHIPPING TRADE FINANCE

BEST BUDDIES

Prince's Trust International

LSE Scholarship evening for students residing in Greece 28 November 2023 (above) and (right) HRH Prince Pavlos of Greece, VP of Prince's Trust International event 14 March 2024.

www.msf.gr three 3-day fundraising & exhibition event 23rd to 25th February 2024 at Stelios Foundation Conference Hall Plaka Athens.

MEDECINS SANS FRONTIERES
ΓΙΑΤΡΟΙ ΧΩΡΙΣ ΣΥΝΟΡΑ

BAYES
BUSINESS SCHOOL

www.bayes.city.ac.uk event 6 March 2024 promoting Scholarships at Bayes Business School, City University of London, for students residing in Greece.

SOCIETY
ΚΟΣΜΙΚΗ ΖΩΗ, LOOKS, ΨΥΧΑΓΩΓΙΑ
ΠΛΑΚΑ
ΤΟ ΒΡΑΒΕΙΟ
ΤΟΥ ΚΑΡΟΛΟΥ
ΓΙΑ ΤΗ ΒΙΩΣΙΜΟΤΗΤΑ

www.protothema.gr Gala magazine 24 March 2024 p84

14 March 2024 the https://princestrustinternational.org/ in partnership with The British Embassy Athens and Corallia presented their Sustainability Award for Europe 2023.
Photos: https://studiokominis.com/

From left to right: Prince Pavlos of Greece, Ioannis & Evaggelos Konstantopoulos winners www.thesportsfootprint.gr, Minister Domna Michailidou, British Ambassador to Greece Matthew Lodge and co-founder Corallia Dr Jorge A Sanchez-P.

STELIOS PHILANTHROPIC FOUNDATION

WWW.STELIOSFOUNDATION.COM.CY

Head office in Cyprus

Markou Drakou 5, Nicosia 1102

Both our offices in Nicosia & Limassol are available to use without charge for fundraising events by other charities.
For more information, please email marios.missirlis@stelios.com

Our offices at Markou Drakou street as depicted in watercolour by artist Liam Wales

STELIOS PHILANTHROPIC FOUNDATION

WWW.STELIOSFOUNDATION.COM.CY

Cyprus - Stelios' parents' birthplace

His father, Loucas, was born in the village of Pedoulas in the Troodos mountains and his mother, Nedi, was born in Limassol.

His maternal grandmother Cleo Missirlis-Potsos was born in the village of Lania. The Foundation owns properties in both these communities and continues to support both areas financially.

Lania

Limassol

Pedoulas

Scholarships 3 x MBA at University of Cyprus:

University of Cyprus

Other Cypriot charities the Foundation supports:

CYPRUS RED CROSS SOCIETY · ΚΥΠΡΙΑΚΟΣ ΕΡΥΘΡΟΣ ΣΤΑΥΡΟΣ

THE CYPRUS ANTI-CANCER SOCIETY

ΙΔΡΥΜΑ ΘΕΟΤΟΚΟΣ Αμερίκος Αργυρίου

Μωρά-θαύματα

CYPRUS ENVIRONMENT FOUNDATION

CYMEPA Οι φίλοι της ΘΑΛΑΣΣΑΣ

ΘΕΡΑΠΕΥΤΙΚΗ ΚΟΙΝΟΤΗΤΑ "ΑΓΙΑ ΣΚΕΠΗ"

Stelios founded the Cyprus Marine Environment Protection Association in 1992

World Maritime Day organised by CYMEPA

Little Heroes

CYPRUS ECONOMIC SOCIETY

April 2022 Lania Village €10,000. A street in the village has been named to honour Sir Stelios Haji-Ioannou.

The Foundation supports Olympic Cypriot sailor Pavlos Kontides. November 2022 crowned European Champion Hyeres Laser European Championship. https://pavloskontides.com/

stelios

STELIOS PHILANTHROPIC FOUNDATION

WWW.STELIOSFOUNDATION.COM.CY

Working for lasting peace in Cyprus:

stelios
BI-COMMUNAL AWARDS
CYPRUS
14TH YEAR
2024

The Stelios Bi-Communal Awards for Business Co-operation between the Greek Cypriot and Turkish Cypriot communities are to promote lasting peace on the island. **Since its inception in 2009 a total of € 4,3990,000 has been given in prizes.** Now in its 14th year, 2024 saw ten winning teams (involving at least one Greek-Cypriot and one Turkish-Cypriot) being awarded €20,000 to each team with a total of € 200,000 given in prizes. This hybrid ceremony took place on 18 April 2024.

Awards for young entrepreners in Cyprus:

stelios
AWARDS FOR YOUNG ENTREPRENEURS IN
CYPRUS
2023

Sir Stelios and the Foundation ran awards for your entrepreneurs in Cyprus for the first time during a ceremony at his foundation headquarters 5 Markou Drakou, Nicosia on 15 September 2023. A total of €60,000 was awarded to the top three entrepreneurial ideas, with Sir Stelios congratulating the winners via Zoom and Rena Panou, Trustee for the Foundation congratulating the winners in person. 2024 awards launch 8 May with hybrid ceremony 5th September.

1st prize €30,000 Theodoros Panayides
www.facebook.com/stavrosrestaurant/

STAVROS
RESTAURANT

2nd prize €20,000 Hasan Siber www.coliveoil.com

co
live

3rd prize €10,000 Eudokia Hadjiadamos
www.Instagram.com/lulukidonuts/?hl=en

stelios

STELIOS PHILANTHROPIC FOUNDATION

STELIOS.MC

Stelios Philanthropic Foundation Monaco
14 Quai Antoine 1er

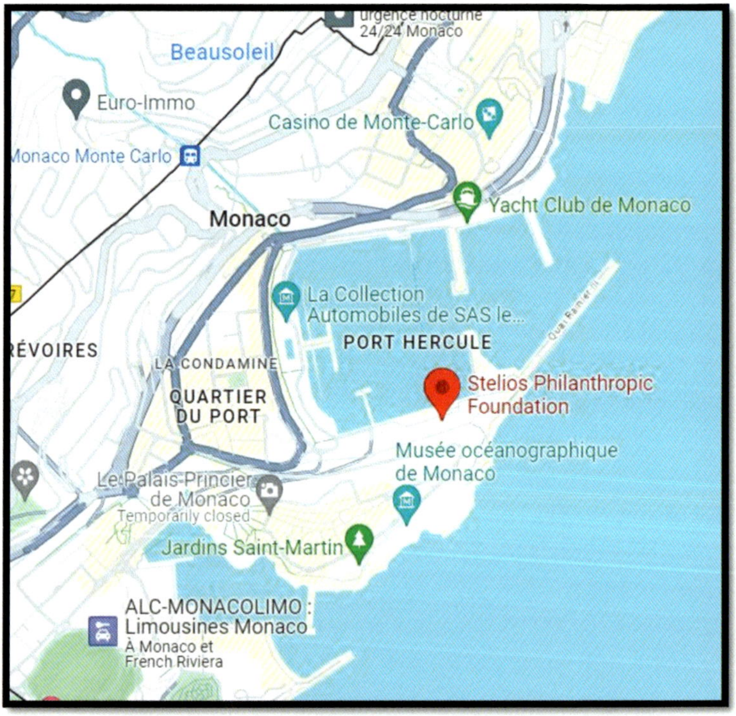

Our Monaco headquarters and the foundation's conference hall is located at Port Hercule on the ground floor of the Ruscino Building. It is available for use by other local charities for their fundraising events. For more info contact Philippe.ewart@stelios.com

Our offices at 14 Quai Antoine 1er as depicted in watercolour by artist Liam Wales

Our work in Monaco and France:

www.comstbarth.fr for common goo
of the island, FFMUR – St Barts
Foundation for Emergency Medical
Equipment and https://station-saintbarthelemy.snsm.org/

WWF & FPA2 annual fundraising dinner:

FONDATION PRINCE ALBERT II DE MONACO

WWF

From left to right: Sir Stelios Haji-Ioannou, WWF International Director General Kirsten Schuijt and HSH Prince Albert II of Monaco.

The WWF-FPA2 charity fundraiser took place on 27 September 2023 with a sit-down dinner and a special charity auction at the Stelios Philanthropic Foundation Hall, Monaco. Sir Stelios and the Foundation matched all donations made on the night which raised a total of 864,000 euros which was equally split between WWF and FPA2 for their joint efforts to protect whales and dolphins in the Pelagos Sanctuary. Thank you to all the generous donors. **In its 11th year now, just under 2.5million euro has been raised for the environment.**

STELIOS PHILANTHROPIC FOUNDATION

WWW.STELIOS.ORG

Our Accounts

Stelios Philanthropic Foundation (UK)

Summary income and expenditure account for the year ended 30 September 2023:

Income from donations from easyGroup:	£16.3m
Total expenditure:	£6.5m
Surplus for the year:	£9.8m

Summary balance sheet as at 30 September 2023:

Fixed assets (properties):	£17.6m
Cash at bank:	£14.8m
Total Net assets:	£31.8m
Charity funds:	£31.8m

Audited by Kirk Rice LLP and filed with Companies House (UK) and the Charity Commission.

STELIOS PHILANTHROPIC FOUNDATION

WWW.STELIOS.ORG

Fondation Philanthropique Stelios (Monaco)

Summary income and expenditure account for the year ended 30 September 2023:

Income from donations:	€1.2m
Total expenditure:	€1.3m
Deficit for the year:	€0.1m

Summary balance sheet as at 30 September 2023:

Fixed assets (properties):	€4.9m
Cash at bank:	€1.3m
Net assets:	€5.5m
Charity funds (incl. Patrimony):	€5.5m

Audited by Monaco auditor Jean-Humbert Croci and filed with the Monaco Government as regulators of the charity.

Note: the total cumulative donations from Sir Stelios and easyGroup to his charitable Foundations in the period 2010 – 2023 amounted to €84 million (euro) (equivalent to £73m).

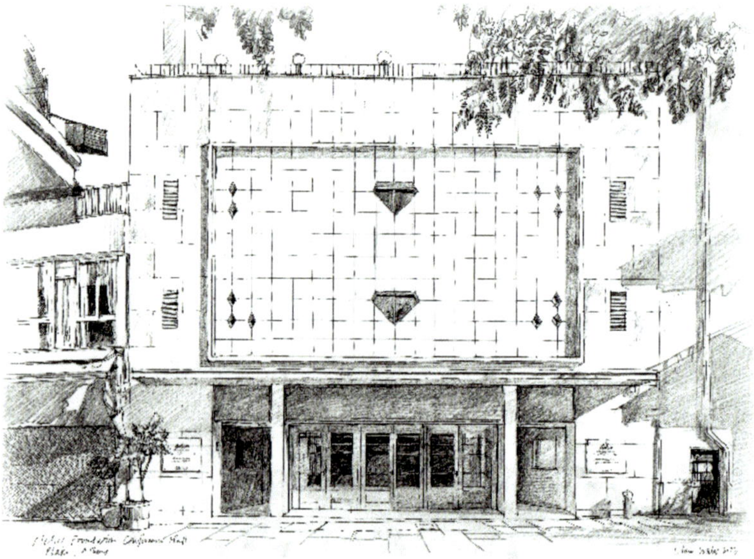

Stelios Foundation Conference Hall,
22 Kydathineon, Plaka, Athens, Greece